And Then It Was Now

The autobiography of
Christopher Guard

Foreword by Brian Blessed

OAK TREE BOOKS

For my children and grandchildren:
Daisy, Rosie, Tallulah, Mae, Jude, Molly and Beatrice

Contents

Foreword

Wham! Bam! Alakazam! This book leaves me gobsmacked. It is a celebration of life, nature, lights, camera, and action! Off we go!

What a privilege to write the foreword for such a remarkable man as Christopher Guard. His book displays great determination, inner strength, a wicked sense of humour, and a love of all that is worthwhile in art. He conveys the sacred fact that art is everything.

A few years ago, a vast array of students at Cambridge University nominated me to be Chancellor of the University. Me! I ask you? The election was great fun; with a gas balloon floating around the grounds with the words "Brian's Alive!" – referring, of course, to the film *Flash Gordon*, and the well-known phrase my character uttered: "Gordon's Alive!"

Yes, the election was great fun, and I almost won. Had I succeeded, I would have replaced Prince Philip, as he had just retired from the post. That's what I love about Britain, anybody can achieve anything. Just think, I was educated in a C-Class secondary school in Yorkshire. A good school, I may add, as my father was a coal miner.

The only thing that I regretted about losing was that I was denied access to the legendary Cambridge Library at the university, which I considered 'heaven on earth'. Had I won, I can honestly say I would have placed a copy of Christopher's book amongst the hallowed shelves of that famous library.

Forgive me, my patient readers, I run before my horse. Allow me to go back in time to the 1960s. During that time a miracle took place; BBC Television Centre was created at White City in Shepherd's Bush, London. It was bursting at the seams with high octane talent. The building was six floors high and boasted well equipped studios, workshops, restaurants, tea bars, offices and wardrobe and makeup departments. Actors abounded everywhere. There seemed masses of work for everyone.

On several occasions I bumped into Christopher. I do mean 'bumped'! I was often quite clumsy. We would both emit a fleeting smile, apologise, and speed away at a rate of knots. Chris seemed to me, at the time, a rather shy young man with a gorgeous twinkle in his eye. We were both on television from dawn till dusk. God! They were happy Halcyon days!

All the actors at Television Centre rehearsed nearby at the Acton rehearsal rooms. The place was affectionately known as the Acton Hilton. It also had a large restaurant and canteen and roomy car park. We had complained for years about the lousy rehearsal rooms scattered about London. Now the powers that be with loud voices and great pride told us to belt up and enjoy the new facilities. We thanked them and got on with the projects at hand.

I first worked with Christopher in *I, Claudius* in 1976. I played Emperor Augustus Caesar and he played my nephew. He was absolutely marvellous. Unfortunately, he was poisoned in the first episode by my wicked wife Livia, portrayed by Sian Phillips. He was badly missed by the whole cast. His knowledge of music was astonishing. He was a born musician and delighted the senses with his expertise.

Forgive me, ladies and gentlemen, as I once more do a time-loop and inform you that the Acton Hilton, that temple of dreams and the actors deeply loved 'Shangri-la', no longer exists! The building is there, yes! But it has been transformed into a scent factory!

It is bloody incomprehensible!

Whoever was responsible for that transformation should be blasted off at the speed of light in an ugly, smelly rocket; flown to the far reaches of the unmanifested universe and shagged sideways by a cosmic Tyrannosaurus Rex!

In 1986, I played the part of Long John Silver in the ten-part serial *Return To Treasure Island*; which was a Walt Disney production, made by HTV (who were renowned for making fantastic and epic serials). It had a great script with thousands of extras and wonderful locations in Wales, Spain, and Jamaica. It was directed by that marvellous man – Piers Haggard.

Much to my delight, Christopher was cast as a twenty-year-old Jim Hawkins! God! He was good! We got on like a house on fire. Consequently, we moulded together wonderfully as Long John Silver and Jim.

In Jamaica, we were located at the Trelawny Beach Hotel and both of us swam in the sea every day and exercised like madmen in the local gym. He focused on fine-tuning his body, whilst I worked on bulk; benchpressing up to 400lbs. We became insane with fitness, inspired in the background by the fabulous voice of Annie Lennox, pounding from the shiny, black cassette machine.

After several hours, we would stop and allow the lads and lasses of the wardrobe and makeup to pour masses of native green oil over our entire bodies. The whole experience was heavenly, and totally atavistic!

Then, lo and behold, we were joined by Piers Haggard and legendary stuntman Alf Joint. Alf was an Olympic gold medal swimmer and champion high diver. In fact, he broke the world record for high diving. Bless the guy, he will always be remembered for his famous Cadbury's Milk Tray advert dive on film and television. He is also famous for his exploits in the film *Where Eagles Dare*, standing in for Richard Burton. In fact, in the last twenty minutes of the film, you can see plainly that it is Alf Joint and not Burton! Still, they wonderfully get away with it. And the film is great!

I digress, back to Jamaica. We lay on our respective towels. Alf, me, Chris, and Piers; staring out at the night sky. The drama of the universe unfolded, with its gracious curve, the Milky Way soaring across the backdrop. Venus, so bright that we felt it could cast shadows in a room. Stars of red, green, blue, yellow, and white. Billions and trillions of them.

Chris whispered, "The whole of the Milky Way must be teeming with life". Yes! Piers laughed. "And it doesn't look the same here as it does in Britain, because we are in the tropics and therefore it appears upside-down"

We all roared with laughter and Alf brought us back to our senses by reminding us that he would be putting us through hell and high water the next day, to perfect our fencing skills for the next five weeks.

Chris and I had a ball! We were like two naughty boys. We laughed from dawn till dusk. He has a huge sense of humour and staggering imagination and vision. In one of the last big scenes in the serial, we hold one another in a tight embrace in deep water as he comforts me in my despair. I can honestly say that it shook the entire viewing public! I owe him a debt of gratitude. He is very special.

Ladies and gentlemen, boys and girls, and happy Tripods from the BBC Special Effects department, I urge you to devour this book and then continue repeating the experience until your minds, hearts and souls are reborn again and again.

Enjoy!

1: What Am I Doing?

I had promised several people, including, I suspect, myself that I would write down some of my life: the anecdotes, my quips and quarrels, the knee-grazing scrambles and the tumble-down hills. A kind of memoir.

"Ooh, you really should write all this down. It's *so* fascinating! You'd make a fortune!"

I suppose I never really felt old enough, although it all began very early for me. I mean, the material was always there, from a young age: the illustrious company, the street-life, the stars-to-be, the hammering typewriter, the TV appearances, the direct-grant grammar school full of Hugh Grants and Alan Rickmans. It was always there. And Mum and Dad, and Flanders and Swann, and Briers and Quilley and Finney, and – well, more of them anon… maybe. If your fancy is tickled enough.

Or not.

Sit up straight lad. Cap on straight lad. Straighten that tie boy.

Now what am I doing? I'm definitely old enough, but still dragging my feet, or rather sprinting to somewhere I can hide, until the fever has passed, and I can get back to street corners with fleeting friends.

I should be writing an unusual autobiography, about when I was interviewed on *The Braden Beat* about the Cuban Missile Crisis and played a young David Copperfield that grew into a young Ian McKellen. I should. I shall not disappoint. Sondheim and Liz Taylor, Gielgud and Elton John – they are all here. And there. I promise.

Digression was always my forte – do one thing and immediately start something else. Jack-of-all? Not really. Slave to curiosity. Off the beaten track again. Breadcrumbs all gone.

I watched a documentary about orangutan rescue last night. Borneo. These amazing, dedicated *hominidae*, fighting against the clock, the buck and the devil's own desperados. Most of the rescued apes are infants, and there they are, a dozen of them in a wheelbarrow, like they'd just been bought from market. Fresh and tasty. "Dozen baby orangutans, please mate, and a kilo of water voles". Yet they were protected, and on their way to be nurtured and mothered and eventually back where they belong. Up a tree. Like Jack Lightning. They don't hang about.

How on earth can they remind me of Dame Flora Robson? Because I should be telling you how, as Betsy Trotwood, she fed me cold BBC chicken soup from the Lime Grove canteen and enunciated so well she spat darts of spittle in my eye. And I pretended to be grateful. All Dover Road exhaustion and love. She was a sweet woman. Innocent and wise.

There were live donkeys among the polystyrene bushes. And Mister Dick. Orphaned, helpless and free. I loved acting then. It was Mum and Dad's craft and I just got on with it.

Didn't expect to walk into school on the Monday morning suddenly to be notorious.

"Oi! Copperknob!"

Jeez, what a shock. Microcosmic fame. Even the teachers were at it.

"You're not at the BBC now, Guard!"

Blimey. I thought better of them. Damned if I didn't.

I lie in this wheelbarrow with the baby apes, each of us with a different rumbling, restless view; a new take on trust. Seven years of learning. What not to eat, what not to do. I've seen it all before, yet it is for the first time. The trees and their leaves and the calling canopy are breaths to my eyes, deep rushes of objective colour. The same for us all, different for us all. Mister Dick had hair like us; long tufts of glory, unmirrored. Totally dependent on Betsy. In the barrow of improbable love. Pure, unconditional parenting. I push against Albert Boniface as we line up.

I was four when I went to full-time school. No nursery. Just straight in. Nine to four. St Peter's C of E Jungle. Perfectly organised chaos. It was the straight rows that freaked me out. I saw them through the glass rectangle in the door. They were like me but symmetrical. I howled, and clung to coat-hooks, and wouldn't

Roofy at work

2

budge until Mum came and got me, took me back to the garden where I had barely begun.

Worms, hollyhocks, woodlice, whole worlds beneath paving slabs. I was lucky. I asked and they answered. Mum and Dad.

And lovely Roofy, who wore way too much make-up and smelled bittersweet and called me "Ducks".

We sat at the felt-topped camping table and talked.

I was three, then four.

And so was she.

We weren't counting.

Mum and Dad were in plays and Dad wrote them too. *The Tunnel of Love* with Ian Carmichael, *The Wind Might Change* by Dad, at the Theatre Royal, Windsor.

That was the raw tapestry in the blue Stamford Brook sky. Woven of grown-up wants and wishes. What they did and talked about, while I discovered red ants.

Oh, and Mum had dated Peter Sellers before she met Dad, and been the only woman to appear in *The Goon Show*. And that was my norm. And hers. Mum particularly loved Spike.

An orangutan tumbles from the barrow and is snugjuggled back in. She does not have to sit up straight. She is allowed to lie limb-curled, neck-draped, semi-prone. Not side-by-side but among. She is allowed to learn *how* to learn. One two is two, three twos are six, eleven elevens are a hundred and twenty-one orangutans. And through her eyes, I see my canopy: a university of sensed understanding.

I had a place at Christchurch College, Oxford, but I didn't go. I was filming in Vienna with Liz Taylor. I smoked spliffs with her at the back of a box, at the first night of the interminable *Don Carlos* in Vienna. Enjoying the canopy, not the view; unable to concentrate on the bellowed procedure.

"Come and *watch*!" implored Liz's mother.

Watch with Mother. It was listening we were struggling with.

There you are. I said I'd keep my promise. Names are dropping like rain from a rainforest sky. I shall try to concentrate better. Stick to show biz, toothsome anecdotes. The special requests. I aim to please.

MAN OF THE MOMENT

With our production of "The Wind Might Change" Philip Guard enters the ranks of actor-dramatists. On page 3 John Counsell discusses the finer points of this union of author and player, and below Philip Guard himself throws light on another facet of the matter.

TROUBLES never come singly.

For instance, not only am I married to an actress, but she, poor soul, is married to me. Not only have we one robust son of four, we have another of sixteen months.

Now these facts in themselves are far from troublesome. But occasionally they converge. My wife and I remain incurable optimists about this converging. Usually our optimism pays off. When my wife is busy, I am often free to assure the boys they are not victims of a broken home—apart from their own vandalism. When I am touring my wife is frequently about to explain to them that I have not gone to sea or to gaol.

Recently a mighty converging threatened. My wife was offered a nice part in "The Tunnel of Love", due in town in December. It necessitated a four-week tour. We were optimists about it.

"You must take it," I said, "I'll manage."

"But supposing something comes up for you," she said, "like doing 'The Wind Might Change' at Windsor?"

"Oh, it won't," I said, trying to persuade myself that this was looking on the bright side.

"All right," she said, "I'll take it. Perhaps it will be a nice near tour like Golders Green and Streatham Hill, and I can live at home."

"Yes, of course it will," I said.

It turned out to be Liverpool, Leeds, Blackpool and Oxford.

"Never mind," I said, "I'm free. And nothing much will turn up."

The next day I was invited to play in "The Wind Might Change" at Windsor. Nothing much. Only an ambition of thirteen years standing to play in one of my own plays. I shut out the noise of a gunbattle in the playroom and bawled "Yes please" down the telephone.

So if a new character, about 3ft high, and dressed in pyjamas should arrive on-stage one night asking for a drink, you will know why. And if I should make a hasty exit to attend to a squalling noise in the dressing-room, that will be either for "wind" or a "change" of an entirely different sort.

PHILIP GUARD

Dad in the Theatre Royal programme

2: But

Dear, oh dear, Christopher! I was with the Royal Shakespeare Company. Well, not really: just the one play in The Pit. Good part, great reviews. Enough to impress the Americans.

Next thing I knew, I was sharing a caravan with Liam Neeson, making a TV series with Deborah Kerr and Jenny Seagrove, and 'Johnny' Mills. I acted like a man, though I felt more like that scruff-tuft orangutan. And I think in some ways Liam did too.

Have I lost you? I think I was 'off' – not on stage when I should have been. Well, how do you know where you are in that building? Trees I understand, elevators confuse me. I got talking to Ron Daniels and missed my call. Calling, more like!

Writing feels like freedom; stage acting can be, well… like saying the same words at the same time, in roughly the same way, for six months in a pit. Or at the Lyric, Shaftesbury Avenue.

Catch me if you can. Dave Clark Five?

Enough. It's a wrap. The lights go down on Studio Two, Lime Grove.

In the cottage in Alpheton, Suffolk, there was no electricity. At the heart of the swinging '60s, we travelled by four trains and a pig farmer's 'taxi' on a Friday night, at the end of another testing Latymer Upper week – surrounded by future captains of the shuddering world – a happy bundled family. Dare I say classless? Dad was ahead of his time and ahead of his head. Ow. It hurt him and all of us. I thank him for trying.

I love him always.

The cottage at Alpheton

There were five of us by now. Our little sister arrived when I was seven. First home birth.

She was named Candida but known as Molly or Milly, or Sis One. A fun, feisty dreamer. She's an animator and novelist these days.

The local lads came by – on scrapped bikes, with mums' haircuts, living on Mars Bars, and most of them were the Cox family. They were searching for us: the unusuals from London and we didn't have long but we ran with them. Their corn was our corn, their clods were our clods and it was me and Dom, my brother – soon to win a BAFTA in *The Go-Between,* as if this were a secret rehearsal. We got off with local girls, trysted in lanes near Lavenham, snogged in pill boxes. Dom was soon to be at the bosom of Julie Christie, but for now, he was at the mouth of a girl called Titch.

Where are you now?

And 'A Hard Day's Night' was playing on my little tranny as I lit the candles. Lennon was born in Suffolk and I met Carol in an avenue by the council estate. She wore a black leather miniskirt and walked straight towards me like a ghost. I died of love for her just being there.

We watched the World Cup final at Geoff – the forester's – house. A modern box, with a TV and jelly and blancmange. The screen was black and white and tiny. But it wasn't really because I saw – we all saw – what really happened. It was huge and in colour.

That's why I quite like losing my sight in one eye. Because I can see what I may have missed before. Because I can nearly see everything. Like Stevie Wonder.

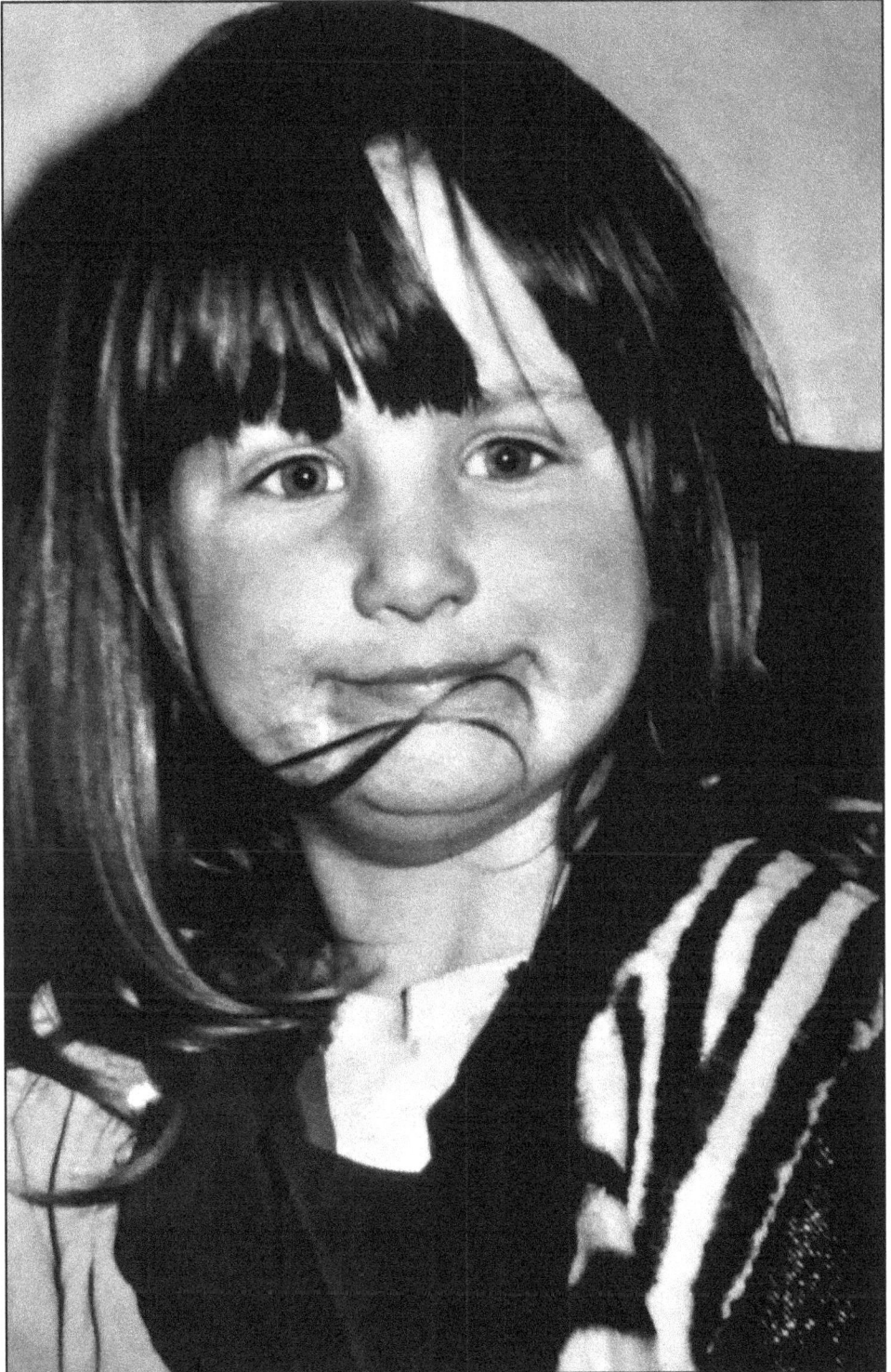

Young Candy

3: Excuses

There are no excuses. It's been months since I started writing this book. There's been a pandemic and all sorts of tribulations. Everyone's squabbling and waffling and promising and regurgitating and, subconsciously, maybe that's been an excuse. Not that I've been idle. I watched Mum and Dad swinging through the trees when they were still fearless and innocent. Long enough for me to learn.

I recorded a solo acoustic album in June, 2021. Mainly songs I had written for others, now reinvented raw and husky. Daughter Rosie says my songs are best as I'm actually writing them, fumbling about, digging diamonds out of ditches. Maybe she's right.

I always felt more rock and roll than Theatre Royal. But what would I know? I painted some pictures, even sold a few accidentally. I mean, I didn't pitch anything. Social media isn't all bad.

I've been running up hills too. Well, one hill in Acton Park, the one near the little pond. It's enough. Not an ocean but, in the chill and sometimes rain, it fills the soul almost to the brim. Enough to make me fret that I should be writing. Always something else. Not an excuse. Not confused. An infusive effusion.

It's the early eighties. I'm filming *Memoirs of a Survivor* with Julie Christie, and my first experiment with a band is waiting for me in a dunghill in Acton. Post-punk band, Some Burglars.

Julie was one of the new wavers, straddling the swinging bridge between wartime and peace, blessed with a smile that personified the hope of a generation.

Dom, at fourteen, completely adored her.

In *The Go-Between* she was all repressed Edwardian sex; in *Memoirs of a Survivor*, she had left Hollywood and Beattie for dystopia. The mood was sombre and the future bleak.

Oddly prescient now.

Mirrored in the same wise eyes.

Outside in.

From Julie Christie to The Windsor Castle in Kilburn. Sublime to sub-something else. The Evening Standard ran a story on it. We had a Friday night residency and an extension to midnight. When the other pubs shut, swarms of would-be sex gods would rock up and have fights in the beer sludge at our feet. Fantastic.

Trouble was, finding the time for it all. Not the energy. Like doing a jigsaw puzzle while running the four hundred metres.

And I was a dad at twenty-four and totally in love with my kids and family. It was a tough stretch, and I didn't always manage it.

So much to do, so little time.

Now that I'm apparently pretty bloody old, I think I made some pretty bloody good choices.

But maybe not in the right order. All at once more like.

With Mum and Dad

4: Play

The Theatre Royal, Windsor published my 'first play' – The Farm Boy – in their programme, *Curtain Up*.

All on one page, hammered out on a Saturday morning on Dad's typewriter, before anyone else was up, at the age of six. It features a surreal cast list of family and neighbours, some of whom don't actually appear in the play, and a unique approach to the English language. The enthusiasm was blinding. All done by noon. First night beckoning. No rewrites, just sheer would-be genius. I suppose I'm bringing much the same haphazard hopefulness to this project, although it seems to have extended beyond a page. The more I plan, the more I shift and fret.

A week later, Titty the cat was sick all over the typewriter. She was actually called Titania, in honour of Dad's role as Puck in the legendary Robert Helpmann *A Midsummer's Night Dream*. But that was before I was conscious and now Titty was a queen cat, not a fairy queen. And 'Titty' was apt because she was forever pregnant and suckling. Not that I knew what tits were. Mum called her own breasts 'bosoms' and so did I. I'm not sure what Dad found more alarming – my spelling, the coddled cat sick deep in the hammer bowels or the temporary unavailability of his typewriter.

None of our pets were neutered, and Lord knows we had enough of them. Jessie, the Doberman-Corgi cross (size of a Corgi, head of a Doberman), used to drag Titty's kittens to her own bed because she wasn't allowed to mate, even though she yearned for sex and motherhood. Then Titty would drag them back again. Eventually, Titty got wise and kept the kittens in the cubbyhole above the stairs. Kind of in outer space, which was perfect because we had named the males of her third litter after the astronauts Colonel Glenn and Uri Gagarin.

Our neighbour, Andrew Selden, who stars as the farm boy in my play, took that as a cue to launch the kittens, like frisbees, at the sofa. Poor kittens, though they seemed to survive the experience remarkably well. Perhaps fame had gone to Andrew's head.

Quick co-starring mention here for the tragic herd of white mice, who fought to the death – except for the one who escaped and got squashed under

First Play

Here is the play by Christopher, the six year old son of Philip Guard and Charlotte Mitchell to which reference is made in John Counsell's article. It is set out and spelt as he himself typed it.

THE FARM BOY—in two acts by Chrisopher Guard

andrew selden	the farm boy	paul howlls,	guntch
dominic guard	as silas	jesy	the farm dog
philip guard	the farmer	ann camble	the farmers frend
mummy guard	the farmers wife	john selden	the millcman
dina smith	there dorty	win selden	the millcmans wife

seen one   the millcman notices

seen two   the farmers cort

seen three   the sherrif rides in two town

seen four   the banddites are kild

seen one   the millcman notices

john selden sez i notess some riders
the farmer sez two his son, go two annuver place
paul sez if we dont go now we wont go a tall
dominic said all right letts go
the farmer said letts go in
guntch said ty him up
guntch said weele get there all right
the miklmans wife sez you orded two pints
the farm boy sez ime tierd
the milkman sez theres some ridersover there.
help help there masked banddites save us
9,pp8ppp she fantes on the gound
sound of hoovesthundering up to the house.

seen two the farmers cort

the bandits ty the farmer up
and then dominic sez letse get in too the back of
the bank and get the jools.
and when theyd got the jools they went out and
got on there horses and they were off   and they
went back and prerpered some supper
arf cold, said guntch
oh it dosent matter said dominic
erars your pork

thanks guntch
itsh all right young fellow.
they righed too the farmers house and bring him
back too there camp
then the farm boy runs and undose his farver
they run home again
thanks son   its all right par
and they went in and had a gaim of drarfts
and the farm boy wone and the farmer gave his
son a penny.

end of act two

act three the sherif rides in too town

when the sherif ridded in too town he tried to
catch the banddids but he just couldent.   and
he went back to the farmers house and told him
all a bout it
well you better try agin
so he did.   but he mist agin
so he told him all a bout it agin.   well he said
weel hafe too wait till too morrow said the farmer.

end of act three

seen four   the banddits are kild

so when sonday came the sherif tried agin and
he shot so mutch that he nerely lost ten of his
boolits and he did get them in the end
and they were poot in too jayl for ten years and
the farm boy went too bed.
and he dremped he was the best sherif in town.

First Play: *The Farm Boy*

the piano. What the hell were we doing collecting all these pets? Mum and Dad were self-employed, life was full and frequently frenetic. Space was tight for humans, let alone the eclectic menagerie.

And there were more to come. So many more. Of which more anon. Wait until you meet Jeeves, the satanic Jack Russell.

Jessie wants Titty's kittens

We were living in – of all places – Pleydell Avenue. Hardly a Dingley Dell, but 'pley' – or play – was about right, covering everything from reluctant piano lessons to Batman boxing gloves.

The latter were a Christmas present from Dad, intended – in the season of goodwill – to discourage us from fighting. A strange approach but the key was the accompanying punchball. This we gave short shrift, and it was not long before I was engaged in a particularly hot bout with Mick, our next-door neighbour, which culminated in Mick crashing backwards through a downstairs window. I'm still in touch with him. Knock down ginger and Fulham forever.

Then there were the everlasting football games at Stamford Brook Common. Or 'the green' as we called it. Dad referred to it as 'the grane', after our less than 'proper' pronunciation. This was just our attempt to fit in with the neighbours; my accent would change in fifty yards, between number twelve and the portals of the park. From 'posh' to 'cockerney'. This was important. We were playing with stars: Rachid Harkouk went on to play for Algeria in the World Cup. We had to fit in. Dad did not. He called us in for lunch from the park gates like Prospero summoning Caliban. Crystal chiming. I would shrink. "Please don't do that Dad. Please be a bit more normal, more street". But Dad didn't care. He had been 'The Queer Sandwich Boy' at school, on account of his wholemeal bread and dates, and he wasn't going to compromise for anyone. He acted on stage. I was a chameleon.

On the day of a Fulham home match, I could hear Mick across the passage between our houses, singing Fulham chants while sitting on the toilet. "We got Jimmy, Jimmy, Jimmy, Jimmy Conway, on the wing…" We only went to Fulham in the first place because of Mick or, more precisely, because of his boxer dog, Robbie.

It was '66. Football was as fab as The Beatles. I used to imagine Martin Peters was George Harrison and Alf Ramsey was somehow connected with Brian Epstein. Posh managers, working class players. Like we were supposedly posh and had to tone it down for the green. We were no more posh than George Martin really, and he wasn't posh at all. Class was a shifting, sliderule of a conundrum. Still is. "You think you're so clever and classless and free". Well, maybe we were – a bit.

Before the love affair with Fulham began, while Dad was hammering out yet another play, Dom, Mick and I would buy Twin Rover tickets of a Saturday morning, affording us free, classless access to any bus or Underground train that took our fancy.

And these were ubiquitous Routemaster days. You could hop on and off at will, sometimes at perilous speeds. So much fun.

I'd started experimenting with cigarettes by then. Dom and I loathed and loved them in equal measure, and they were a mistake really, but a breathless, winding hurtle to the top, back seat of a bus for a Number Six was liberation itself. What you couldn't do back then! On the tube trains, we'd jog trot casually from carriage to carriage, hurling open the doors and banging them behind us as the wind roared. Not to be bad or delinquent. Just because we could.

One autumnal Saturday, Mick's mum insisted Mick took Robbie – who was even more neurotic than Jeeves, our (wait for it) dog-to-be – on our latest tour. After hitting the end of the line at Amersham, and criss-crossing Circle Line platforms until we were dizzy, we were headed down the Fulham Palace Road on top of a 220 when Robbie started to heave the gorge. A hasty retreat was beaten, and we tumbled onto the street, while Robbie continued to vomit in the gutter.

But what was that other noise, beyond the petrol roar and heaving guts? On the other side of the street were hordes of shiny, happy people. Festooned with rosettes. "Can I have your thing?" Mick enquired of one and, sure enough, he became the owner of his first piece of official Fulham FC merchandise. All silk and pleats. The vibe was palpable. We were hooked. No more Twin Rovers. No more Saturday sojourns for Robbie. It was the terraces forever. The double over Leicester at Christmas, Sniffer Clarke, George Cohen – late of World Cup chart domination – Johnny Haynes, Bobby Robson, just a few old pennies to swing the turnstile, glossy programmes, soon to go colour.

It was all part of the mid-'60s spine tingle. And, at twelve, almost too much to bear. Even Bond girl, Honor Blackman, supported Fulham. And Dad had played opposite Connery's wife Diane Cilento in a movie called *The Angel Who Pawned Her Heart*. So cool.

I've been a hopelessly besotted Fulham supporter ever since and suffer pangs of guilt whenever theatre rehearsals are compromised by football fixtures. My best excuse was a tooth abscess so that I could meet Dom at Euston Station, and travel to Maine Road for the dreamy FA Cup victory over Birmingham. Afterwards, we partied at George Best's club, Slack Alice's. George was there, being grumpy.

As for the rehearsal, it had been due to end at one, until a late decision to keep us on after lunch, so we could hang around "just in case we were needed". I've never learned much from hanging around so I made an executive decision and gave the best method performance of my life, even breaking into a real sweat from the 'pain' and taking several minutes to recover – not until I was a hundred yards up the road. I wasn't missed. Not really. And it was worth it for the grin on Dom's face at the barrier.

Dad hated football culture. He was athletic, and competitive in his own way, but gangs were anathema to him. He had broken away from a puritanical background and an instinctive mistrust of culture. This philistine mix was deeply irksome to his sensitivities and spurred him on – despite the disapproval chiming in his ears – to win the RADA gold medal and startling early success.

How and where all that began to go wrong, hell only knows. The socio-cultural landslide certainly didn't help but it was the maternal intransigence

Mick and Robbie

that cast the longest shadow. Dad went from loathing to loving his mother in a sad and sudden way that was unpredictable and unsettling in equal measure.

After he'd left home when I was fifteen – following a horrid nervous breakdown – and when I was asked for the umpteenth time what had happened to him, and told how talented and inspiring he was, I eventually lost the will to explain. All I knew was that, as the oldest, I got the best of Dad – when he was still in love with Mum, and they laughed like drains, and the house was full of the most extraordinary mix of people, all embraced with the same vulnerable open-heartedness.

Dad's work rate was phenomenal and, at his peak, when he was starring in his own plays, all things seemed possible. He was stubborn about his work, and fell foul of some powerful people, but that wasn't the real problem. My theory is, he was simply born a few years too early.

The nub of it was what we still loosely call rock and roll. Having only just broken away as a young firebrand himself, within the blink of Brando's eye, a new generation was flooding his world like a tsunami.

Dad's best pal was the dashing actor/singer, Dennis Quilley. I loved his visits to the house. He sang and played the flute and ate like Henry the Eighth. Just his appearance at the front door made my adrenalin rush. Heaven in the hall. But he was kind of old school. Donald Swann, of Flanders and Swann – with whom Dad wrote a musical called *Wild Thyme* – was definitely old school. As was Mum's patron, Joyce Grenfell, who supported her early appearances in review. Review was basically stand-up.

Mum – or Charlotte Mitchell as she had rebranded herself – was a poet, actress, wife and zookeeper. She also wrote all her own material.

And darned socks.

Another visitor to the house was Albert Finney, married briefly to Mum and Dad's friend, Jane Wenham. I thought he was just fine, crawling and whooping down the hall at Christmas, dressed in a native Indian headdress. But Albie represented a tribe that Dad was uneasy with. The naturalistic breed of actor descending relentlessly on the West End from the industrial towns of northern England. There was no animosity: far from it. But Dad had a problem with people not doing things properly, in the way RADA had taught him – the 'correct' pronunciation, the way to stand and use your hands – even at home, in day-today life.

This seemed to stem partly from how he felt about his 'lower middle class' mother, his family's narrow world view and the way in which they had initially disparaged the performing arts. It was an overreaction on Dad's part. He could have been and done anything: he was agile of mind and body, but something was strangling his soul. Maybe he just had too much to prove. Maybe it was

Possessions

Possessions
they are without grace
how they shout about the place.
How is it that they never tire?
"Insure us against theft and fire!"

I would rather
stay in bed
and index treasure
in my head.

Possessions, a poem by Mum

winning the talent shows on the pier as a boy with his beloved sister Nancy, then having to hide their prizes from the parents. And hide their joy.

Meanwhile, Richard Briers had moved in two doors up from us. He was a few years younger than Dad and had a laissez-faire and gentle confidence about him. Dad took over from him in Ayckbourn's *Relatively Speaking* in the West End. Maybe Dad felt it should have been the other way round. Either way, I was so proud of him and his star dressing room. I certainly didn't feel like first reserve when I took over from Peter Firth in *Spring Awakening* a few years later. It was a pleasure to fill his shoes.

Five years after Dad left – for northern Scotland – I was at the Old Vic in Peter Hall's first season as Director of the National Theatre. This was 1974 and Peter's new ethos epitomised what had happened during the '60s, from the days when Olivier was king and Norman Wisdom was the top cinema box-office star to the era of Finney and Osborne.

Our Old Vic Company – assembled to perform *The Tempest, Romeo and Juliet* and *Spring Awakening* – was just about as eclectic as you could get. Although Peter struggled to apply his beloved democracy to a company on starkly disparate wages and with decidedly unequal opportunities, his achievement in hauling together this astoundingly diverse group of talents was worth a knighthood in itself. Gielgud – at seventy – was returning to the role of Prospero, and Dad's best mate, Quilley, now a golden National boy from the Olivier era – was alongside him as Caliban. But Peter was a maverick. Stalwarts were all very well but he had also cast a bunch of mercurial hippies in key roles and offered Beryl Reid and Jenny Agutter their first tastes of the Bard. Oh, and just for good measure, Arthur Lowe was on board.

One upshot of this admirable leap of faith was that after the first night of *The Tempest* – which, on account of John Bury's lumbering set, Gielgud had dubbed 'Theatre in the Way' – Michael Feast, who thus far had provided a delightful Ariel, took his role too much to heart, and literally vanished. The apparent cause was high spirits, a tumble or two, and a bout of his bête noire, depression.

Strangely, this was also what afflicted my father. Maybe Shakespearian sprites are particularly prone to it. Of course, manic depression is called bipolar now, which makes me think of bears stranded on floating ice – just about as depressing as it gets. Manic depression described the foul affliction pretty well.

Michael – 'Micky' – simply didn't turn up for the second night. Plucky understudy, Stephen Williams, was rushed on in his place, never in a million magic wands having believed this would really be his fate. He was in good shape but a bit hefty for a fairy and could only just about squeeze into the taffeta. All went well until the scene in which Ariel pretends to be a harpy and descends from somewhere precipitously high onto a dining table replete with shiny plastic chickens and wobbly goblets.

Unfortunately, the guys in the flies had not been advised of Ariel's overnight weight gain, causing the substitute fairy to plummet at about a hundred miles an hour and nearly break his legs on the table. Under normal circumstances, the lords are dumbstruck and terrified. By the time Stephen had verified the health of his legs and reminded himself that he was made of air, we had just about stopped laughing and reminded ourselves how terrified we were. The following night, Stephen was lowered so slowly he started his speech with his legs still dangling five inches above a chicken. The moment he said, "You are three men of sin…", his descent resumed. Plop. Respect, Stephen.

By the way, most of these lords' scenes are pretty boring, and I had the misfortune to be playing Francisco, a part which – wisely – is usually cut. Francisco has only one short speech, which is even more boring than most of the lords' speeches. Out of deference to the Bard and unintended cruelty to me, Peter had decided to cut nothing from the play. Even the last-minute rubbish that had been conjured by the Bard's co-writers. My speech at least afforded the audience an opportunity to clear their throats for twenty-eight seconds. It was as if they had been rehearsed. The coughs would start at the very moment I said "Sir, he may live…" and end with uncanny precision at "…he came alive to land". By which time I had died again.

Forty-eight hours earlier, Sir John had died.

Or so Peter thought.

The technical run-through started at ten o'clock and lasted until some indeterminate time, probably long after opening night. Instead of lots of airy-fairy lighting effects and gauze, the magic of this Prospero involved chains, trucks, voluminous costumes, and the rare employment of the infamous Old Vic trapdoor. Late in the play, Prospero is tying things up: generally pardoning, freeing and blessing everybody.

The high spot of the maestro's shenanigans is the revelation of lovers, Ferdinand and Miranda, joyfully playing chess. In our production, they were in fact underneath the stage, cunningly positioned on a sort of dumb waiter. I don't recall the precise engineering details but the plan was for the trap door to open just as they were elevated to stage level, whereupon they could live happily ever after and we could all bugger off round the pub.

Sir Peter was at the back of the stalls, making sure he could hear everything (except me) and Sir John was – incorrectly – standing on the trap door. The outcome was that Sir John, perhaps anticipating the demise of his loyal fairy, also suddenly vanished, landing – yellow tights akimbo – on top of Jenny

Agutter, Rupert Fraser and the unfortunate chess set. Pale, and beaded with sweat, Peter hurtled from the shadows – even faster than Stephen Williams had shot from the sky – yelling "Sir John, Sir John!" Sir John found his way back to the stage almost as fast, no damage done, elegantly flapping and more concerned for young Jenny and Rupert than his own old self.

Micky's infamous absence led to a sort of show trial in the green room at the top of the theatre. Peter had clearly made up his mind what to do next but had to navigate some entrenched opinions first. Most of the youngsters were unphased: we'd got through it, it was cool, look to the future.

But Quilley and Joseph O'Connor were unhappy. Unprofessionalism was not to be tolerated. Look to the past.

Peter was a master of political diplomacy. It was his defining glory.

In the end, Micky got off with a two-hour 'half'. In other words, he had to arrive at the theatre an hour and a half before everyone else. And everyone else had to stop taking drugs. Ho ho. It was not my finest hour, but I still recall the modest limerick I ascribed to the crisis:

> "An irregular actor named Feast,
> In attendance has lately decreased.
> Though O'Connor said "Out!
> He's a rake and a lout!"
> This actor has not been released."

As good a summary as any I suppose.

The wondrous Arthur Lowe, who played Stephano in *The Tempest*, kept himself utterly to himself. I don't recall him addressing a single word to anyone.

Ever.

Sir John was utterly forgiving of Micky, as he was of me when I reminded him where we had last met.

Mum and Dad had been in his theatre company at the Lyric Hammersmith in '54 and I would sometimes be left at the stage door in a large pram. I was six months old and given to rowdiness.

One afternoon Sir John enquired of Mum, "Charlotte, have you got that wretched baby with you?" Twenty years later, I confessed.

I confessed to Sir John again as Marius in a TV movie of *Les Miserables* in 1977. Whether as Prospero or as Gillenormand, Sir John forgave sublimely.

***

Life at the Vic could be chaotic, but it was once we were on the road, taking *The Tempest* to Bristol and *Spring Awakening* to Nottingham, that the hippies really came into their own. Peter Firth, twenty, radiant and glorious from Broadway conquest in *Equus*. Veronica Quilligan, just seventeen, plucked like a shining, shameless shamrock to play Juliet. Julie Covington and Dana Gillespie, fresh from *Godspell* and *Jesus Christ Superstardom*. David Dixon, Ford Prefect to be. Patti Love. Mike Kitchen. Bryan Brown, Aussie whizz-kid who went on to play opposite Tom Cruise in *Cocktail*. The list goes on…

On the subject of cocks, Peter Hall's preference for cutting nothing had allowed Bill Bryden's innovative *Spring Awakening* to be presented in full uncensored glory, including the controversial borstal masturbation scene. Bryan was game for anything, and it fell to him to initiate the wanking contest by exposing himself downstage in front of some very affronted customers. Several of them would usually leave but only once it had dawned on them what he was actually doing.

I wonder what Bryan's audition had entailed. He wasn't shy. But this was the era we were in. Experiment, shock, pushing the boundaries, love, peace, danger.

And that season embodied it all. Marijuana was not the enemy: it was one of our co-stars. And we all delivered onstage. That was the bottom line.

I think Joseph O'Connor regretted kicking up such a stink over Mickey. In the end, he kind of capitulated and just shook his head a lot. It was the norm for soothing smoke to swirl through the corridors of The Oxford Playhouse or Bristol Hippodrome. Maybe he became permanently, passively stoned. Better anyway than the dreaded booze which was soon to claim a couple of veteran Olivier company members. Casualties of the revolution. *Turn and face it. Ch-ch-ch-ch-ching-ching.* Bums on seats.

The thinnest edge of the fractal wedge was the so-called mobile tour of *Romeo and Juliet*, featuring Peter and the sublimely splendid Michael Kitchen as Romeo, opposite Veronica, with Beryl Reid playing the Nurse. We were supposed to be "taking culture to the shires", but it was a deliberately low-budget affair – hence its mobility – and it was somewhat embarrassing to roll into Basildon to be greeted by makeshift banners announcing, "Beryl Reid and The National Theatre in Romeo and Juliet". We were meant to be a theatre co-operative, not a star-studded variety show. Why not throw in The Tiller Girls for good measure? We did our best, but we didn't really live up to the billing. It should have read "A bunch of desperados attempt to perform Romeo and Juliet". Actually, we did it at the Vic for a week, and it went OK, but it was, for all director Bill Bryden's genius, perhaps a little unloved.

What was loved was the pub, which was our hub in most towns. The one up the road from the Vic stage door was home, and others were sought and adopted on a bespoke roll. Veronica, who at seventeen really could look thirteen, the right age for Juliet, could also talk her way into any pub in the British Isles. It was so obvious she was underage that this became, in a gloriously Irish way, the very reason she couldn't possibly be. I mean, why would she be trying to get served in a pub when she looked five years too young unless she suffered from some rare genetic predisposition to age very slowly? So, give us a whisky!

You just didn't argue with Veronica. Beryl Reid certainly didn't. And Veronica was great to work with. As Melchior and Wanda, we had to enact a violent rape scene. Her focus and fearlessness were fantastic. We met again forty years later at St Paul's School, where both our daughters had obtained scholarships after going through the state system. Magic. Veronica pitches up at my music gigs now. And "time falls wanking to the floor".

To give us our due, our digs were often shite whereas the pub offered respite and comfort. We became increasingly like a touring rock band. David Dixon took his guitar everywhere, and Mike and I often played it. Most strategically important was our ubiquitous soundtrack, *Band on the Run,* by Wings. It summed us up, in fact to the point where we all thought we *were* a band, and Wedekind and Shakespeare but minor inconveniences. The boogiebox would beam out 'Bluebird' and 'Jet' wherever we went, shimmer-booming down every incense-infused corridor. This soundtrack was our soul: it fed us and made us better as performers.

A word for Gerry Ryder, master of the penny whistle and seeker-out of generous hostelries. Gerry took eccentricity to a giddy new level. Highly intelligent, gawky, in love with Cheshire and possessed of a medieval singing voice and a rare gamut of traditional folksongs, he was neither modern nor fashionable and looked decidedly rum alongside the god-like Firth, beautiful Agutter and majestic Gillespie. But in a way he was our talisman. He adored beer and darts and snooker and was like a gatekeeper to another world.

We had been at the Northcott in Exeter and had three days off before returning to the Vic. I suggested a dash to my beloved Coverack. Peter hired a car and Gerry insisted on coming too. Once he'd divested himself of all available cash – which took about two hours in the Paris (the pub), he adopted his favoured fundraising technique and played the penny whistle so passionately that, either out of pity or admiration, someone bought him more beer. I never fathomed how this worked, especially in surly city hostelries.

Anyway, we spent three days swimming, singing, drinking, not sleeping and generally careering around the headland. Most of the time, nobody had a clue where anyone else was, either corporally or metaphorically, particularly on the last night when we found our way by some miracle to Mears beach.

We were around a fire, on the grassy cliff above the rocks, with various locals and lunatics, and Gerry was playing his whistle, when suddenly his shanty squeaked to a halt, replaced by Gerry's voice seeming to plunge into another dimension. There was a tragic chill in the air as we beheld, fifteen feet below, spreadeagled in a rock pool, the limp, groaning actor. An ambulance arrived eventually and, next morning, we headed back to London by train, Peter having driven the hire car into a concealed rock on the verge of a very narrow lane and writing it off.

Abetted by his supreme relaxation techniques, Gerry had only broken his forearm and was able to appear onstage as the deeply innocent Otto in Spring Awakening almost as soon as we got back to the Vic. A plaster cast and two nicotine-stained fingers told the tale. No one noticed.

5: Break

I'm missing Pleydell Avenue. Always will. I still walk down that road sometimes; it's not far from here. Can still see Richard Briers through the window of Number 16 and hear Mick's Yugoslavian mum yelling at him in the hall.

"Why you go football? Take Robbie!"

So let's go back again, to where all this diversion and confusion began, to where The Beatles got rock and roll, and how that generation set off in a new direction of innocence and experiment. Learning instinctively like schools of whales communicating in new voices at different depths, not manic, but riding the rollers, and barrows of apes, rolling through the canopies, relaxed in the eye of a storm, calm in high motion. Hanging from Mum as she swings and points – eat this, try that, stay close, trust… Different highs and lows. Love-driven.

And I'm still 'racing at sums' with Albert Boniface at St Peter's.

Bernard Braden was a star. But then so was Mr Bayliss. All one to me. Albert Finney was a star, and so was Roofy. Mr Bayliss, the class teacher who was so concerned for the future of the world he took the time to explain the Cuban Missile Crisis to a room full of nine and ten-year-olds.

Lanky Herbert Marshall promptly organised a game of war in the playground at break, machine gun noises and "Who do you want to be, Russia or America?" Fucking hell, it was a change from Germany and Blighty, but my blood froze. I hated all that war shit. Batman boxing gloves: fine. But not sub-machine guns and nuclear fission. "Over you go, rat-a-tat-tat, what the fuck is that?" "A rat eating your leg mate. Just the fallout." I digress? Not really.

Dad was a peacenik of the best kind. Did three months in the Scrubs for not joining up after World War Two ended. Conducted his own defence. Brilliant. It led to him working for the Howard League for Penal Reform. Befriending prisoners, helping them when they came out. It could be unnerving having a GBH customer for Sunday lunch. Steve was back in pretty sharpish. But Johnny Cox was a success story. True Eastender: sharp suits and winkle-pickers. I loved him. Mum and Dad took a lot on. Often against the tide. Headlong.

Mum, by Peter Sellers

I was lucky to be encouraged to think. It was and is my survival. Just as an orangutan is taught to relate to its immediate environment, I was taught to relate to the universe beyond. Bit high-faluting? Maybe. But the '60s was genuinely a great era and I'm so pleased I got some of it. Bernard Braden was at the forefront of political satire and had his own show. It was where Esther Rantzen cut her teeth. He was also a family friend and was so impressed and wryly amused by my Mr Bayliss-inspired commentary on the Cuban Crisis, I was invited onto his show, pre-recorded. Here was this nine-year-old being so anxious and earnest it almost took the horror out of what nearly happened. Nearly. The audience laughed anyway.

Peter Sellers' stand-in, Vic Galluci, was my stand-in on *Memoirs of a Survivor.* Mum had dated Sellers, appeared in the Goons, knew Spike. George Martin worked with Sellers and the Goons, The Beatles loved their humour. George Harrison produced movies by the Pythons, natural successors to the Goons, and Lennon famously said, "The only thing we're serious about is not being serious."

And here comes the strangest little irony and crossing of the lines and generations… with Dad and The Beatles at the heart of it.

6: Song and Dance

Dad balked at The Beatles and even referred to them as yobs – a moniker he also bestowed on me in certain moments. *Songs for Swinging Lovers*, Peter, Paul and Mary and *West Side Story* were as groovy as our record collection got. Mind you, *West Side Story* was breakthrough for me. I remember Mum and Dad raving about it after the first night in London and bringing home the cast album. The rhythmic stuff I adored. Like wrestling with a tiger on the moon. And Dad loved it too. But *Revolver* was a different story. Like I said, he was born just a few years too early. There are correct ways of being different.

Revolver, Dad bought me for my twelfth birthday – a guitar too. Oh joy! There *is* a heaven. It was also the year I played David Copperfield on TV and 'grew up' into a twenty-six year-old Ian McKellen.

Breaking news… I just learned – now, in 2021 – that Episode Three of that *David Copperfield* still exists; at least a recording of the recording does. All the official early episodes were wiped. The British Film Institute says, "David is played in adulthood by *Ian McKellen*, and in childhood by twelve-year-old *Christopher Guard*, who is excellent in the surviving third episode (in which he appears in every scene) and its unedited studio footage, which shows his assurance when even experienced actors required retakes."

Blimey. I suppose that almost makes up for the rest of my stuff being wiped. I didn't feel like a hero. I was just getting on with it. It felt as normal as learning what leaves not to eat in the rainforest. Know your toxins.

For an interview with the local paper, I was photographed in a 'Lennon' cap – a style Lennon had borrowed from Dylan. And there were two Dylan tracks on *Blowin' In The Wind,* the Peter, Paul and Mary album that had somehow found its way into the family record collection. Something was happening in my spine and loins. Although Dad and I still sang Gilbert and Sullivan at the piano, this was something else. Sexy art. Head and soul. To this day, the blues, folk and rock are my staple. Can't act without them. Can't breathe properly. My best acting auditions were always after a cathartic bellow in a rock dive.

After grade five, I abandoned classical piano, and didn't go back to it until I discovered song writing, and chords written as guitar tabs. These I then transferred back to the piano like an opened-out, horizontal guitar giving up its mysteries. I learned to make it sound dynamic and sweet. Instinctively. And I began to understand what the heck I'd been trying to play all those years. The nocturnes and études. I'd hear some of them on the radio and I'd think, "I know that tune". Well, of course I did – I'd been fumbling through it for years with the uninspiring Mrs Dollar at my side. Ticking boxes, while Mick and StoodyWoo and the gang peered through the front hedge laughing, and I ached to be at the 'grane' playing football until dusk fell. How horribly uncultured of me. But not really. I didn't want to be correct, I wanted to enjoy music.

Dad tried to learn guitar with me, but it hurt too much. He was pretty nifty on the piano, but the stinging dents in the virgin fingertips took him by surprise, even though he was using a borrowed classical guitar with soft, low-lying nylon strings. I was on a purchased beast from King Street Music Store, with steel strings set up like an instrument of torture.

Not for wimps. I persevered while many fainthearts hung their birthday guitars on bedroom walls and never suffered again. Dad lasted three weeks.

Once I knew E minor and A minor, I was off. 'GuineaPig Farm', a paean to my fantastically fertile cavies, was an early 'hit'. I loved the kaleidoscope of rhythm, tune, words and chords, even if I was only using two. The possibilities. The juggling. The urgent desire to create a song transcended the pain, and I wore the calluses with pride.

We listened to the mint copy of *Revolver* together, one Saturday morning. Relaxed and breezy. No plays or cats. Just me and Dad. I so wanted him to love it. He was my hero. He did. He loved 'Eleanor Rigby' and 'Yellow Submarine'. But not 'Taxman' or 'Dr Robert'. Too much 'prang-prang' as he called it.

And then along comes 'Tomorrow Never Knows'. Well, it sure didn't. Not an iota of connection here. Dad looked affronted. We thought there was something wrong with the record. Seriously. That's how ears were tuned back then. Nicely. We returned the offending purchase to the Spinning Disc in the Chiswick High Road, only to be persuaded by the proprietor – Smiling Beard – that track seven on side two was *meant* to sound like that. Of course. Oh dear. Ho ho.

It all came together perfectly when, as if he'd known all about our trip to the Spinning Disc, the restless sculptor of 'Tomorrow Never Knows', John Lennon, somehow conspired to include my dad on the recording of 'I Am the Walrus'. Yep. How daft is that? Dad had played Edgar in a radio production of *King Lear*, which happened to be on air just as John, George Martin and co were looking for extra noises and backing vocals for the outro. And what do you know? There's Dad's voice, clear as a bell, diction to die for, during the "*umpa, umpa stick it up your jumper*" section. Dad even gets credited these days. Totally fab. The '60s were like that. Analogue magic.

The dream is not over.

I'm in the Klimt bar of the Vienna Hilton. It's 1976. I'm chatting with Stephen Sondheim. We're working on the movie of *A Little Night Music* with Elizabeth Taylor and Diana Rigg.

It's the second time I've worked with Diana. We played Venus and Adonis on the radio, though it was too late by then to find our way onto a Beatles album. We would meet again in '96 on a movie partly financed by Eddie Van Halen. What a sweet bloke. On crutches, with little Wolfie, his son. Why crutches? Mix of booze and stage antics, he said. RIP. Thinking of you Valerie.

There was nothing rock-and-roll about Stephen Sondheim. He wore brown cords and tweeds and swept his hair disinterestedly to one side. He smoked cigarettes and drank whisky. He's probably the brightest man I've ever met. In a wry, shy, razor-sharp way, he has a sublime mix of emotional and intellectual intelligence. His eyes would roll and his lids slowly blink as he illuminated vast truths alongside sprinkles of minutiae with equal attention to detail.

Stephen had been encouraged to use marijuana for medical reasons because the whisky he adored didn't always agree with him. In the gloom of that Viennese bar, there was something ironical about sharing thoughts and anecdotes with the man who had co-written *West Side Story*. That show turned me on to something beyond classical music. Something blue and sexy. Yet Stephen prided himself on his pure, traditional roots, a preference for opera and a mistrust of rock and roll.

When we were recording the cast album of *Night Music*, Stephen wandered lugubriously in from the control room and announced that I was the only one singing in time. We were performing the tricksy, multi-layered 'A Weekend in the Country' and I was amongst Broadway and Hollywood royalty: the elegantly brilliant Larry Guittard; his fictional love rival, the extraordinary Len Cariou; Hermione Gingold; Diana, and of course Liz, apparently aspiring to be Judy Garland.

Recording booths are different from open stages. Less margin for embellishment. I think my Gilbert and Sullivan sessions had come in handy. That and some of the more experimental prog rock I'd listened to. The Mikado meets Jethro Tull. The King Crimson Pirates of Penzance.

One cloudy afternoon, when we all had nothing better to do, several of us adjourned from the sprawling lobby to my by now deeply unexciting room, and Stephen Sondheim came along too. We'd been in a swanky Viennese

A Little Night Music poster

hotel (the Hilton was posher back then) long enough for it to have lost its honeymoon appeal. Here were music editor Steve Livingston and his young wife Sandi, me and my girlfriend Lesley Dunlop, I think Larry, and probably one or two others now vanished in the haze.

We smoked a joint or two and giggled a bit and, before the afternoon had totally unravelled us, Stephen suggested a game. He loved games. His New York home was full of them. Not snooker or baseball, but fiendishly delicious games for the brain. You can see it in his work. The perfection of knots unravelled, puzzles solved, 3D jigsaws completed in a blaze of triumphant dramatic irony. The illusion of simple desires, the profundity of the apparently trite, the sweep of Sophocles, the playfulness of Oscar Wilde.

And all put to a glorious fine weave of incomparable music. An embrace of perfection. OK, plaudits done; Stephen has had no shortage of those. And anyway, I was a Beatles fan at heart.

The game on this occasion was as simple as it was fraught with pitfalls. I suspect Stephen suggested it partly because he had such a cool-uncool way of kicking it off. Shall I start? said he, eyes blink-rolling. Sure. The idea – and you might have played this – is to say, "I have never…" and then reveal something you've never done. And you must be obsessively honest.

Of course, the game's success depends on the experiences of the players involved. If you've never brushed your teeth or picked your nose, you're likely to score lots of points, one for each person who *has* either brushed or picked or both.

Stephen instantly took a commanding lead by announcing that he had never worn 'blue jeans' or picked up a guitar, which for a forty-something American in 1976, seemed nigh on impossible. Especially for a songwriter. But it was true. And we never really recovered from that early deficit. Besides, something gruesome happened to take my eye off the ball.

This was a proper Hollywood movie with a big budget. It bought my first little house. But unlike Liz Taylor, I had no guarantee I'd ever earn that kind of money again so, after a few weeks of splashing out our silly 'per diems' – paid in cash – on embarrassingly expensive bottles of wine and lavish Austrian fare, we took to shopping at the local supermarket and saving a fortune. This went down like a pile of cold sick with the staff, who were accustomed to rich people, not actors more used to BBC wages saving up for a small house. A few days earlier, having checked the wad of stashed schillings in the bureau drawer, I became convinced that some of it was missing. This I reported to the reception desk, they passed it on to hotel security and I proceeded to forget all about it.

Until…

With cello and dog collar

While I was desperately racking my brains for something that I had *not* done, but that Steve and Steve and Lesley and Sandi and probably Larry and the figures in the haze may have, the phone rang. The mix of the frustrating game, the spliffs, the supermarket red and the view of Viennese raincloud had caused something akin to a coma so that, when the voice on the other end announced in clipped, commanding tones that I was speaking to the hotel detective, it felt like being raised from the dead by a grenade. I must come to your room immediately. Shit. Thai sticks were like Class A in Vienna. I might be jailed for life. Several lives. Is there honey still for tea? Help!

I did my best. No. No, you can't. No one in the room took much notice. I had *never* been phoned on a Sunday afternoon in Vienna by a hotel detective when the room was full of marijuana smoke. No score. Fuck. "What?… No, my girlfriend is ill… No, she doesn't need to see a doctor. She's fine. Except she needs complete rest. I'll come down… What?… No, don't. I found the money". This was like two episodes of *Fawlty Towers* that had yet to be written. "You want us all to leave?" Sandi had cottoned on. "Yes. Probably. Hotel detective. Wants to see me downstairs. Lobby. Yes. Thanks. See you at dinner maybe". Waft, amble, depart.

I felt pale but had probably turned green. Facing a detective at teatime with nothing in your stomach but wine and smoke is not for the fainthearted. Why the fuck did I say there was money missing? There probably wasn't anyway. I'd have happily given him all of it just to shut up and go away.

We're in the middle of the vast lobby, with the two resident violinists cranking up the Strauss. Help! People are eating piles of torte and drinking gallons of porcelain tea. Being stoned at least enabled me to stare unemotionally into my inquisitor's eyes, denying all and playing dead. Braindead. Like a vertical, wide-eyed possum. The ploy worked. He left in the end, disgruntled, evidently disappointed at not having found an excuse to fingerprint and arrest an impoverished chambermaid. Gaoling Stephen Sondheim would have been more stimulating. Not that that would have happened. We probably had some kind of diplomatic immunity. The Viennese government had invested in the film.

While all this tomfoolery was unravelling, the writer of the finest comedy film of all time was plying his trade in the hotel room of my fictional opposite number, the beautiful and incorrigibly flirtatious Lesley-Anne Down. Her boyfriend was Bruce Robinson, creator of *Withnail and I* and he was over for a sort of working holiday. While Lesley-Anne was out filming, Bruce would hammer at his typewriter while guzzling brandy and compromising the hotel wine vaults. Boy, could Bruce drink! And boy, was it worth it!

At the end of a hard day of being a genius, Bruce's bronze metal bin would be inspected for damage by Lesley-Anne. Just the one empty brandy bottle and two empty wine bottles. "Brucie, you naughty boy!" Two geniuses on the same floor, one taking medicinal herbs, the other just medicating. David Wimbury was our second assistant director. He went on to work as a producer on both *Withnail* and *Life of Brian*. Cool shit saloon.

Diana was the coolest though. This was Emma Peel waltzing in cream-cake, Oscar-winning dresses. She waltzed me round the Theatre an der Wein. It didn't look as if she was leading, but despite my innate sense of rhythm, as a dancer I have two left feet. Well one left foot actually. On the right.

Diana's rule was either lead or catch up. And that was a rule for life. I liked her a lot. We just kind of got each other.

Another visitor was Republican Senator John Warner. No relation to the film brothers; in terms of artistic talent, he'd received a rather paltry serving at birth. He was married to Liz Taylor. The trade-off seemed to be that she would get into politics and he would get into acting; which was a bizarre idea since neither was suited for either. Warner pursued lovely screenwriter Hugh Wheeler like a lugubrious bear on heat. Hugh sidled up beside me on set one day. "Just keep talking", he said. "John Warner wants me to write him a fucking film script. He can't act and I don't know anything about cowboys or World War One air pilots". I obliged with some circuitous drivel about cellos or something and eventually the bored bear withdrew. His trip was fleeting. And anyway, Liz was still far more interested in her ex, Richard Burton.

It was Hugh who suggested I give Liz a call. She was the only one staying at the legendary Imperial Hotel, where breakfast cost more than a two-bed flat in Chiswick; and she had hurt her leg. This was genuine but paranoia had set in among some of the New Yorkers – fair enough, given Liz's reputation for absenteeism. In fact, she was as good as gold throughout this shoot and was genuinely a bit accident prone.

"She likes young people, and she's missing her kids", said Hugh. "Must be lonely stuck on her own at the Imperial. Call her up". We'd only been in Vienna a few days and I'd barely recovered from the shock of getting the gig in the first place. I'd met Liz once, at a singing rehearsal, but that was with other people, not alone. Calling her up cold was daunting. She answered, "Oh sure! Hi Christopher! Well, why not? Come right on over! See you at seven".

Blimey.

There were only two of Liz's entourage still in tow: a dry South African secretary, who's name I'm afraid I forget, and the gloriously camp hairdresser, Arthur, who had just received a consignment of grass from his mother.

Liz was sat up in a mini four-poster bed daubed in a pink nightdress. In her right hand, a glass of champagne, and in her left – well, guess what? We all had some of both. 'All' being Arthur, me, Lesley and one or two people I didn't know who turned up later. It's a bit hazy, apart from the scariest bit.

There was a six-octave upright piano alongside Liz's bed. It had been brought in especially so she could practice 'Send in the Clowns'. I knew why. A couple of days earlier, music editor Steve had smuggled out Liz's first attempt to record the legendary song. Instead of talk-singing like Glynis Johns, she had actually attempted to sing like Judy Garland. This was inadvisable. Definitely room for improvement. Hence the piano.

But the addition of the piano was not an improvement for me. In one of the inevitable hiatuses, some bright spark mentioned that I wrote songs and played the piano. "Oh, my son does too!" chirped Liz. "Ain't you gonna play us something?" Help! All eyes were on me. I was trapped. "What you gonna sing?" In a crimson-cheeked daze, I ghosted through a ballad called 'Wave to Me'. All pretty straightforward except that three feet away, sat up in bed, two spliffs to the wind, violet eyes mesmerised, smiling gleefully, was the most famous woman in the world.

There was a genuine bonding. Innocent and playful. And when Liz heard that Lesley had worked with Burton the year before we grew closer. Lesley had played Mary Churchill to Burton's Winston in a BBC special directed by Herbie Wise.

I had met Burton one evening. He was sober and talked of little else but drinking but had the grace and presence of mind to recall that his first West End acting job was understudying my dad. "Guard? Guard? I knew your father". Well, well.

"How is he? How does he look? What does he talk about?" Liz asked all about her volatile soulmate. Shyly at first: then more boldly. She missed him a lot. Missed a good laugh and a good row and a good Welsh shag. We did our best to fill an unfillable void. Not literally.

One night, she whisked us off to the scene of my first meeting with her, the Theatre an der Wien. Fans hurled themselves at Liz's limo like she was Elvis, which was fantastic fun, and almost compensated for five acts of Verdi at his grumpiest. Liz's visiting mother, Sara, had insisted on attending the first night of *Don Carlos*, a depressing opera that seems to last roughly three weeks and comes a close second to the lobby detective in my top ten Austrian horror stories.

Once Liz, Sara, Lesley, Arthur, me and the scary secretary had been inserted into a box, the entertainment ensued. Liz spent most of the time out of her seat, round the back, drinking champagne and toting on Arthur's mother's herb. I was getting tired of bloody marijuana to be honest but, by now, its omnipresence had entered the realms of farce. It seemed to follow us wherever we went. Like sachertorte and violins.

Despite Sara's beseeching, Liz only ventured out whenever the singing stopped. After each bout of mournful bellowing, the audience clapped for nearly as long as the aria had lasted and upturned faces lit up as Liz enthusiastically applauded what she had just been blithely ignoring.

Meanwhile Arthur and the sour secretary were arguing about nothing in particular other than that they hated each other. Don't ask me why. Ask a dog or a cat. When the entourage was larger, their squabbles had probably been absorbed into the general mayhem; exposed like this it was lucky that opera tends to be pretty loud, even when it's quiet.

More champagne had been called for and, as the little back door flew open, revealing one of the ubiquitous *Rauchen Verboten* signs on the wall opposite and smoke billowed from our 'cabin,' a waiter lurched forward with a champagne bucket on a huge silver salver. Forget *A Little Night Music*, this was rivalling *A Night at the Opera*. It was all too much for the waiter. The bucket slid and fell, glasses smashed and Liz broke into a fit of giggles. "Elizabeth!" breathed Sara with graceful ferocity. I think she wanted to wrestle Arthur to the floor, punch the secretary on the nose and stop Elizabeth's pocket money for a month, but she kept her counsel like a female Jeeves. The butler; not the dog.

I'm probably being unfair to *Don Carlos*. To be honest, I remember very little about it, eclipsed as it was by the extraordinary sitcom being played out in the box above.

It was like a reversal of when, as kids, in the '60s, we'd go to Television Centre to watch Mum as a regular in the sitcom, *Not In Front of the Children*, with Wendy Craig. Rehearsals could be tense, long-winded affairs requiring the warm-up man to appeal to the audience to laugh again at the retakes. And again. Hence the forced guffawing. Not canned, just bad laughter acting. At *Don Carlos*, Sara was like a cool-*down* girl, imploring us to realistically shut the fuck up. Not in Front of the Audience.

A few weeks later, long after Sara had gone home to recover, perhaps by way of apology for the billowing and bellowing, Liz had secretly bought us tickets for something completely fantastic. As if by musical osmosis, our National Theatre soundtrack caught up with us in Vienna.

Paul McCartney's *Wings Over the World* tour, bypassing Basildon, had arrived at the Wiener Stadthalle. Bingbloody-go.

On the day of the concert Steve, Sandi, Lesley and I had made a dash for the Austrian Alps where we were busy making a snow sculpture of Len Cariou and drinking mountain man soup. It was only when we phoned in to the production office on our way 'home' that Liz's surprise was sprung and Steve completed the drive like a cross between Ayrton Senna and a teenage yeti.

Regarding the snowman, I like to think it is still there. If anyone deserved a monument it was Len – or Loo Caroo as he became affectionately known. No-one could roll his eyes like Loo – the personification of gusto. I provided the snowman with a crooning Loo-style singing voice. Maybe the echoes are still there too.

We settled into our seats just as the opening riff of 'Jet' rang out. 'Jet' with lasers. Oh yes. First time lasers had been used on this scale in a rock concert. I looked along our row, half expecting to see Peter Firth and Gerry and Veronica. But it was Liz and Arthur and Arthur's nemesis, and for once they weren't squabbling. No way you squabble during 'Bluebird'. Only regret – we didn't get to meet Paul afterwards. It had been mooted but just didn't happen. Another time. *Band on the Run* was released on December 5th, my birthday.

I remember the effect that meeting Macca had on Trevor Eve. It was like he'd been tangoing with angels. Trevor lived near to us off Strand-on-the-Green and had been playing Paul in the West End show *John, Paul, George, Ringo and Bert*. Paul had simply rocked up one night and called round at Trevor's

Flabbergasted: Larry, Chris, and Trevor

dressing-room. It took a lot to impress Trevor but he was kind of flabbergasted, especially as Macca had been complimentary about his impersonation.

Funnily, when I shared a dressing room with Trevor – at The Lyric in 1977 – the legendary Hal Prince, who directed *Night Music*, came backstage to see me. I think Trevor felt a bit overlooked, but – you know – all things come to those who wait.

Waiting was a popular pastime in Vienna. Viennese Sundays could stretch a yawn like no other day on earth. They were always cloudy, even when the sky was blue. They hung like ectoplasm on a ghost train.

One Sunday morning, we'd gone to the Wurstelprater – the fairground – complete with legendary ferris wheel – yes that one, the one in *The Third Man* – because another legend wanted to ride on it. Lee Remick was married to first assistant, Kip Gowans. One of those sweet, hybrid opposites-attract UK/US marriages. She was only over for thirty-six hours and begged us to tag along with her to the fair.

The word legend has been done to death – it means virtually nothing now – but let's use it one more time like it's a virgin and hasn't been squandered on Reality TV stars. Lee was delicate, deliciously funny and shone like a crescent Venus. For once, a funfair lived up to its name. Fun as fuck and as fair as angels. Like we were all walking on air. Lee had that effect. Suddenly, it wasn't Sunday anymore and the grey sky was blue. Over all too soon.

When Lee had to leave us, the ground didn't seem so fair anymore so we wandered into town in search of nothing. Anything but the torte-bound, Strauss-strapped, time-warped Wien Hilton. And bang, as if lured by Orson Welles himself, we drifted up an unlikely side street and found ourselves outside a small but well-stocked joke emporium, a scherzladen! Complete with humourless proprietor.

We invested in plastic dog turds and disappearing ink, called in at a supermarket for more bargain wine and were back at the hotel by five. That evening, having watched hotel guests negotiate realistic twirls of poo, too embarrassed to complain, we accidentally-on-purpose outraged a stuffy headwaiter with flicks of ink on his snowwhite shirt. By the time he was complaining to reception, the ink had vanished. "You may behave like this in New York, but not in Vienna!" "I'm from Stamford Brook, mate". Pathetic I know, but we were prisoners of luxury confinement and our mental health was paramount. Where wit was redundant, good old practical jokes would have to serve. Man, did we laugh! And as Steve and Sandi would say, "Miss you guys".

I had a strange relationship with musicals. As a songwriter, I felt increasingly pulled towards bands and, as an actor, towards movies. I wanted a career like

Bowie or Sting, not Michael Ball. And that's kind of what I got – in a less world-conquering sort of way. "There's time yet", he mumbled to himself…

Night Music was my last musical theatre venture. I appeared in the satire *A Hymn From Jim* directed by Colin Bucksey and written by *Rocky Horror* man, Richard O'Brien, playing a bisexual heartthrob pop star who murders his boyfriend with a gold disc. We recorded a couple of Jim's supposed hits and I performed one at a mocked-up *Top of the Pops*, replete with swoony teenage stage-school girls; but that was a short television film, not musical theatre.

Harry H Corbett – Steptoe junior – played my manager. Smoking untipped Senior Service cigarettes, he was restless, almost haunted, and very kind. I wish he'd hung around more after filming. He'd have a swift half in the pub opposite Ealing Film Studios then off he'd fly, flecked with ash, every inch a human being. Harry was a talented, serious actor. But you can't legislate for where the breaks come from, especially with mouths to feed. Maybe he was haunted by what he might have been. Popularity can be a hard ride.

Funny that name Jim: it was my nickname for a while because of an alleged resemblance to Jim Morrison.

Then it cropped up again in *Return to Treasure Island*. Perhaps a swansong musical beckons? *A Hymn From Jim Hawkins*. Come on baby, light my parrot.

The *Bouncing Back* cast

I worked with Colin Bucksey again on an extraordinary star-studded production called *Bouncing Back*, written by the creator of Rock Follies – Howard Schuman. I play a slick psychotherapist who devises a mocked-up game show, designed to give 'victims' a chance to get revenge on their tormentors by humiliating them in the game. My 'patients' were Roger Lloyd-Pack, Caroline Quentin, John-Gordon Sinclair and Eleanor Bron.

I'd pranced about and crooned a bit at Latymer – especially in the *Jantaculum*, the yearly free-for-all of a review – but Flashman in *Tom Brown's School Days* was my first taste of remunerated singing. It was an odd piece, not only because of its eclectic cast and some soon-to-be household names, but because of its myriad roots.

Here you had a show co-penned by Joan Maitland, who had shadow-written extra verses for Lionel Bart's *Oliver*, and directed by Peter Coe who had previously directed *The World of Susie Wong* and of course *Oliver* itself. Joan was feverishly ambitious; this was her baby now and she wanted *Tom Brown* to be every bit as box-office-breaking as *Oliver*.

Drafted in to write the music was Chris Andrews who had been a pop star, notably with *Yesterday Man*, and hovering in the wings were MAM (Management, Agency and Music Ltd), who managed Englebert Humperdink and Gilbert O'Sullivan, and were also hoping for *Oliver*-size spoils. Ironically, making up the numbers as a 'boy from Rugby School' was none other than a puppy-faced Simon Le Bon. No one, least of all him, knew what awaited him but maybe MAM would have done better to sign Le Bon and sod the show.

We recorded a cast album, which is now a rare and coveted slice of vinyl, only for the show itself to be taken off almost before the wax had dried. The Cambridge was a bastard of a place to fill.

Joan had a nervous breakdown. I'd only ever seen her in a blonde wig before. Suddenly she stopped wearing it; the red lipstick too. She threw a party aimed at reviving the show, but nobody turned up except me, my brother and one other boy. The sight of Joan's meagre wisps and bloodshot eyes hurt the heart.

I ended up in a clinch with their French *au pair*, which was not very respectful of me but, by this time, we'd heard the cast recording nine times and were desperate for solace. Joan's young partner was furious and phoned my mother. I was nineteen, for heaven's sake. Roy Dotrice singing 'What Is a Man?' to a chapel full of choirboys had had an unintended effect on my loins.

I shared a dressing room with actor/singer and future astrology star, Russell Grant, who insisted on being called 'Mother', and had a photographic memory. One day, in the empty stalls, he predicted I would be a writer. Well, maybe he got that bit right after all. Russell and I were to meet again when he was resident starman on *TV AM*, and I was being interviewed by Anne and

Nick to promote *Return to Treasure Island*, the HTV-Disney series I made in Jamaica and Spain with Brian Blessed. But more of that later: I'm flying ahead of myself. In fact I'm not sure whether, at this rate, 1985 will arrive at all. Though I'm told it did.

The thing about *Tom Brown's Schooldays* that truly changed my life had nothing to do with the show itself: I contracted pneumonia and pleurisy. Singing and smoking and generally getting hot and sweaty in a theatre rammed full of other people doing much the same provided too fertile a ground for skulking viruses.

As I was sitting in the pub after a show one evening, a searing pain wracked my lungs like walking into a sledgehammer. Every breath hurt like being sawn in half. I was hot and cold and hotter and colder. Like a polar bear in the Everglades or an arctic orangutan.

The show was over. Flashman was floored for real. I was rush-taxied home, the doctor was summoned, drugs were proffered, shots were given. This was viral. Double viral. High fever. Hallucinations.

I wanted to be in the garden of Pleydell Avenue with Roofy. Slowly and curiously just playing, not getting paid to play. Amateur. For the love. It was too much. I didn't train for any of this. Just learned as I rolled. The dancers were tough. Dancers are. I felt more like some deluded romantic poet trapped in a factory farm. Opening my lungs to sing every night, then filling them with tobacco tar. Should never have smoked. After Dad left I was on twenty a day within months. It got me through my A-levels. That and *Led Zep II* on my Boots stereo. Stereo was a thing then. Ow. Why? Ow. One last agonising breath, one more lightning bolt through the ribs, then white. Silvery-white. And out.

As a boy, I'd had vivid dreams. Especially when I had a fever. Sometimes I'd be stark-staring awake, bolt upright in bed, with the light on. One recurring dream involved a red tie about a foot below the ceiling. Dad would be sitting beside me, large as life and clear as day but I was off my rocker. The tie was one of those elasticated little boys' ties, inoffensive in itself but the stuff of horror for me. I was tripping. Like I was in a Salvador Dalí painting. Way before LSD was anyone's drug of choice.

The tie was alarming because it just hovered, kind of bland and threatening all at once. Someone had a theory that I was a highwayman in a former life and had been hung in my teens and the tie represented the noose. I like the romanticism of that but, frankly, I couldn't give a monkey's what it was meant to be: I just know it scared me shitless.

Even worse was when Dad was trying to comfort me and, every time he smiled, his big, strong teeth turned luminous green. "No! Dad, don't do that!" "Do what lad?

It's OK. It's OK!" Jeez.

The other recurrer was when Dad would be shot into outer space, beyond the pull of Planet Earth, lost and lonely but unable to get back. The chill of missing him and fearing for him are with me still. I think this was a glimpse of the future, or a deep subconscious understanding of Dad's soul. Because he did leave us, if only for Scotland, and he *was* stranded, and he never did come back.

Mum told me later that the doctor had turned a worse colour than me that night. She thought I'd died. Well, I kind of had. I did have a bit of a death wish. I knew the cigarettes were fucking me up, but I loved them. They soothed me and gave me confidence. I was still wet behind the ears really. And anyway, I just wanted to do what The Beatles and The Stones and everyone else who was cool did. Smoke! Consulate. Cool as a mountain stream. Yeah, really. The Marlboro Man died of lung cancer. The Number 6 that I smoked were known affectionately as nails-in-the-coffin.

It didn't help that I'd taken thirty-six hours being born (sorry Mum), and developed bronchitis as a baby, and had always been troubled by chest stuff. Ears too. The Ear, Nose and Throat Hospital was a second home for a while. And it all made no sense because I was strong and athletic, just prone. Flaming mass of contradiction. Why couldn't I just fucking well be normal? I still have to watch out for smoke and dust and sudden temperature changes. Basically, I'm asthmatic but I don't use inhalers and can still run a thirteen-second hundred metres. The smog of '53 didn't help much either. Mercifully, khaki-coloured air, along with legal asphyxiation, were soon to be consigned to history.

I recovered fast. Almost as fast as I'd fallen ill. Onstage again ten days later. But smoking was never the same. I tried but it didn't work anymore. The scar tissue saved me. Even joints I learned to resist because of the tobacco. This was a drag when I was at The National. Or rather it wasn't. Refusing a spliff was bad etiquette and not inhaling was laughable. I ate the stuff instead.

Strategically, the most important backstage department on *Tom Brown's Schooldays* was wardrobe. There were mountains of costumes and an avalanche of dancing boys – some growing fast. Hitching and last-gasp stitching were requisite. It was a good job for a would-be actor looking to get theatre experience. And there, smiling benignly and weaving manfully was art student Alan Rickman. Yes, *that* Alan Rickman. As if he knew exactly where he was going and had all the time in the world. Normality personified.

On the subject of normal, I was reading about steppe bison last night, and how they're being reintroduced to Blean Woods in Kent as a part of a plan to increase biodiversity. Bison used to be all over the UK. They help by felling trees, eating the bark, then leaving the rotten 'carcasses' as homes and snack bars for sundry invertebrates. And they create open glades too, for cavorting lizards and even druid wedding parties!

Wild East, a charitable foundation seeking to rewild parts of East Anglia, is doing something similar, promoting beavers, and even talking of bears and lynx, both of which once roamed our land. The idea is to get back to normal. Not to a pre-pandemic capitalist norm, but to a natural balance that makes it possible to live safely on the planet in the first place. A kind of green socialism. I think Alan would have approved. He was a natural socialist, a kind, democratic humanist, and for all his success he never lost touch with his roots and sense of proportion. The last time I saw him was just two years before he died, at a schoolmaster's funeral. We talked of art and art rooms and didn't mention acting once.

7: Mel, Hugh and Barnaby Who?

Alan Rickman was a few years ahead of me at Latymer and had often dreamed of being an actor, though he tried his hand at other things before he recognised that it was his calling. I was the first of that thesp generation to get started – with parts in *David Copperfield*, *Great Expectations*, *Dixon of Dock Green* and other work that dovetailed into the school holidays. And my brother Dom followed soon after, with his BAFTA-winning performance in *The Go-Between*.

Latymer was not an acting school: it was proudly academic. Hall walls were stiff with Oxbridge scholarships and exhibitions. But, while music was a bit of an afterthought – certainly in the curriculum – and drama was a once-a-week affair at most, the Gild drama group and its junior 'feeders' the Apprentices and Journeymen were hugely influential and much loved. And the ambitions for the school play were way beyond the call of extracurricular duty.

How all this evolved I'm not sure. My sorties into the professional world certainly had nothing to do with it, but during the '60s, as the country generally loosened up, the variety show *The Jantaculum* and the school play were vital hubs for exhibitionists, talented eccentrics and anyone who just fancied a crack. In the case of *The Jantaculum*, this included teachers, frequently in drag, and a laissez-faire that transcended the world the school was beginning to leave behind. The grizzly clatter and yell of the school cadet corps had gone within two years of my joining Latymer and, by the time I hit the second-year-sixth, girls were included in the school play. *Francha leale toge*. The Godolphin Girls' motto. Free and loyal art thou. That worked.

There were splinters and cracks. It was inevitable. Wonderful Wilf Sharp, maverick Head of English, seemed way out of touch as he berated the inclusion of miniskirted Godolphinites in pretty well anything. Now, of course Latymer takes girls throughout the school.

And there were moments of levity. One day, we noticed Wilf's testicles had slithered out of his Y-fronts and escaped through a hole in his Terylene slacks. They were just sort of lying on his chair while he discussed *The Wife of Bath*. What's so funny?! We didn't have the heart to tell him. I mean Chaucer *is*

The Jantaculum: Jollity Farm

meant to be funny. And in places it's downright pornographic. Ribald as fuck. Of course we were laughing. Sail on, dear Wilf.

Without Sir Peter Hendy CBE, the dancing and prancing would have fallen apart. Maestro of all things practical, Pete's back-stage insights and ways with committees were on another level. *The Jantaculum* was a perfect place to cut his teeth. He's now head of Network Rail.

I found my way on to a sixth-form committee and helped argue away the need for sixth formers to wear school uniform. Deep down, we wanted it replaced by kaftans and afghans but negotiated a compromise.

'Moderately flared trousers' became officially tolerated, and even delusional young teachers invested in these – usually on the short side and terminating just above the nylon socks.

Inevitably, rules were bent.

Bell-bottoms as wide as puddles enveloped feet, concealing illegal boots; ties were fat and floral and scarves purple and record-breaking. My scarf certainly was. Mum had knitted it to my specs, and it was taller than me.

I also took to sporting a grey, fitted RAF jacket with silver buttons, which a friend of Mum's had worn as a young conscript. Carnaby Street was ablaze with wartime memorabilia, embraced in paradoxical fashion by the pipers of peace. Once *Sergeant Pepper* hit the consciousness, that was the only way to go.

I thought I looked great.

Mister Terry, the second master, thought otherwise. Out of school he was sweet as pie and known to me as George. But inside it was war. When everything about you drooped and flopped, Wilf's scrotum included, the only option was to avoid him at all costs.

He was popularly known as 'The Grease' and expected everyone to look like him, coiffed and terribly tidy. "Would you call that hair shoulder-length?" "Well, some of it, sir, yes".

"Don't be silly. Get it cut".

Fuck.

I'd rather have cut my ears off than expose them to Godolphin girls, not to mention the gales blowing up the school subway. There were side entrances into the school, and a precise knowledge of The Grease's schedule helped. But he always got you in the end.

Colin Turner, English teacher extraordinaire and king of all things dramatic, advised me to sharpen up and become a prefect if I wanted to avoid suspension.

So, I did and ended up in young Hugh Grant's classroom.

I was doing well with my schoolwork, so it seemed unfair to wage war on my appearance. But I had a particularly rum gauntlet to run. Ever since that first TV outing, my profile had remained uncomfortably high. "You're not at the BBC now, Guard!" And certainly not on *The Old Grey Whistle Test*.

Someone just reminded me that our dear headmaster Ken Sutcliffe was Sir Ian McKellen's uncle. Two Lancastrians. I'd completely forgotten. How strange. The Grease was Ken's fixer, while Ken exuded warmth and sagacity. Typical of his avuncular approach was an announcement he made to a full school assembly one Monday morning: "It's come to my notice – ahem – that some of you boys have – ahem – been smoking marijuana… Don't do it lads. It doesn't do you any good… ahem." He pronounced the 'j' in marijuana. Coming from anyone else this would have elicited smirks from some loafers at the back. But it didn't. Ken was loved. He was like Mr Barrowclough in *Porridge'*, painfully sensitive and wearing the mantle of authority with the conscience it deserved.

The clothing conundrum was epitomised by a line in the annual school journal outlining dress codes.

"The school cap is not mandatory for sixth-formers but may be worn if preferred."

Hilarious.

I imagined the fabulous Paul LaneRyan, who looked about thirty-two, placing a cap on his impressive Mungo Jerry-sideburned head, before driving his Dad's Hillman Avenger to school. What Paul actually preferred was nodding off in Ancient History lessons.

Our teacher, the charming Mr Fella, was new and looked all of twelve. He was from Cyprus and spoke English so fast we couldn't understand a word he said. There were only about ten of us in the set, and room for thirty in the classroom. We spread out like we were social distancing fifty years ahead of a pandemic. Martin Shipton would sit right at the front, just inches from the incomprehensible Mr Fella, contorted in implosive laughter, swaying like one of those wobbly toys that rock low but always return to vertical.

I'm not sure if Hugh ever got to wear purple loons. He was eleven when I was his form prefect in 2H. A singular mix of charm and disarming cheek. He had a vibe, no question, even then.

And he was a Fulham supporter too, so he was alright by me!

We would meet sometimes, a few years later, on the terraces, near the famous green pole at the Hammersmith End.

Misty Night at the Cottage by Christopher Guard

The last time I saw Hugh in the flesh was on a Piccadilly Line tube train from Heathrow. I got out at Turnham Green, and the rest was history. We were on our way back from Barcelona, where we'd been attempting to make a schlock Anglo-Spanish movie called *The Stabbing* having been cast as a pair of swashbucklers. Hugh was still a while away from *Four Weddings,* and serious nonsense like this was well paid if nothing else. Really it was stuff for juvenile leads ('juves' in industry jargon), a genre in which we were both stuck – in my case even at the age of thirty-two. We shared an agent and, once Hugh had been cast, my name had come up as a suitable foil. I'd recently been swashing a lot of bucks in Jamaica and in fact even in Spain and was now living with my young family in Cornwall.

Unfortunately, having left Coverack – supposedly for two months – on the Monday, and having given some building work the green light, I was home before you could say "adios" or "dos cerveza". There was some kind of falling out between agent and producer, and director and casting director, and God knows who else. Hugh and I went to the gym a couple of times, drank some *cerveza* and discussed his girlfriend Liz Hurley's recent outing in a Dennis Potter play.

I'd also been in a couple of Dennis Potter plays so, as long as we were speaking English, Potter made for good conversation. At dinner with the Spanish agent however, it was agreed to speak French, which Hugh speaks fluently and which I speak with a great accent but not much else. I never quite knew who said what or why or to whom, but it was all pretty awkward and after some heated phone calls to London, we beat a retreat. Building work cancelled. In a French accent.

The next time I was in London, I spotted a retro film poster with lots of young English people on it, and Hugh somewhere near the centre. It was *Four Weddings,* and that – as it transpired – was that.

Hugh had said he'd considered getting out of acting and concentrating on writing, as had I, and then this immaculate script comes along and meets its kismet. Hugh had been in a comedy troupe: his timing was impeccable. Two boxes ticked. Glamorous and funny. Transcending The Pond.

Fame is like that.

You wait, you doubt, you wonder and then, youch!

It was no more predictable for fellow Latymerian Mel Smith, nor indeed for my brother. And as for Alan, older than Mel and me by several years, he took forever to take the plunge, working as a dresser for Sir Ralph Richardson, running a graphic design studio and of course stitching Simon le Bon's trousers. "If it be not now yet it will come – the readiness is all".

Mel was one of the most extraordinary people I've ever met. He was a year older than me, but we caught up in the sixth form, where I – supposedly on account of my academic prowess – had arrived a year early. If cigarettes have any benefit, it's the edge the nicotine induces. Remember, I'd never have got Ancient History A-level without Player's Number Six and Led Zep basslines. 'Dazed and Confused', 'How Many More Times' and a pack of ten and I could motor through an essay on Medea murdering her children with a surprising zest for life.

Zest or not, I was too young for the sixth form really. Mel, like so many others, looked like a man already. Some boys were going bald before I'd even started shaving. We were all growing our hair like fury, either as long and straight as possible or as big as possible, Afro-style.

Mel made the most of what he had, as he did with everything in life, and looked like a cross between hopeful hippy and canny turf accountant. I remember seeing him for the first time in the school corridor – an exotic, bouncing, intangible mix of beauty and beast, with sensitive brown eyes and that defining underbite. I never knew quite what to make of Mel. And neither, I suspect, did he. Like Alan, Mel had working-class roots. His Dad was from Geordie mining stock and opened one of the first licensed betting offices in the UK – two in fact – in Chiswick, *Fleming and Smith Turf Accountants*. The Fleming was Granny, Mel's mum's mum, keeper of the purse. She ensured Mel was never short of a few quid. I'd never even seen a ten-pound note until I met Mel.

Mel and Alan, and even Hugh and me and Dom to some extent, were what Latymer had originally been designed for. Not as a public school, which is effectively what Thatcher forced it to become, but as a direct-grant grammar school, providing a good education for people who couldn't afford it. None of the members of the little thespian crew who emerged at that time had much to do with money or privilege; for all our posh roles Hugh, Dom, and I were from pretty basic backgrounds. Alan was pure working class, and won a full scholarship, while Mel was but one generation away from a career in coal mining. Like my dad, he came from a studiedly unartistic background; his parents were simply hard-working, good with numbers and ambitious for their children.

Mel's dad's betting offices – apart from providing a Saturday morning income – were perfect rehearsal spaces. At just seventeen, Mel had already turned producer and director, organising extraordinarily ambitious productions at venues like the LAMDA theatre and The Cockpit. He would push and prime us like pros, his energy and guile often outstripping that of the professional shows I was involved in.

His crowning glory was the first ever theatre production of The Who's *Tommy*. Mel had burst through the school gates on the morning of the album's release in a state of high excitement. These were the great days of vinyl, when possession of a record and its glorious sleeve could be a passport to unprecedented friendship and influence; social upheaval even. Clearly Townshend had envisaged a dramatic production at some point. Like its predecessor *Jesus Christ Superstar*, it was a rock opera; but as with so many things, and unbeknown to a wider world, Mel had got there first. Roles were at a premium. Girls and boys queued desperately in the corridors. That deaf, dumb and blind kid sure played a mean school hall.

Mel and I are both Sagittarians, born two days and one year apart, and we received the same make of guitar for our 1970 birthdays: Hoyer. Not content with being captain of rugby, an astute gambler, an entrepreneur and a director, Mel created another persona as a singer-songwriter. Briefly he and I became Flotsam and Jetsam and played the Troubadour in Earl's Court the same summer that Bob Dylan rocked up there.

Around the time the idea was also coming to Billy Connolly, Mel discovered that jokes and impromptu rambling vastly increased our standing. As we meandered through another of my Donovanesque offerings, you could feel the audience gagging for more of Mel's caustic tomfoolery. I was too sincere. There's a difference between deadpan and plain dead. Mel had the populist touch; he favoured covers over originals and told old jokes like no one had heard them before. I wanted to be the next Bob Dylan, not the one we already had. Mel just wanted a full house.

Our musical partnership was thus short-lived and while I was summoned to appear in the BBC Play of the Month, *Macbeth*, Mel secured a residency in a pub on Richmond Bridge, where he sang Loudon Wainwright III songs and took the piss. I was Third Apparition.

"Be lion-mettled, proud, and take no care who chafes, who frets or where conspirers are".

Not a bad dictum for Mel actually; he led from the front and lived fearlessly to the full. And his material was certainly funnier than mine.

Ironically it was partly Mel's fear of being typecast that steered him away from acting as a profession. He was a fantastic Falstaff in *Henry IV Part One* which also featured me as the ill-fated Hotspur, dispatched in a loud, clumpy fight by Doctor Hilary Jones MBE's Prince Hal.

Hilary looked like a film star. Like Hugh and Mel, and apropos of nothing really, he was also from Chiswick.

Chiswick was a sleepy backwater back then, famed mainly for numbering Tommy Cooper among its residents. Tommy's son, Thomas, was in the same

Chris as Hotspur, age 16

school year as my brother. It was not until the mid-'80s that Chiswick became flash and artisans' cottages incurred insane mortgages in return for a W4 postcode.

Mind you, the wide pavements are impressive and, before this pandemic, they still seemed like vast extra-terrestrial casting suites, festooned with show biz types watching casually for the next opportunity across the rims of cappuccino cups.

By the way I'm not writing this book because of the pandemic. It needed to be written anyway. I think I had COVID-19 two years ago, in early 2019. It certainly answered the job description. After a band rehearsal at AB Music Academy in Acton, where people gather from overseas with eclectic regularity, I developed a satanic round-the-clock, rib-shattering cough and a fever that made pleurisy seem like a mild pet allergy. I didn't feel right for six weeks and put it down to flu and being much older than I was when I'd had pleurisy. But now I'm not so sure. Maybe it *was* COVID-19 and maybe, like Mel, I'd simply got there first.

Inevitably, I saw less of Mel after he went to Oxford. While my singing Flashman was terrorising the boys of Rugby School, Mel was busy becoming president of the Oxford University Dramatic Society and patronising every racecourse within a day's drive of New College. Mel had a passion for gambling. I went to Dover races with him once and lost a pound on a flat race – on Eric at 20 to 1. Mel did warn me but the odds were too tempting in a three-horse race. Eric led all the way and finished last.

I made up for it at White City Dogs the following summer. I'd been in Coverack experimenting with Buddhism and astral planes and drinking Spingo in The Blue Anchor in Helston and was convinced I'd developed psychic powers. Spingo was an in-house brew reputed at the time to contain hallucinatory wood alcohol. I'd happily lost all track of time and, when I returned to London, the television seemed like it was an extra-terrestrial cyclops hell-bent on destroying my brain.

While I was in this delicate condition, Mel made one of his now less-frequent swing-bys at Pleydell Avenue. Honk honk. The familiar cry of Mrs Smith's Mini. Next thing I knew, I was studying form and betting on the tote, while Mel was down the front waving wads at the tic-tac boys.

Miraculously, and it amazes me to this day, I picked six winners, with an almost saint-like precision. Mel was gobsmacked. My theory is that it was because I didn't give a shit, divested as I was of all material desires. Ho ho. It's more likely because I'd bothered to read the little form book and got lucky. Good story though, and not the last time I would accredit hazard to some kind of visionary prowess.

Mel was also renowned as a heavy drinker. Alcohol, that ubiquitous drug of choice. Adored. Powerful. It emboldens and disarms, usurps and destroys; without it some careers would probably not have existed.

Bowie was a self-confessed alcoholic. When I saw his Thin White Duke at Earl's Court, he sang just two songs before plucking a large glass of blood-red wine from the wings. It was divine. The light, the thinness, the richness, the contrasts, the style with which the thin man quaffed.

Fast and devoutly. He was one of us. Not just a cocaine and milk man, but a robust, ribald Englishman. As much Geoffrey Chaucer as Lindsay Kemp. A transcendental, trilling, thrilling trouper. No one really knew he was an alcoholic.

Mel wore alcohol like he wore his clothes. It was necessary. It kept him hidden, calmed him down, warmed him up, made him happy, made him mad. Not just a drug but a whole culture. He taught me how to sink chasers after pints. I'd never heard of that before. I often threw up. We just drank everything.

Mel's Uni friends talked of being 'Smithed'. Well, I knew what that was, though not by name. In the end, you just had to hide or pretend not to be in or to have caught rabies. A day with Mel was like the antithesis of a Sunday in Vienna. A rollercoaster, no fun fair required. And all inevitably fuelled by alcohol.

A typical scenario would be, after a skinful at The Ravenscourt Arms the night before, before you've had time to say Bleary McSheery, honk honk. "Help!" "What? You said ten to eleven!" "Did I? Oh shit." "Chris darling…?" (this is Mum calling) "I said I would, Mum." "But…" Hurtle, tumble, slam, rush, slam, roar… The White Hart.

Bar football. Mega jukebox. Vinyl singles. Mel pays for ten. Buys the first two rounds of keg beer. Always keg for Mel. Dylan, The Who, Dylan again – 'Positively Fourth Street' – The Eagles – 'Desperado' – very apt that, Mel loved the tune, something for me – Thin Lizzy probably… "The Boys Are Back In…" "Game of darts?" He lets me win. And again. "Wager?" I win two bob. "Another pint?" Now Mel starts winning. "That's OK. Owe me… double or quits?"

By the time we leave, I owe Mel a fiver. "Lunch?" "Well… er…" Restaurant in Holland Park, zoom, roar. "I'll pay". "Er, I can't afford…" "Don't worry, pay me back when you can." Scoff, slurp. Bottle of wine… "Fancy playing guitar?" "Well, I've got an essay to write…"

Mel had made the genius decision to study science subjects in the sixth form, cutting written work to a minimum. He never seemed to be behind with anything. His passion was theatre, so he studied Physics. How smart was that?

I wanted to mix Biology with English and History but that wasn't allowed back then so I had to write reams on the Corn Laws and *Ulysses*, which had nothing in common but their girth.

Mel wasn't fat. He was actually just shaped that way – round and big-boned – and for all the quaffing and scoffing, what his body didn't burn up, his brain certainly did. He was a nimble dancer too, and unlike me had several feet, both left and right, and could choreograph like Lionel Blair.

Years later, I met Griff Rhys Jones in Hospitality on the eighth floor of Television Centre, on the night of *Children in Need*. "I used to be you," was my opener. "What?!" he chuckled. What I meant was that I'd also been Mel's other half and had some insights into the job description. Of course Mel and Griff were big stars by this time, and their partnership was almost a national institution, but the notes Griff and I compared were similar. We both loved Mel but had had to run a giddy gauntlet. Griff had given up booze, I would stop and start, Mel just rolled on. "You live and then you die," was his maxim. It's that simple.

Hang on. I got side-tracked. The restaurant in Holland Park. What happened next was probably this: sun was coming out, so grab the Hoyers, zoom, screech, back to Pleydell. "Chris, Chris, where are you going?" "It's OK, Mum, I had lunch."

Mum had Shirley Cain round for coffee, so that was OK. Shirley played Mrs Gargery in *Great Expectations* when I played Pip. That was the year after *David Copperfield* and featured my first screen kiss. Francesca Annis. Now where have you gone, Christopher? I'm being Smithed! Time and space no object. Tardis Mini. Hurtle. Mel's house next. On the Great West Road. Guitar. Money. Off licence on Faucenburg Road. Near the family betting office. "Hi Dad. Bye Dad!" Half a bottle of vodka. Soar.

Richmond Park. A clement hill beneath a tree. Some Bob Dylan. Then some Mel Smith. We blues-tuned the guitars to E so we could play easy bar chords the wrong way round. "Sail me into yesterday, there let me drink my fill, where the poor man and the leper boy divide the kingdom's will." A Mel original. It was good actually. Dylan meets Richie Havens. The day should have ended twice already. So little time and so much to do. Pub by the river. Barnes. Coach and Horses. I'm losing the will to live. Or is it the will to die? More beer and darts. The only sign that the excesses are affecting Mel is his mood. More acerbic, more cutting. Here we go.

Later, we met a couple of other mates – heaven knows who – at Capability Brown's on the Brompton Road. Trendy restaurant where they knew Mel well. Ferocious feasting. Full works. Ended up buying the bottle of Hine brandy. And then driving?! Apparently.

Maybe Mel phoned his girlfriend next. Jane. They had a row. Again. Then Mel burst into tears. Dropped me home at Pleydell around midnight. Ow.

The following morning, we played tennis at Ravenscourt Park. He was even good at that. Mel didn't do hangovers.

He captained the rugby First Fifteen on Saturday mornings.

Sometimes Mel would temporarily run out of cash and call in the never-nevers. Probably on a Tuesday after double Ancient History. "But Mel, I haven't got a hundred and forty-two pounds."

"Give me what you've got." Groan.

The last time I saw Mel was three years before he died, in the same Chiswick church where I'd last seen Alan Rickman. Mel was doing a favour for the Chiswick Arts Society, with a bit of cabaret for a select audience in the pews. He sang Flanders and Swann's 'The Hippopotamus Song', and we met in The Tabard pub beforehand. It was pouring with rain and our dear friend, Chris Gull – dentist to the stars and sometime Barbara Streisand impersonator – was keeping a kindly eye on us.

Mel's dependence on alcohol was massive. The whiskies were hurled down like a Highland Games event, barmaids were befuddled by the rate of demand and my ten-year-old Tallulah was greeted, shall we say, somewhat halfheartedly. Mel was firmly from the WC Fields school. Preferred his children not so much fried or boiled as not on the menu at all. Fair enough. The mix of show biz and family is not for the fainthearted. You always forgave Mel. Because when he was sober, or just not too drunk, his humanity was second to none.

One wonders what might have happened if Mel had carried on at the Crucible, Sheffield and not been headhunted for *Not The Nine O'clock News*. Would people still have said, "you know Mel Smith? Wow!" in the same way they would allude to Alan or Hugh. It's strange knowing famous people before they're famous. Before their names startle and impress. They're just the same. Just as talented. Just not famous. It's everyone else that changes.

Mel hated it at first. Fame, I mean. From being this restless, powerful figure behind the scenes, he was suddenly 'the fat one' in a television comedy show. Seemed ridiculous really. But there it was and, borne on a tide of booze and genius, the doors opened and Mel fulfilled his dream of directing Hollywood movies. Rubbing shoulders with the glitz.

I wonder. Maybe, without the white dust and black limos, Mel's career might not have been as cosmic, but I think he was a great theatre director in the making and could have ended up running the Royal Shakespeare Company or National Theatre. Who knows?

Certainly, Mel's career at Oxford was not about academia. He directed some luminous productions, including a remount of *Marat/Sade,* which he'd originally directed at school. I went up to play guitar for him. Sat on stage strumming jazz nonsense while the inmates of the asylum staggered around me. And as I watched them, deranged and directionless, I began to wonder about my own direction too.

Mel was kicked out of Oxford after two years for attending more race meetings than tutorials, but he'd already achieved his goal, which was to become president of O.U.D.S. and sow the seeds of a career in show biz. We very nearly passed each other heading along the M40 in opposite directions.

The best thing to happen in '75 was Fulham getting to Wembley, even if they did lose. On paper, it should have been playing Lucentio in *The Taming of the Shrew* with Zoë Wannamaker and a pre-*Brideshead* Jeremy Irons. But we kind of lost that match too.

Jeremy had yet to star in *Playaway* on children's TV, let alone in *The French Lieutenant's Woman*. Our polite production was designed for the opening of the new Regent's Park Open Air Theatre and was thus very traditional, not at all the rock and roll romp it could have been. Due to a blazing summer and the wrong cement, we had to relocate to the Roundhouse, which was a ridiculous space for a proc arch plod. But it was either that or cut our losses and quit; an option I tended to favour, along with a replay of the Cup Final. With Fulham winning.

Following a disjointed tour, the play made little impact in London, and left me wondering if I'd made the right choice going into show biz straight from school. I contacted my friend and mentor, Colin Turner, who was delighted to help me reapply for Oxbridge – Christchurch College, Oxford in fact – and I resat the exams later that year, back at school, at the age of twenty-one. The interview swung it. That and one essay that I wrote on *Wuthering Heights*. I was offered a place. But the fates were already spinning their threads.

Within months of me meeting Christopher Butler, the English don at Christchurch, Hal Prince and Stephen Sondheim had summoned me to the Park Lane Hotel. "Just wanted to check you hadn't turned into an aging character actor", grinned Hal. "See you at work!" And that was that. Money was short. Mum was doing OK, but Dad was gone, and the offer was too much to refuse. Not to mention the company. So, I never did go to Oxford. And neither Mel nor I ever got a degree.

8: I Wish My Name Was Dick

Dom, my brother, was the most reluctant Latymer thesp of all. He has his own chapter partly because he is my brother but mainly because he's fucking great and because we escaped from Millwall football ground in an ambulance.

Dom, our sister, Candy, and I had acted in little homemade adventure films after Dad inherited a 9.5 mm camera from his parents. Dad's parents had used it to make interminable travelogues of their interminable holidays, usually featuring someone standing motionless by a tourist attraction, smiling dead-eyed straight into the lens for anything up to two minutes. I mean – why…? Just take photographs and save us all. Yes, that's Granny, and that's a sphinx. But which is the more animated? The pyramid probably. Dad upped the ante. Invested in new, state-ofthe-art 8mm equipment. It was just a question of time before Playpen Pics were straddling the globe.

Pirates? Humbugs! was shot entirely on location in Coverack and featured Dom as the good, laughing pirate, in a Chelsea Pensioners tricorn hat, and me as the bad pirate with a greasepaint Errol Flynn moustache. An entire holiday was disrupted by the filming schedule, canoes were hired, props purchased from Brenda's Stores and wages paid in double 99s and trinkets from the Seine Loft gift shop.

Dom had a unique relationship with the camera, frequently collapsing in fits of giggles and taking a decidedly method approach to his role, while I was all one-take blood and thunder. The blood really was tomato ketchup. That was the 'joke': the bad pirate was following a trail to the laughing pirate's red sandwich.

Weeks later, reels of glossy celluloid would be cut and spliced, and film shows held for friends and family, accompanied by Prokofiev or Stravinsky on the Grundig TK23 and Dad's live commentary in the dark. Sometimes, the brittle edits would snarl and rip and Dad could be found manfully juggling the wriggling footage as the lights came up. Worth it though. Playpen productions were in demand, and we were not to disappoint.

Maiden Mislaid soon followed, shot in Suffolk, and starring Candy. Then *Blood of the Legion,* a desert romp set in the sand dunes of Oxwich, south

Wales, also starring Candy and featuring Dom as the baddy this time: Ben Zedrin. It's all on DVD now – silent and strange and wonderful.

So where is all this leading? Not to a BAFTA award, surely. Dom's sometimes lukewarm enthusiasm for yet another Playpen Pics epic reached its nadir when he stood on Westminster Embankment dressed as a policeman, head buried in his arms, stubbornly refusing to play ball, let alone Police Constable whatever-his-name-was. It didn't help that I was gagging to play the delinquent burglar. The faster I ran away, the less likely I was to be pursued. Dad attempted to bribe Dom with several hot dogs from a nearby van, and they were duly eaten, but we got nothing in the can, and the production was abandoned. Much as *The Stabbing* was abandoned years later, and I said goodbye to Hugh on a Piccadilly Line train; this time it had been the District Line in stony silence. Some things are not meant to be. Great art is like that. Ask Police Constable Ben Zedrin.

We didn't have a TV. Well, we hired one at Christmas, and that was so unbelievably exciting I would dream of it while I was at school, imagining it sitting there in its glory, inanimate like Granny in front of the Taj Mahal, all square and sexy, in *our* house! Our usual daily fare was radio. *The Clitheroe Kid* or *The Peter Goodright Show* at 7:31, after the news; then Dad would read us a chapter of something weighty, like Dickens, then lights out.

For visual entertainment, the go-to was cinema. Cinemas were everywhere. We had four in Hammersmith. Not sliced into Screen One, Two, Three and Four but whole. Like whole-nut chocolate. Not halved or crunched, but nuts! Whole hazel nuts! Whole cinemas, with at least one balcony, seating up to fifteen hundred or more. The Gaumont, the Regal, the fleapit Essoldo on the Broadway. One afternoon, we were at the Commodore watching *Tarzan Goes to India* and probably licking peach sundaes, when a jolly lady turned and spoke to Dom. "Hello little boy, and what's your name?" "Dom" "Tom?" "Dom!" "Don??" "Dom! I wish my name was Dick". Dom had drawn the short straw in the name department. Christopher was none too common when I was born but became more so during the '60s. Maybe on account of Christopher Lee popularising biting and Christopher Plummer singing about flowers. Dominic though remained pretty rare, and Dick would definitely have been more convenient. To make matters worse, The Singing Nun had had an unlikely pop hit with 'Dominique', the chorus of which sounded like a tribute to knickers and did Dom no favours in the school playground.

I remember, years later, talking to Hayley Mills and Leigh Lawson's little boy at a party. He had been called Ace which, being the first born, I suppose was fair enough. But he told me, in dark tones, *sotto*, on the landing, "My name is Ace, but I want to be called Jack Robinson!"

I only played David Copperfield because someone had happened to say to someone, who happened to say to someone else, "they're looking for someone and they haven't found him yet". These 'someones' were actor friends so we were kind of in the mix already, but there was never a plan.

Dom and I weren't at drama schools, we just happened to inherit the tools. How and when the parts blew our way was down to fate. There was no great ache to be actors. Besides, we were both somewhat compromised in the thespian department.

My Achilles' heel was asthma. Dust, smoke, grass pollen, the usual suspects. Or I'd get over-excited playing football at the park, then the temperature would suddenly drop, and I'd get wheezy and tight. Breathing is an actor's lifeline and I had to work hard to control it.

Dom's Achilles' heel was his stammer. Not part of the job description for RADA, in which Dom had no interest anyway, but the stammer fed into a style and presence that the screen adored. Dom's fates came roaring via another chain of mouth: a wondrous, winding whirligig of events that no one could have anticipated.

Years earlier, Harold Pinter had adapted *The Go-Between*, HE Bates' atmospheric tale of lost innocence and Edwardian sexual hypocrisy, for the big screen. Joseph Losey was to direct. So finely balanced is this story that every last detail had to be right. The location – wide open, paradoxically claustrophobic Norfolk; the weather – an uncommonly hot English summer; the cast – two stars were essential to raise the budget; and pivotally, the boy. The Go-Between himself, at a fleeting stage of preadolescence, wings still wet from the chrysalis, subconsciously aware of love and sex and what lies beyond, struggling from one form to another.

Easy. Get a good actor. Play it. Act it.

Probably while Dom was laying into his second Embankment hot dog, showing as much appetite for the camera as a rare, nocturnal monkey, Losey and Pinter were abandoning the dream for another year. Time and again they'd been thwarted. Right stars, promising boy, locations available, diabolical weather. Or right stars, great weather forecast, no boy... and no boy had been the problem more often than not.

To make the shoot feasible, they had to start with swathes of blazing summer still ahead. 1970 was turning out like so many previous attempts. Losey would rather have packed up and gone home than compromised. So near and yet... Two highly eligible superstars in Alan Bates and Julie Christie, gems like Margaret Leighton and Edward Fox lined up to support, the promise of an idyllic, hot August in Norfolk, the clock ticking and... no Leo Coulston. No eponymous anti-hero. Until...

The king asked the queen, and the queen asked the dairy maid, could we have an actor for this wondrous slice of film? Well, in fact Mum's mate, Tenniel Evans, had been up for the Michael Gough part and got wind of their predicament. Tenniel wondered if I might be suitable. Copperfield and Pip. I'd earned a spur or two. "No way. Too old. Sorry". "Dom?" Dom? Mum hovered. "I'm not sure if he… I don't know. I could ask him". And she did. And Dom said "OK", he'd go up for it. Not with any huge enthusiasm, but with an intangible, silent something stirring inside. A muted, "Wow!" Well, just maybe…

Dom barely spoke a word at the interview. His stammer got the better of him, as did a natural diffidence. But what Losey spotted was a shining intelligence and a raw honesty which were exactly what he'd been looking for. It was a simple case of "I'll know it when I find it". Like falling in love. The die was cast.

The early days of shooting were tricky, but Losey had total faith and Dom quickly discovered imaginative ways to control and even utilise his stammer. Friendships were forged with co-conspirator Richard Gibson and with Julie and Alan; and as Dom's confidence grew so his talent blossomed and two months later, he had created a performance that was to win a BAFTA award for Best Newcomer.

Dom was a star. Reluctant at first but utterly deserved. A starring role in Peter Weir's *Picnic at Hanging Rock* followed, plus the lead in *Absolution,* with Richard Burton.

Dom grew in height and reputation and girls inevitably followed. Several at once at some of our Pleydell Avenue bashes. Weeping and pining and scrapping like early Beatles fans.

The Daily Mail ran a headline: "The boy who acts better when Fulham win". It certainly helped. Along with neighbour Mick, we were besotted. Craven Cottage held us in thrall; with an intangible magic so different from television and film sets – rough and live and unpredictable. Some were appalled by our devotion. Dad included. He just didn't get it. Open terraces invited major pitched battles pre-match. I bet Liz Taylor would have enjoyed it though. Her pal Michael Jackson pitched up at the Cottage years later and he certainly did. Football is mindless in good ways too.

Dad was well pissed off. Having broken away from philistinism, here were his sons dragging him straight back. He only came to one game. Away to Southampton in '67. There was a fight on the local train on the way home. As punches were thrown dangerously close to his face, Dad just stood there, bolt upright, like Granny standing in front of Nelson's Column, staring at me with a huge question mark across his face. I didn't know – truly. We were hooked; to the wide, misty, old Thames at night games, and the dazzling virgin-green turf in August. To the eclectic crowd, to the clank of the turnstiles, to the rivers of beer eventually. It was an escape. It meant nothing and everything.

Here's that Millwall ambulance story. The terraces were preferable but, as Dom was half-way through a film-shoot, for safety's sake we opted for seats. There was no home/away segregation back then. You just used your nous and sat or stood accordingly. When Fulham scored late on, an already irascible crowd presaged the storming of Capitol Hill by fifty-odd years and vaulted the railings at the far end of our stand. A delirium of monkey-booted fuckheads then proceeded to kick through whatever was in their way. Thermos flasks, transistor radios, women, children.

Skinheads – or 'peanuts' as they were briefly known used much the same technique at The Rolling Stones free Hyde Park concert in '69. My cousin Pippa was over from Canada, and we went together. Ferdinand and Miranda. That time it wasn't Fulham supporters but cross-legged hippies admiring the distant butterflies Mick had just released for Brian. The peanuts invaded like they were wading through shallow water. Kick, stomp, kick. Not as close to us as the skinheads on the train, but close enough for discomfort. Donald Trump would have been proud. Lucky Mick missed that. He'd have been very depressed. Like he was when he watched the grizzly Altermont footage.

In a moment of inspired panic, Dom and I headed somewhat more delicately across the seats behind us and did a sort of synchronised Fosbury flop into the directors' box. I think we knew one or two of the incumbents. Maybe David Hamilton. Not sure. More of him later, I imagine. "My brother's making a film – insurance – can't risk injury – continuity!" It worked. We were bustled to the rear of the box – no 'Verboten' signs – down some steps, into a yard, then into an ambulance that was about to head for the Underground station – an inevitable hot-spot for post-match warfare. We got there ahead of the monkcyboots but didn't feel entirely secure until a District Line train shuffled into Stamford Brook station an hour later.

Why? Why risk life and limb? Well, quite.

9: We Know Something You Don't Know

This short chapter is loosely about girls. In an abstract sense. As a sort of mystery. Nymphs and sirens.

Carol from Lavenham, Moira from Dundee, and first loves at the age of seven.

Actually, I've said "short" without the faintest idea how long the chapter's likely to be. It's a big subject, dreaming.

I'm in the girls' playground at St Peter's. No nursery; straight in at the deep end. The theory seemed to be that the company of older girls is more soothing than having your head banged on the water fountain by Danny Judd.

This was true up to a point but, sugar and spice notwithstanding, some girls found the teasing of small, lost boys irresistible. Like cats with mice, they could taunt without mercy, until the heart pounded, and the cheeks flushed and all four-year-old attempts at valiance were in vain. No water fountain required.

Tradition is paramount in playgrounds. The games, the chants, the secrets. A time-honoured opening gambit would be "We know something you don't know!" sung roughly to the tune of 'ner-ner-ner-ner-ner', but more jaunty and definitely more unsettling.

OK, so it's my first day in the playground. I barely know a soul. I'm irrelevant: just another boy with a wonky fringe and a cow's lick. I nearly choked on the free milk because it was warm and had some creamy scum on top, and the mandatory government red vitamin capsule went down *not* a treat.

So now I'm already compromised and not at all keen on Mrs Croke, the playground monitor, who looks like a warthog and can't speak without shouting.

When two girls loom large overhead in pleated skirts and ponytails, singing the aforementioned "We know something you don't know!" chant, I can't fathom whether to applaud or to inspect my socks again.

As it is, after a second rendition, I yield and say,

"What?"

To which the reply is, "What what?"

"Um – what do you know that – er – I don't?"

Maybe it was something important like a solution to the Cuba Crisis. The answer was simpler than that. Pressing an index finger to the ends of their noses, they said simply "Nose!" and flounced off.

I think the idea was that I was being nosy but, since it was their idea not mine, this seemed unlikely. Maybe they were just repeating the word 'knows' but that didn't add up either. Maybe I was just confused, which was absolutely the plan.

In the heady world of sexual politics, it was a perfect manoeuvre. Strike first, employ the element of surprise, take no responsibility for your actions then flounce off.

Looking back, what my four-year-old self was feeling but couldn't articulate was, "Fuck off".

Perhaps for the best.

I would probably have got the cane on my first day at school, setting a new world record. Like the last boy to be hung in Helston. At fifteen. For stealing a sheep. Maybe he'd seen it all in a dream. Red ties on the ceiling.

I kind of recovered, but I'd been forced to palate an unbearable truth: that girls really do know something I don't know, and 'twill ever be thus. For that I thank the flouncers. Best get it over and done with.

"When I was seven, in primary school, I looked across the classroom, I fancied you, I fancied you, when anybody says your name, I feel exactly the same". Song called *Seven*. Blues chugger. 2012.

Kiss-chase was obligatory, like skipping: a sort of cross between tag and sexual harassment. You didn't have to fancy the girls you kissed – and when I say kissed I mean peck, on tiptoe – nor they you. The first time I risked it I must still have been four. Maybe in an attempt to compensate for not knowing things I didn't know in the first place. In a flurry of rosy cheeks and wild evasion, up a dead end near the locked-up shed, where you had no choice. A breathless girl flattened against the black, flaky palings, wild eyes challenging you to proffer a peck.

The fun was in the chase. And the unfathomable.

As the days rolled on and I settled, I grew to like the St Peter's co-ed mix of social mismatches. In those days, most parents didn't travel miles or pretend to be Catholic to get their kids into the school of choice. You just went to your local primary.

I walked to St Peter's, at first with Diana from next door, then on my tod. Half a mile at the age of six was nothing. There were no Chelsea tractors backed up outside the gates, just humans ambling and shuffling to school. Some may have been in wheelbarrows, wide-eyed and legless. Or am I just imagining that? I'm sure, at least, that there was an air of the precipitous unknown.

It's a shame I didn't fancy Diana. As my next-door neighbour, she would have been the ideal girlfriend, but she was the marrying type… and I wasn't ready for that.

It was the exotic hard-to-gets that called my tune.

By the time I was seven, I'd developed several crushes. Jaqueline and Connie lived on St Peter's Road, one of the streets of working cottages that ran from King Street towards the newly installed A4 extension. That, by the way, was a total drag. I can just about recall being walked from Stamford Brook to the river down long silent avenues before whole roads were sliced in half and the A4 flyover – a 'wonder of the modern age' – descended like a writhing snake.

The same extension necessitated subways between the two Latymer playgrounds. This meant that, on the way to the dining hall, you could pick up the cry of "Spew!" echoing ahead of you underground and turn on your heels. Stew was an ocean of gritty gravy featuring a rivalry of inedible lumps. If it wasn't chips and arctic roll forget it.

But these were the all-boys days to come: 'house shoes' and procedure. At St Peter's, I walked home for lunch.

Roofy, Chris, Diana and her sisters

64

Jaqueline had a brunette ponytail and Connie's was blonde. They sat next to each other, polite and resourceful, with three-hundred-and-sixty-degree vision and a penchant for beautiful pencil cases. I sat to their south-west and, when I was looking at them, the ponytails would shimmer.

Some of the cottages on St Peter's Road and Black Lion Lane housed anything up to eight people – two parents, a grandad perhaps and loads of children. Connie's family was like that, except that her dad was in prison. Probably just for being poor. No one mentioned it. The kids were kind that way. She looked a bit underfed, as did Bob Sutton.

The Suttons all wore each other's clothes, sometimes at the same time, hand-downs and jumble-sale snips, drab and ill-fitting. They were a bit smelly sometimes too. Not that anyone cared.

Julia on the other hand, lived in neighbouring St Peter's Square, a sweep of elegant four-story mansions featuring Vanessa Redgrave and Lord Aberdare. She spoke differently from Connie, but there was no snobbery. It was the vibe of the age. Class-ridden, but not divisive. Not among us St Peter's kids anyway. It was more important how many marbles you had, who had the all-conquering conker and if you would swap two Eden Kane bubble-gum cards for a Helen Shapiro.

Whatever it was that Julia had, she knew it, and that in itself was enough to kill from a hundred skips. She oozed class. Nothing to do with upper or lower or sideways, just the indefinable 'that'. Her hair was daffodil yellow and endless, and her eyes were misty blue and, for all her self-possession, she blushed like an ocean dawn, nostrils lightly flared, lips stopping just short of a smile. Kiss-chase was a duty. This was love.

Julia and I lost touch when I moved on to the Latymer Prep at nine, and she was wafted across to Putney High. I caught heart-stopping glimpses of her at bus-stops but it was years before we spoke again. By then, we were seventeen and in our respective sixth forms.

Thanks to the 'revolution' it was OK for sixth formers to be out and about at lunchtime, which for me signalled a uniquely hectic hour. I was connected to several disparate social groups, and had my work cut out fitting them all in. First up was the ABC bakery, with Shipton and Buckingham just because they made me laugh. They were natural satirists, drifting up King Street with flaky sausage rolls and chocolate éclairs, roaring mercilessly at suburbia.

Next it was the bench in Ravenscourt Park, with fashion icon Steve Humphreys and the cool boys, for an immaculately rolled joint and a reoriented view of our immediate future – which for me and Steve was the hilarious world of Lord Palmerston. Surprisingly engrossing after some gold Leb.

Next, a dash to the smoky depths of the Ravenscourt Arms to join Mel's jocund crew for a pint of Watney's.

And finally, to the Two Twenty Café for lunch – a home-made burger and 'Get Back' on the jukebox. One day, mouth agape afore a hasty bun, I was arrested by a vision in the steel and glass doorway; it was Julia. In Putney High purple and a crisp, slyly revealing white blouse. How weird. She was now a teenager, sultry and self-aware, and yet the way I felt had its roots exclusively at St Peter's. What I mean is, she was the same but different. Morphing from child to woman and back again. Nostrils flaring, she caught my eye. I was seven again. And didn't she know it.

Nothing had changed. Black Sabbath's 'Paranoid' was spinning on the jukebox.

Godolphin girls were our natural allies and would gather outside the school gates after school and appear in school plays or Mel's latest groundbreaker. Miniskirts in June, afghan coats in December, big hair and high intelligence. They were fond and forgiving. What did Julia have to bloody well turn up for? Putney was another continent. Putney girls didn't migrate. Corona girls, yes. That was the stage school just up the road. Tina Charles – popstar to be – used to sing along with the Walker Brothers in the Two Twenty. But that was delightful. Just basic glitz and glamour. Julia had me by the soul.

She was dating someone else. Vince. A classic rock-star style hippy. Like a cross between Brian Jones and Marianne Faithful. I used to see him coming out of Stamford Brook station, no doubt on his way to St Peter's Square to impress Julia. I had no idea where he came from. I didn't care. But boy did he irk me. He was older than Julia and channelled all his energies into definitive cool. And he was probably great in the sack. Or wherever they copulated. The Moroccan futon probably. Well, he must have had something going for him. The one time I asked Julia out, she said, "I'd love to but I'm really hung up on Vince", in that middle-class hippy way of hers. Depressing. I was obsessed.

We did have a snog and cuddle once, but it was in the afternoon, my Osram bedroom lights were on and there were other people in the room discussing the Vietnam War. Not conducive to a life-changing event. It was time to move on.

Smoking was requisite for a girlfriend. Not necessarily hash but certainly cigarettes. Or 'straights' as they were known. Foul though they were, they signalled risk and adventure, and that included sex. Cigarettes were glamourised everywhere you turned: in movies, in ads, in the hands and mouths of rock stars, in screen-goddess photo shoots. They were a natural companion to partying and, for me, pretty well everything else. I smoked two before going into school each morning and usually had one on the go when I went swimming in the sea. But even when Godolphin girls smoked, it could be some months before the consummation devoutly to be wished actually occurred. A bit like that Richard Beckinsale-Paula Wilcox sitcom, *The Lovers*.

Once you were sixteen, losing your virginity at Latymer was more important than owning Led Zep II, or what car your dad drove (in my case none), or a star part in the school play, or bell-bottoms with a flap, or getting Mr Clamp to say: "The Rank Organisation". (He pronounced his Rs like Ws). So some of us sought the comforts of a conventional relationship. Pairing off as though for life. Wed and accounted for. Slurred vows of devotion at one of Jane Le Boot's parties. (Jane was somewhat off the rails. I met her again a few years ago at The Park Club in Acton. She was sweet as pie and utterly *re*-railed).

I was still inventing ever more elaborate ways of pretending that virginity was a thing of my past – which it wasn't – when a friend of my mother's came gloriously to the rescue.

When Dad left, rotten though it was for all concerned, it meant a new lease of life for Mum. She was grieving horribly and sometimes I used to sit up all night consoling her. Tears and smoke. But money needed to be earned and Mum was a talented actress. She'd taken a back seat when Candy was born, while Dad, to ensure that school fees were paid, had taken a regular job with the BBC Schools Drama Rep. Not his favourite gig, but it did at least mean he could appear as Edgar on 'I Am the Walrus'. Now that he'd gone and was still struggling with the effects of his breakdown Mum courageously re-entered the world of light entertainment. Her books of poignant poems, like *Twelve Burnt Saucepans*, were published and popular but hardly paying the mortgage. Sitcom was a much more remunerative option.

Stop Press. Quite timely, in fact, as I'd just got to 'sitcom' – and all true. I've just been sent a link to an archive site where some dedicated spark has discovered me in an episode of *The Young Ones* called *Cash*. The young ones' farty neighbour is watching TV and, in a parallel to Lennon happening to turn on the TV and hear my dad as Edgar, here the TV she's watching has been randomly turned on to me reading *The Phantom Tollbooth* for *Jackanory*, at 4:25 on January 30th, 1984. And it was the one and only repeat. So, it must have been meant. Mustn't it? I wonder if I get any money for that. Or Dad for his Edgar.

Mum certainly got money for *Not in Front of Children*, thank heavens. As she did for *Black Beauty*, a hugely popular series, with a great theme tune that got into the charts. Cool Mum. Another plus was that Mum, Charlotte Mitchell, although given star billing, rarely had much more to do than wave goodbye to the young heroes at the beginning, fret a bit in the kitchen, then welcome them home at the end. Oh, and pat the horse. So it left her

Mum in *Black Beauty* with Stephen Garlick

with energy for single-parenting: my sister Candy was seven years younger than me. Nevertheless, some help was called for, and it came in two very contrasting forms.

To provide some security and all-round companionship, it was agreed we'd get a dog. Yes, a guard dog. Although guinea pigs were still breeding in the garden, and a cat was skulking around somewhere, we hadn't had a dog for years. Theoretically it was the perfect enhancement for a household prone to leaving windows open and doors unlocked. Two Jack Russell brothers were interviewed, and we chose the one with – shall we say for now – personality.

The first mistake was getting a dog at all. We were all too busy really, but it happens every time. The lure of the new. I don't remember calling animals 'cute' back then but we said "Aaah!" a lot as if there was something particularly endearing about pissing on the floor and biting the furniture. I wrote a song about that, years later. Different dog, same conundrum. 'Bad Dilly Dog'.

The second mistake was not choosing the gentle, retiring brother. Like choosing me instead of Dom. The nice dog went home in its box, while Jeeves – as he came to be known – settled in immediately.

The third mistake was calling him 'Jeeves', at least in imagining that he would afford us the same level of domestic reassurance as the famous butler. He had come to protect us after all. The house had been mildly burgled twice already, so the logic was impeccable. What was not impeccable was Jeeves himself. Male dogs are always a challenge. Over-sexed, male Jack Russells are the stuff of nervous breakdowns. But I'm running on too fast. Jeeves gets his own chapter in a minute. And quite right too. He's best kept as far away from everyone else as possible.

Dilly Dog by Christopher Guard

And so, to the other contrasting form. A friend of Mum's suggested an au pair – someone to cook, particularly – for when *Black Beauty* had run late or the car back from Stockers Farm was snarled up in traffic. And to cover some light domestic chores like feeding the cat. She suggested interviewing some girls up in Dundee where she was on tour. Good working stock. Keen to see London. All heart and willing to learn. That sort of thing. She shortlisted two and, rather than waste money on train fares, she simply described them over the phone. Again, the one bursting with personality and *joie de vivre* got the gig, and soon Moira would be taking up residence alongside Jeeves, me, Candy, Dom, Mum and the rest of the Pleydell inhabitants. Moira was nineteen, dependable, a good cook and very good at looking after people. She got off to a perfect start.

I was fifteen when she arrived, soon to turn sixteen. I was dating a nice Godolphin girl and working hard at school. My virginity was still begrudgingly intact, but I'd made my peace with that, and was – for now at any rate – happy to channel my mojo into schoolwork. I loved the first year sixth. Colin Turner taught us *Othello* brilliantly. It came totally to life on his watch and I wrote great essays while Led Zep boomed and the Golden Virginia burned low.

In a dormitory reshuffle, I'd been given the big bedroom and Mum had made a nest downstairs. She didn't like to be reminded of happy days with Dad too much and I certainly welcomed the space. Even the flock wallpaper – Dad's take on boudoir sophistication – I embraced happily. It had a Biba vibe and went great with the genius hippydom thrumming and floating from my speakers.

So much music. I listened without prejudice. I wasn't in to all that rock snobbery. Loved The Stones as much as The Beatles, Donovan as much as Dylan, and deliberately bought obscurities like Black Cat Bones and even unhip shit like an Osmonds album. Why? Because of 'Crazy Horses', of course. Donovan albums were particularly fab. Decca knocked them out dead cheap – for ten and sixpence in fact – and songs like 'Sunny Goodge Street' were up there with the best. And the album *Stand Up* by Jethro Tull, with a sleeve that really did stand up. Forget downloads and streaming, this was real treasure. Wonders of the modern world. My room developed the ambience of a louche private members' club, more by evolution than design, although I did like to install red lightbulbs of an evening.

Because we lived just a Ravenscourt Park stroll from school, girls and boys would drift across to Pleydell, during 'free' periods or after four o'clock, almost as if by osmosis, and a bit of smooching and spliffing might develop, but all pretty mild fare. Nothing to rock the house. Chilled and curiously charming, we were perceived as a fashionably liberal household and, at first, the new regime seemed to be working rather well. Mum was making old friends new again, or just making new friends, Dom was on the crest of a wave and Candy had a group of friends who rolled and giggled through the house like a babbling brook: Candy at the front, Jenny, Debbie and Shirley loyal and breathless in her wake.

And then trouble. Well, not really at first. And for me, what you could perceive as some kind of progress, but like a lot of things in life it wasn't planned that way. I'd never seen Moira in a romantic light. She was too old for a start. Nineteen was ancient. And though she had bright, flashing eyes, masses of healthy brown hair, great teeth and a glorious giggle, I'd just never seen her like *that*. And anyway, as the oldest, I was a strategic part of the evolving status quo, supporting Mum both emotionally and practically. Not that I did much housework. None of us did. Mum wasn't house-proud anyway. We were clean and tidy enough for purpose.

I'm not keen on the Bohemian tag but, compared to Mrs Wilkie, I guess that's what we were. Maybe retrospectively the word galls because of my problem with 'Bohemian Rhapsody'. I know – it's brilliant; I just can't stand it. Sounds like five unfinished songs bolted together on a wet Tuesday afternoon. I loved Queen's first album but give me Curved Air any day. They played at our school dance. It was their last small gig. Copeland on drums. Sonja! Gracing the same rostrum that was inhabited on Monday mornings by the Grease.

Moira prepared breakfast in her pink quilted dressing gown. I don't know if she meant me to know she had nothing on underneath but a flash of inner thigh near a kitchen table leg was enough to suggest as much. I know something you know too. Or maybe she was just fulfilling her duties and that included – subconsciously or otherwise – seducing the oldest son, in time honoured tradition. Maybe she had always understood that to be the implicit agenda. Of course she hadn't. For all her breezy worldliness, I don't think she was capable of agendas. That was what I liked about her. She didn't play games or calculate, she just went with the flow, and had a flirtatiousness she couldn't help. She'd just forgotten her pyjamas. Or nightie. She'd been in a rush. Fuck it, I don't know. Some things just happen.

In the evening, while she was running a bath, I would wade through an essay on *Oedipus Rex* then phone Kate to arrange another innocent tryst. One day, after I'd neatly stacked my essay and as the bath gurgled down the plughole, Moira gave me a look on the landing. Not the au pair. Moira.

Booze is nearly always a prerequisite for romance. They go together like love and marriage. One evening, at a loose end, homework done, I fancied an underage quickie at my local, The Raven, and asked Moira if she wanted to

Me & Mum

come too. She did. She was good at drinking, and it made me less likely to get questioned about my age. Blind eyes were more easily turned in 1970.

Moira liked barley wine and could down several without the slightest hint of inebriation. Unless you count the knowing chuckles. An hour later, she was sitting alongside me on my bed, still no acknowledgment of what was about to become inevitable. A kiss, a fumble, a vague dawning that maybe this really was goodbye virginity – not in the way I'd envisaged, but maybe in a way that it had envisaged me. Our clothes stayed on, as I dithered and she sighed, until eventually, and this really does sound like yesterday today even – she said, "Do you nay find this a wee bit frustrating?" I mumbled, "Yes" and she abruptly left to have a portentous bath. With bubbles. I knew what came next – not more frustration, but the wondrous opposite. There was no going back now. I crept across to her bedroom and lost myself in the folds. Phewph. Thank heavens. She was plump and fun and just what I needed.

This soon became a regular feature of existence, and my schoolwork went from good to extraordinary. Straight As across the board in my end of year mocks. And mainly thanks to Moira. I was able to renounce virginity in the corridors, even if I'd kind of cheated by submitting to an older woman from Dundee rather than seducing an academic beauty from Barnes. And sex, along with drugs and rock and roll, suited me perfectly. These were halcyon days. I wore horns and halo with equal aplomb. Thanks Moira. Where are you now?

And then came the crash. The nemesis of the rake. It was shit what I was doing. Disloyal to Mum and dishonest to us all. And yet it seemed so innocent and reasonable; and it was just a sign of the times anyway. But we got too casual. Almost as if Mum knew what was going on and didn't care.

One Friday night, after a trip to The Raven, I fell asleep on top of Moira, and she fell asleep too. She didn't seem to mind. She was comfortable and I wasn't heavy. Then the lights came on. Mum hadn't heard us come in. I wasn't in my bed. Where could I be? Ask Moira. Oh dear. "Christopher, would you go back to your own bed please?" Oh God. I unglued myself and retreated. There was nothing more to say. Ignominy. Hurled from the Garden of Eden.

Mum was no prude, but this wasn't right. We all knew that. I was warned off, Moira too. She was allowed to stay on as long as it never happened again. Fatal. It didn't. For three weeks. My schoolwork was suffering. Seriously. What a mess. Then we got caught again. Just that one more 'just this once'. After some barley wine probably. Bloody booze. Bloody pleasure. Infernal flesh. As King Crimson wisely crooned, "Confusion will be my epitaph".

Moira was given her notice. It was for the best. We couldn't trust ourselves. It would never be the same again. Bugger. She got a job quickly enough. Mum helped her with that. For another actress friend. In Earl's Court. Gave her good references. The friend had daughters. I tootled over there sometimes on my Maxi Puch. But Moira was changing. She was tougher somehow. More cynical too. I didn't blame her. Nothing lasts forever. At least you knew something I knew too. I have never… well, I have now.

Before finally getting onto Jeeves, who had the sexual appetite of Rasputin, I want to go to Suffolk. To Carol. I mentioned her before. She was from the council estate in Lavenham and was also older than me. Before Moira. And maybe what follows is how love should always be.

Carol was a modern, country girl and I was the unlikely actor boy from London who stayed in the funny old cottage two miles across the disused airbase tracks, with no mains drainage and oil lamps for lighting. We sold the cottage soon after Dad left and there was little time left to enjoy its cosy, windswept vacancy.

Dom and I, and my friend Len, were allowed a few days farewell feral freedom in late summer. We went to the youth club in the old wool hall in Lavenham and danced with the locals. The next day we went looking for them, and they for us. Len was six feet when he was twelve so, at fifteen, now sporting a bum-fluff moustache, he was able to lie about his age and buy cider. This we ferried across by bike to an open-minded household on the council estate. Their most recently purchased single, 'Give Peace a Chance', was played *ad infinitum* all afternoon so everyone was in a very agreeable mood by the time Carol looked by at four.

She was way out of my league. Sheek, elegant, like a cross between Twiggy and Dusty Springfield. Black leather miniskirt, petite matching jacket, natural poise, other worldly. She danced. I tried to. I told her my name, she was intrigued. Maybe I was as exotic to her as she was to me. An actor? And from London. Across the divide. I didn't feel exotic. I had two left feet, a crap bike and had run out of cider. To my amazement she agreed to meet me at nine in the avenue to the north-west of the common.

Dusk fell as she shimmered into view, a teen wraith, gliding towards me, feet off ground, chill descending, blood rising, until we were within unbelievable touching distance. We talked softly, hugged, and agreed to stay in touch. That was all. I called her name a million times as I cycled home across the old airfield. An East Anglian angel with two O-levels, a beautiful bum and immaculate taste in hairspray. If I'd fainted and careered into a ditch I wouldn't have cared. Len was jealous and punched me in the ribs several times. Dom was OK. He'd been snogging Titch in a pillbox and had the thirteen-year-old love bites to prove it.

The following week, a letter arrived, explaining Carol's problem with our age difference and how many miles away I lived and her sudden preference for an older bloke with a Triumph Herald. My heart sank like a stone, but the dream lived on. Because that's all it ever was.

Jeeves on the other hand was not a dream. He redefined stark staring reality.

10: Jeeves

So, the moment has arrived. Even the title makes me quake. A whole chapter devoted to one small dog. The biggest small dog I've ever known.

Dad is compact and spry. Even now. Perfect choice for Puck. But he left a dad-shaped hole and attempting to plug it with Moira and Jeeves was bizarre to say the least. Dad was irreplaceable so why bother even trying?

Mind you, Jeeves was compact too. And shared Dad's energy and sex drive. In fact, now I think about it, there is a sort of symbiosis going on here.

And ironically Dad settled in Dundee, where Moira was from. And their laughs were not dissimilar either. At different pitches.

Hang on.

Was this all a fix?

I remember walking to school as a tot, convinced I was an experiment that everyone was in on except me. You can see where Sophocles was coming from. Smirking, knowing choruses watching doomed protagonists playing out their destiny with no control over anything whatsoever.

Maybe that's all those girls in the playground were. A tragic chorus, reminding me that however I played my hand I was fucked.

That was certainly Mel's philosophy.

Solum fac id et fuckit.

I'm procrastinating already. I was so looking forward to the Jeeves chapter, like we were so looking forward to getting Jeeves in the first place, but now it's arrived I'm a bit overwhelmed.

To Jeeves or not to Jeeves – Jeeves as a verb – I wonder. Covers a multitude of sins.

The thing is, it's just too easy to be mean about Jeeves. It wasn't his fault he was born with criminal proclivities; it was our fault for not understanding him.

Possibly.

Whilst I think about it, here's some of the song I wrote about Dilly years later. Dilly is still with us, and is the most patient old girl, but as a puppy, like a lot of border collies, she was a frigging nightmare. Just by being a dog.

Chris and Diana walk to St. Peter's

"She chews the legs of tables,
She chews the legs of chairs,
She bites electric cables,
She takes them unawares.

Then round about six-thirty,
As I stagger down the stairs,
I'm the one who gets the shock,
When will this destruction stop?

Bad Dilly Dog, this is my home.
Bad Dilly Dog, leave my stuff alone.
Bad Dilly Dog, give me a break,
Bad Dilly, bad Dilly Dog, for goodness' sake".

Better with the tune but I really did mean it. End of the tether stuff. Even good dogs have bad days.

Unfortunately, in Jeeves' case, there weren't really any good days. Just lots of good stories.

And even then, only after a significant gap for recuperation.

The first to spot a problem was the cat, Titty's successor. She was called Snowdrop, because she had a white splodge on her nose, but was otherwise a featureless void. Untypically of a Pleydell creature, she was spayed. At least as far as I recall. She certainly didn't give birth to any astronauts and showed little or no interest in anything really, least of all the opposite sex. Her redeeming feature was a sort of witless, abiding contentment.

Until Jeeves arrived. Poor Snowdrop. One feverish pursuit round the kitchen and she lost the will to live. "What the hell was that? That orange and white thing with teeth and one inside-out ear. I thought this was rodent territory, apart from me and the humans. Guineapigs, gerbils, the rabbit, not a problem. But Jesus fuck, when's he going?" It was a life sentence. It took Jeeves just ten seconds to force Snowdrop into the washing-up bowl – an unlikely retreat for a cat because it was full of water and Fairy Liquid but at least it was near the window, which was far enough ajar for her to squeeze through and exit. Jeeves by this time had eaten the rest of her Kit-e-Kat and pissed on anything he thought she may have had a claim to. Like her blue blanket.

Nice one Jeeves.

Snowdrop never recovered. She spent the rest of her life miaowing at the back door to be let in, and then immediately leaping into the washing up and miaowing to be let out. Whatever she did and wherever she went, all she could see was Jeeves. Even if he was down at the park biting a great dane. And herein lay another problem.

Jeeves was a) fast and b) small. Even when he was an elderly eight, people would sigh and simper when they met him at the front door as though he were still a puppy. This suited him fine. No mug, Jeeves. He'd play the idiot for a moment, then either piss on their coat, hump their calf or more often than not vault the front gate and sprint to the park. "Dog's out!" That was directed at me, partly because I could run nearly as fast as Jeeves and partly because I harboured a vain desire to train him.

Chris and Jeeves

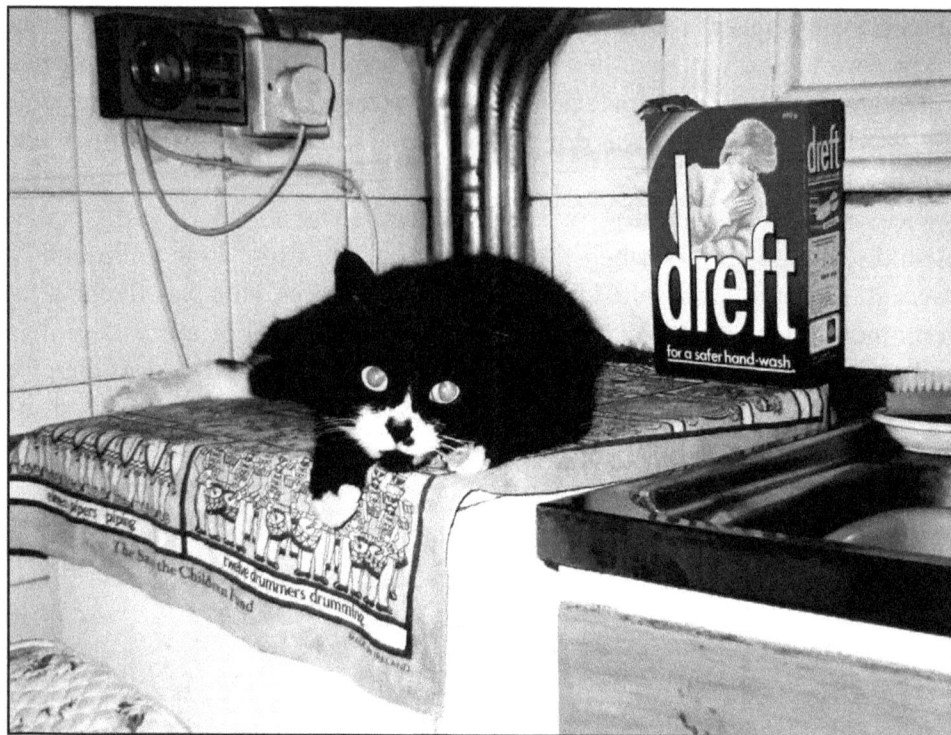
Minty Tat, a later arrival; I couldn't find a picture of Snowdrop

Thing about training dogs, especially males, is you do have to translate your undying love into some kind of consistency. In my dreams it might have been possible, but the household was too erratic, everyone running this way and that – and Jeeves was a supreme opportunist. Years later, I trained a dog called Jack, whom we got from a rescue centre, and had had a rotten life. It kind of worked but it was exhausting for us both and he always preferred drifting down to Shepherd's Bush market to inspect fruit to watching me cut the front hedge.

I was usually in the middle of an essay when Jeeves escaped: at a pivotal point, like debating whether Iago was sexually jealous or just a bit of a dick. Actually, you could ask the same of Jeeves. Never thought of a whole thesis on him, but the material is there in depth. So small and yet…

Jeeves could do more damage in thirty seconds than a scatter bomb. 'Jumpers-for-goalposts' would be squirted on, large defenceless dogs attacked from below and, if there was time, a quick shit was irresistible – in the summer as near as possible to a picnic or, in the winter, on another pile of shit. Frozen shit. Like he was making a shit snowman.

As soon as I was within a yard of him, he'd roll over on his back and grin cheesily at me, as if to say, "Fair cop, guv' but, you know, dogs will be boys".

Or bastards. I'd cradle him home like a baby, whispering curses in his ear, begging him for mercy. It never came. He was too quick, people were forever at the door, Mum was too expansive, my sister was only eight and Dom – well, he did share the duties – but, in some kind of masochistic way, I felt a noble calling. As if Jeeves and I were predestined to sprint to the park together. Eventually, I went by moped instead and brought him back in the front carrier. He looked as if he enjoyed that. Or maybe it was just the wind blowing his lips back.

Jack Russells were not an official breed back then, not as far as Cruft's were concerned anyway. So, they didn't include bite-the-great-dane's-balls in their small working dog disciplines. Or snap at the postman. Or hump Auntie Vera. Or chase the cat into the washing-up bowl. Shame. It would have been progressive and certainly challenging. Jack Russells did eventually make the grade but, by then, it was too late for the likes of Jeeves. They were bred as ratters, pure and simple, and if there were no rats, bellbottoms would do.

I was walking home from school one summer's day when I spotted Jeeves sneaking out of the front garden. The gate had been left open, probably by an onion seller or a knife grinder or The Singing Nun and, instead of turning right and legging it, Jeeves had spotted suitable quarry on the opposite pavement. An unassuming man in assuming trousers found himself wishing he was wearing drainpipes, as Jeeves leapt out from behind a Ford Cortina, snatched hold of one of his voluminous flares and proceeded to wring the life out of it. The man was backed up against a fence, frozen in terror. The only motion was the breeze in the lime trees and Jeeves' gyrating neck muscles. The only sound, apart from a silent scream, was Grrrr. And Rrrrr. And Gerrrrrr. In my imagination, I crossed the road, confessed ownership, apologised, scribbled my name and address and arrested Jeeves. In reality, I thought, "Fuck it".

I'd had a shit day at school. Mel had called in debts for a meal we'd had the previous week. I hadn't even wanted to go. And I certainly didn't agree to sharing a lobster. To soften the blow, he said he'd waive the fifty quid I owed from the game of brag, but could he have the twenty for the lobster and dessert wine. I didn't drink any fucking dessert wine. And he ate most of the lobster.

So, it was Mel's fault I didn't cross the road to help the stranded man, and Jeeves' fault for starting it in the first place. I had an essay to write on the fucking Corn Laws, the Grease had told me to get my hair cut – again – and I'd seen Julia coming out of Stamford Brook station with Vince. I was a dog too. And I had my rights.

Wendy saved me. Wendy Craig that is. Mum played her neighbour in *Not in Front of the Children*, and Wendy was the star. A relationship they mirrored in life. She often popped round to see Mum. Real neighbours. Wendy was full of fun and loved a giggle. She offered me a Rothman. I looked at Mum. Officially I didn't smoke though everyone knew I did. Mum nodded. Yeh! Smoking with the grown-ups. Virginity next.

I looked out of the flock-bedroom window, through the sun-speckled trees, 'Sympathy for the Devil' on the deck. The man had gone, and no doubt Jeeves was at the green. I wandered downstairs. In fact, he was in the sitting room with Mum and Wendy, eyeing Wendy's legs and eating some cake. Never did discover what happened next.

Jeeves wasn't a psychopath; he just didn't understand the British legal system. Why he felt the need to assert himself so relentlessly I never really knew. He was at his best on a lead when I took him round to the Queen of England pub, a dull, old-fashioned place in Stamford Brook.

Mick Shanley used to drink there with uncles twice his age. His brother was Kevin Shanley, who invented the famous Queen Di haircut. One day, Mick crossed the road a bit too slowly and got run over. He didn't seem to mind. He was like that. Took everything in his stride. How lovely. To have no ambition but to dress and walk like your dad.

Jeeves liked the old pub vibe. Just blokes together. Maybe he could smell the lack of ego. So why all the swagger at home? Was he just defending the patch? Keeping fit? He certainly didn't know he was small. He thought he was taller than me. If he saw a giraffe, he was at least that tall. Not that he ever did. Not as far as I know. Or maybe it was the libido. He had enough opportunities with the opposite sex, but he preferred tall leggy types and this may have added to the frustration. He certainly never seemed to relax. His threshold of boredom was even lower than he was. Nearly as low as Dad's. Dad never seemed to relax either. Mum used to wish he'd go round the pub sometimes, instead of writing three plays a day. Play darts. Be boring.

One of Jeeves' favourite ways of relieving boredom was by adopting the flying squirrel pose and masturbating on the hair carpet. His eyes would narrow and his ears flatten as the dreaded moment approached, and he wasn't at all pleased if you caught him at it and dragged him into the garden. In the end, we gave him a sausage-shaped cushion to clamp on to. Partly because of the effect the hair carpet was having on his willy. Out of its pouch, the willy would become irritated and swell up like a small pink balloon, marooned on the wrong side of the pouch. I would then cradle Jeeves down to the vet at Turnham Green – it's still there – with a towel draped across the embarrassment. One look and the vet would bounce us to the front of the queue, ahead of the ferret and lucrative parrots. He didn't want Jeeves hanging around. Especially in that delicate condition. Quick jab and things would settle down. Decorum restored. "This way with your ferret, madam".

Jeeves loved balloons. So much so that, at Christmas or birthdays, he would burst several and swallow them whole. The bangs didn't bother him. He was a sociable hooligan at heart and was happiest in company. He liked to reach out to others, let you know he was there for you. All dogs do it, cats too. Squirting and pooing is code. Telling jokes on lampposts, writing essays on trees. It's what animals do for conversation.

One afternoon, I'd nipped round to Stamford Brook station for the late edition and was buried in some football scores near a large plane tree. Jeeves was on the lead but, for once, he'd stopped yanking at it, and I'd almost forgotten he was there. As I dragged myself away from "Midget Mark nods shock equaliser in mudlark" (verbatim) I became aware of a wide-eyed woman at my elbow.

Even by his extraordinary standards, Jeeves had excelled himself. In an attempt to share his opinions with an Alsatian, he had done a handstand and was actually managing to shit on a smell at least two feet up the tree. And – and I mean it – what was in fact emerging from his arse was a green balloon. Genius. The woman smiled weakly as though in the presence of deity. One or two others stopped out of admiration or disgust, or both.

I shouldn't have interrupted. As I pulled Jeeves away, or down, the green turned to brown, and Jeeves shat all over his back. Kung Fu poo. Fucking hell. Midget Jeeves poops green balloon in shitstorm. Enough. This is more scatological than Mozart. Cosi fan Jeeves. The Magic Jeeves. More than enough.

Let the triumph of the story be Macduff's. Macduff was Candy's rabbit. We'd had a rabbit before. Barney Warbit white, red eyes – who was completely massive. In the summer, he would melt and become six feet long; cramping his own style. In the end he dug an escape tunnel into the next-door garden, a great Colditz-style shaft beneath the fence. You half expected to see him the next day roaring round the green on a motorbike like Steve McQueen. But he was never seen again. Funny that. Most of our pets were homers, and certainly survivors, the white mice notwithstanding. Oh, and the goldfish who ended up on the carpet when Jeeves got locked in the sitting-room on a hot day and drank their water. Even they had the will to live. And they certainly weren't going anywhere.

Macduff wasn't as big as Barney Warbit but he was all bloke. Handsome, grey-brown thing, well-tended by Candy and no pushover. Jeeves trod with care. Macduff stood his ground. One day, I watched Jeeves saunter down the garden, nonchalantly threatening. He wasn't meant to be out. Macduff was sat snoozing in the middle of the lawn. Jeeves growled. Macduff growled back. Jeeves pulled a nasty face and raised his hackles. Shit! I was about to run to the rescue, when the rabbit leapt three feet into the air, hung for a split second, then caught Jeeves broadside with an almighty kick from his vast feet. Jeeves tottered and reeled. Macduff went back to sleep. Jeeves looked over his shoulder to see if anyone had been watching. This was the height of embarrassment. Beaten up by a rabbit. I pretended not to have noticed and Jeeves tiptoed back to the house in search of easier prey.

Unwitting balloons and demented cats. By now, Mum had taken to calling Snowdrop That Fucking Cat, which was not very nice, but I know how she felt.

Much like I did about that fucking balloon.

Jeeves was happiest in Walberswick, on the Suffolk coast. He went on holiday for a week with Mum and Candy and a schoolfriend called Lorrie. I didn't go. I was probably too busy shouting Carol's name from my careering bike.

Jeeves ran all day along the shoreline until he was totally exhausted then slept all night in a caravan. That was all he needed probably.

The simple life.

Plenty of fresh air. A good night's sleep.

We're all the same.

Jeeves with Dom

11: High Time

This is clearly the moment. Or as good a time as any. I've just done a Zoom interview for the *Who at Hoylake* event, for my friend, Erica Lear. With Dee Sadler, who played opposite me in *The Greatest Show in the Galaxy*, written by the brilliant Stephen Wyatt. Dee and I were anachronistic hippies based on Jim Morrison and his girlfriend. Bellboy and Flowerchild.

Strange to think that, in '88, all things hippy were deemed sad and ancient. So much so that my daughter Daisy, on seeing continuity Polaroids of me in purple flares and a *Sergeant Pepper* jacket, cringed in agony and swore me to secrecy. "Dad in flares. Jeez. Please don't show my friends". I waxed philosophical about the vagaries of fashion. Turn to the left, turn to the right and all that. But I respected her rights. Lefts notwithstanding. On one condition. I bet her that by the time she was fifteen she too would wear a pair of flares. Well, that raised a laugh. The bet was taken with a shrug and a smirk, and Daisy still owes me a meal for two. I won ahead of schedule. Within two years, she was packing a bag for an overnight when I spotted something unmistakeable flopping from her case. It was a flare. The age of Lenny Kravitz had arrived.

Dance-rock crossover bands. The Manc vibe. Oasis reinventing Lennon. Festivals exploding across the nation. It was like the Isle of Wight all over again. Dads, kids, mums, grandpas, babies, dogs – all roads led to mud, lighters, crêpes-on-the-run and glory. I loved it. The original bands were either rediscovered or reinvented while the new ones paid exquisite homage. Radiohead hove into view. Björk materialised. I joined Indians in Moscow as lead vocalist with the brilliantly innovative Stu Walton and Pete Riches, writing lyrics to their loops and samples and playing The Marquis in Oxford Street. Indians had appeared on *The Tube* and *The Crankies*. It doesn't get cooler than that.

That *Dr Who* should unwittingly have been in the eye of this storm, two years ahead of itself, was only to be expected. The whole point of Who is not so much to travel through time as simply to ignore it. It's what happens, not how long it takes. *The Greatest Show in the Galaxy* was a twenty-fifth anniversary celebration, with a bigger budget than usual. Producer John Nathan-Turner was directly involved and hand-picked his cast and crew: Ian Reddington; Danny Peacock; Peggy Mount; Chris Jury; Jess Martin; TP McKenna; Alan Wareing – comics, singers, impressionists, thinkers, dreamers – an eccentric, diverse troupe in a strangely fated show. Dee said she'd have done it for nothing, and I think we all would.

The powers at the Beeb had been moaning about *Doctor Who* for a while. Seems extraordinary now, but its popularity had waned, and it was sidling inexorably along death row. Within a year of the *Greatest Show*, *Who* was no more. Our four-parter was greeted with confusion more than anything but, as with flares, concept and context are like sliding doors. This was literally timeless. In, out or otherwise. We were doing it just because. Stuck with it. By some strange other-worldly glue.

Jess Martin suggested I wrote a song for the show, 'The Psychic Circus'. I recorded the demo on my four-track analogue Portastudio and composer Mark Ayres produced the single. It wasn't taken up by BBC Records. But then neither did it go away.

Bellboy

The show nearly wasn't made at all, because of asbestos at Television Centre. Just as our contracts were about to be cancelled, we were farmed out to Elstree Studios and installed in an un-soundproofed marquee. A real circus tent for an unreal circus. The stars of *Eastenders* and *'Allo 'Allo* would float through the legendary gates in their limos while we – reprobate outcasts in a struggling show – battled against planes, pigeons and, in Ian Reddington's case, a portcullis that landed on his head. It was only a pretend portcullis but it still hurt and Ian fell to the floor in a heap and lay there as if dead for long enough to make the point that it wasn't in his contract to have portcullises dropped on his head.

One of the stars at Elstree was Richard Gibson, who was in *The Go-Between* with Dom and in the BBC serial *Tom Brown's Schooldays* with me. He spent much of his spare time trying to become a background extra on *Eastenders*, nimbly sneaking on set when the floor manager wasn't looking in a bid to introduce Herr Flick as an unlikely patron of the Queen Vic. The Queen Flick maybe. He never quite managed to appear in the show but the floor manager came close to a nervous breakdown. Richard was and still is a master of the improbable.

Mark Ayres nobly archived *Who* material throughout the nineties. When I worked with him on a pop music project in '96, he was writing film scores and recording the singer Lesley Garrett. His star was ascending and *Who* seemed almost like a sideline. Until the BBC Electronic Workshop played the Royal Albert Hall and Glastonbury Festival. Suddenly, Mark and the backroom boys were centre stage. And then it felt like it was always meant to be that way: it was just a question of time.

The DVD of The *Greatest Show in the Galaxy* was released in 2012. Some of us were reassembled for interviews and my 'Psychic Circus' song was remixed and included as an extra. "We know what you're thinking, we never go away, for the pleasure of your company, it's a small price to pay". And this morning there was Flowerchild, aka Dee Sadler, in front of her webcam, recalling the clay pit where we were chased by the kite, and the baking Weymouth sand, as if it was days, not decades, ago. Well, maybe it was. Time is at best an illusion. I'd not planned this book to coincide with lockdowns, but they sure give timelessness an added dimension. I'm not the only one forgetting what day of the week it is.

I had first connected, or rather disconnected, with *Doctor Who* from the very beginning. I was one of the original behind-the-sofa kids. We had no TV, so we legged it round to Francis and Jason's to catch Episode One, *An Unearthly Child*. No iPhones back then but we sure knew about this shit-scary new show. That was playground power. Swifter than Telstar.

'Telstar' was a record by the Tornadoes, used as the theme tune to *Scales of Justice*. The early '60s loved outer space. The first satellite station had recently been installed on Goonhilly Downs, near Coverack, where we first went on holiday in the '50s. By steam train.

We only went because Coverack was one of the few villages in the UK with a vegetarian guesthouse; otherwise, we could have ended up in Weymouth. Or Walberswick. Or anywhere. Anywhere out there on Planet Vegetarian.

Freakish fad back then.

Remember how Dad had been The Queer Sandwich Boy? Marconi made his first transatlantic phone call from Goonhilly. There are camels there now, on a farm. And a sign saying 'Cornish Camels'. It took eleven hours on a sleeper train to get to Redruth, and another two hours of driving, to reach Coverack. So that we could be timeless, transported. That's how the Lizard peninsular, jutting into the ocean, surrounded by stars and porpoises, made us feel.

First visit to Coverack, 1955

Francis and Jason's dad was the great landscape painter, William Bowyer. In those days, he was teaching to make ends meet, and painting in a bedroom. On Friday nights, he would play darts and drink beer at The Cross Keys, our local pub, that pub where Mum wished Dad would go and relax sometimes. Bill was always hungover on a Saturday morning, and Francis and Jason had to be charmingly unctuous if they wanted him to agree to something. Luckily, on November 23rd, 1963, they had wangled it so the TV could be on in the late afternoon, and Dom and I joined them to be scared witless by a fifty-five-year-old Doctor, who looked like your grandad with toothache. Mean, irascible, preoccupied. Your original anti-hero.

Patrick Troughton, the Doctor's second incarnation, had played the pawnbroker in *David Copperfield*. When we worked together on that production, I remember him squinting at me from behind the shop counter in the corner of the Lime Grove studio, near the stairs that led down to make-up, which was handy for my next change. Then dash to the next set.

These mid-60s dramas were filmed like live TV, only pausing to run short pre-recorded 16mm telecine sequences. Editing was time-consuming and costly so, even as the sequences rolled, we had to keep going like it was a theatre performance. Grab your coat, grab your hat, make the set in seconds flat. Make-up to match telecine – bit of sweat, some dirt, whatever – then stagger into Betsy Trotwood's garden where the multi-cams were prowling like Daleks, finding focus as we hit our marks, every move pretimed to perfection in a draughty church hall the week before. Patrick was a combination of stubble and silken bedragglement, skulky and mistrustful, but with a hint of elusive gold. Earthy otherness. He was a good replacement for William Hartnell.

Was *Doctor Who* sexy back then? I think the fear certainly was. The unknown. And the androgynous Girl had something about her. But the Doctors? Not really. Hartnell was deliberately and obsessively cerebral. I guess Patrick had a swarthy allure about him but again no time for romance. Maybe Tom Baker started all that. Bit of a rock star. Fine line between eccentricity and electricity. He crossed it.

I first became aware of sci-fi as a genre when I saw *Planet of the Apes* – the original, at the Commodore Hammersmith. With Charlton Heston in a loincloth instead of a robe. Dad had this cool trick whereby he would pretend he was taking us somewhere boring, like the Commonwealth Institute, then suddenly turn sharp right before the 27 bus stop and march us up the Attic steps of the local cinema.

It didn't matter what we saw. I just loved the whole vibe of the place. The sweet smell of aging velvet, the darkness, the obliging swing of the seats, the hot dogs, the trailers especially the trailers for an X-rated film. How great was that? Imagining how nightmarish *Whatever Happened to Baby Jane? really* was.

Not having a TV was a luxury. It made the cinema seem even more exotic. And Dad always discussed everything with us, especially the thought-provoking stuff like *Twelve Angry Men* at the Classic, Baker Street.

Planet of the Apes seems like a load of impossible tosh until the brilliant denouement. Shit! It's Planet Earth. I wandered home reliving the plot from a fantastic new perspective. That's sci-fi at its best.

That and anticipating the future. When Conan Doyle was allowed to escape from Sherlock Holmes, he conjured superb glimpses into the future. *The Lost World* is the precursor of *Jurassic Park*, and *The Poison Belt* anticipates city streets in this current pandemic. So, in a way, does Doris Lessing's *Memoirs of a Survivor*; the film version I made with Julie Christie is creepily prescient now. And, of course, Mary Shelley's *Frankenstein* was the mother of them all. It's that thing of asking yourself, "What are we *actually* doing? And where will it lead?" Out of time. The inevitable. Wrote a song with Indians in Moscow in the early '90s called 'Hell's Harvest'. "*As you sow, so shall I reap; it's just a question of time*".

Doctor Who is science fiction, but not in the classic sense. It sits at the heart of everything – past, present and future and reserves the right to travel as it wishes. It doesn't so much anticipate the future as ignore time altogether. So that all time can be present. On your TV set on a Saturday evening.

It deals with timeless moral issues too. The Daleks are the epitome of fascism, dehumanising and obsessed with power. That particular monster is uncomfortably present right now.

Whenever I've put a toe into the waters of sci-fi, I seem to have entered a world of universal devotion. Even when I provided the voice of Coggy in *Tripods*: one day's work thirty-five years ago – was a small price for immortality.

Is *Lord of the Rings* sci-fi? Or is it fantasy? Maybe Freddie Mercury knew the answer. He certainly struggled with reality. Me too.

My involvement with *The Lord of the Rings* was yet another trail of chance and happenstance. I was roped in, along with other actors with a radio pedigree, to play the character, Merry. I did a lot of radio in the '70s. Flavour of the month at Broadcasting House for a while. Lots of juve lead parts. Melchior in *Spring Awakening* for the legendary John Tydeman, and Adonis opposite Dame Di Rigg's Venus. Radio was a cool gig, because, as with *Jackanory*, which I appeared on several times, you didn't have to learn your lines – just read them like you meant it. I liked the imaginative leap. Loved reading to my kids. I liked microphones too, liked the relationship with their simple power.

Working close to them and playing with nuance. As if you were talking into someone's ear. Voicing a fulllength animated movie felt kind of destined.

The director was Ralph Bakshi, whose claim to fame was *Fritz the Cat*, the first X-rated full-length animated film. The producer was Saul Zaentz, who made *One Flew Over the Cuckoo's Nest*. Bakshi wanted the entire script recorded before he even started creating the drawings, so we were assembled at Bray Studios: among others, my brother Dom (we worked together several times), John Hurt (who I'd worked with on *I Claudius* – though we'd only briefly crossed paths) and Annette Crosby, Victor Meldrew's future wife. The marvellous Martin Jarvis had landed the role of Frodo.

On the second day, there was a distinct chill in the air. And no sign of Martin. Cripes. Was he OK? Yes, sort of, but he'd been relieved of his duties. He was one of the great voice artists of the age, but where was he now? At home. Paid but not played. Too old they thought. Too sonorous. As Pippin and Merry, Dom and I were doing the silly voices we usually reserved for our kids – cheeky high-pitched chirrups, throw-away stuff – but Bakshi seemed to think we'd set the hobbit benchmark. As I sat down with a coffee, he looked at me and, without ceremony, said in his Brooklyn drawl, "You're Frodo!" Blimey. And I was too. Sorry about that Martin. My wages were doubled and all for putting on a silly voice.

One thing they didn't pay me for was the tune I wrote for Frodo's 'Merry Old Inn' song. Oh well. Must have been my round.

Playing Legolas, and about to hit legendary status, was Anthony Daniels. The year before, he'd made a low-budget little movie called *Star Wars*, playing C-3PO. Another case of spontaneous stellar projection. You truck along, you do your best, then along comes fate and suddenly it was always meant to be that way. From the BBC Drama Rep to Hollywood red carpet in the arc of a rollercoaster. Cue the knowing chorus and the canny casting director.

Bakshi worked feverishly for two years, using an extraordinary mix of Disneyesque animation and rotoscoping, before eventually re-assembling us for overdubs. (Rotoscoping involved filming genuine Spanish extras for the battle scenes, then tracing them into the animation cels). Not that we were overly concerned with the reason. It was another two days' money, the footage was looking great, and the atmosphere was almost celebratory. There was even talk of a sequel.

John was still called 'Hoit' by Bakshi, despite his increasingly brilliant career and, by way of redress, he was up the pub most lunchtimes. Red wine suited John. He drank and smoked a lot – but always within his limits – and was a consummate thespian. He had the chameleon instincts of Bowie and the rich voice of a Shakespearian. He could do anything really. And laugh through it all too. A unique chuckle-roar. Wisdom and defiance. He didn't care what Bakshi called him. He was a free spirit and nothing would phase him. "Hoit!" Drawl off a sprite's back.

It was interesting how the animated characters turned out. As if Bakshi had morphed our disconnected voices into the fully-fledged hobbits, and there we were somehow within the lips, eyes, and facial movements. Not a representation, but an audio-visual projection, so that Frodo actually looks and moves a bit like me. He seems to, to me anyway.

Maybe sci-fi fantasy is so popular because it has no preconceived bounds. It is literally the stuff that dreams are made of. It traps you in a timeless vortex where Frodo and Bellboy and Coggy never die, and fans believe in you forever. It transcends all the Plays of the Month and BBC Classic Serials, the Theatre an der Wien and earth-bound swashbucklers. Transcends Liz Taylor and Julie Christie. Even when you pitch up at *Doctor Who* conventions, thirty years older and feeling the force of gravity, the sight of the glossy pics of an earlier, timeless you, the sweep of permanent ink as you add your squirl, a dedication to someone who refuses to grow up? It's a curious sensation, not being allowed to die. Bless that rickety rocket and all who sail in her.

Shakespeare's The Tempest is sci-fi. Moral retribution acted out through the vehicles of magic and other-worldly beings. Ordinary as a police box one moment, wild as endless space the next. The Doctor as Prospero. Discuss.

In Chapter Three, I mentioned being 'off' at the RSC; not foul and smelly, although I may have been that too, but not onstage when I was meant to be. By a weird coincidence, the actual line that greeted my entrance was "What kept you?" – the joke being that most of the characters were tearing around like blue-arsed flies so nothing was keeping us at all. The hiatus simply provided a different take on being kept waiting. By being somewhere else. Nobody noticed.

I loved Cyril Cusack. He played the villain, Antonio, in *The Tempest* and flatly refused to play the part 'villainously' despite the urgings of an irksome assistant director. While Peter Hall focused on the sexy stuff with Caliban and Miranda, 'Irksome' had been given the task of making the lords' scenes interesting, which is impossible because they're innately boring. "More villainous, Cyril! Louder!", Irksome would implore. Cyril blithely ignored him and played the part with a wonderfully dry, smiling otherness that made him sublimely evil. If you're playing a baddy and being treacherous and murdering people, you don't have to remind the audience what a shit you are. In fact, the nicer you are, the nastier you are. "And what's he then that says I play the villain?" (Wrong play, Christopher).

Anyway, the lords have three main entrances. First, when they're a bit pissed off but still *compos mentis*, second when they're beginning to go a bit loopy, and third when they've gone completely bonkers. Cyril's dressing room was at stage level and, as all his entrances coincided with mine, he'd asked me to "give him a little knock" shortly before we were due on. Perfect.

The lords would appear from various directions high up on the heavily raked stage, before making their way downstage and boring the audience. In his second appearance, Antonio has a touch of fever but appears calm and is facing downstage. In the final appearance he faces upstage, slashing at imaginary monsters with his sword and groaning a lot. One night, Cyril got the two scenes the wrong way round and, as everyone else was already a long way downstage preparing to be boring, I was the only one far enough upstage to notice. I shuffled sideways several feet before muttering, "Wrong scene, Cyril!" With consummate sangfroid, he popped his sword back into its scabbard, gave me a little wink and arrived where he was meant to be just in time to be villainous. Cyril was so cool. For the real nutjob scene, he re-choreographed his slashes and growled rather than groaned. And of course, as ever, nobody noticed. Except me.

My sister Candy is a brilliant animator. And she writes illustrated novels too. At a time when digital was blossoming and anything was becoming possible, Candy preferred a more Bakshi-esque approach. She invented an award-winning, semi-autobiographical comedy series called *Pond Life*, deliberately keeping the drawings low-fi, scripting it all herself and directing a hand-picked cast as no one else could have done. She even used my mum and brother to voice some of the characters, and me to write the theme and incidental music. This was partly out of loyalty but also because we were simply more likely to "get it".

The material was drawn directly from her own growingup, featuring recognisable schoolfriends and even a Jeeveslike dog. The mum – played by Mum – is, well… Mum. Sort of. The dramatic license is impeccable. Set in a dull, go-nowhere, suburban world, Dolly's mother is not the creative spirit Mum was, but the nuances are there – the mother-worries, the vicariousness, the angst. Luminaries like Emma Chambers and John Thomson are in the mix. But to play her alter ego, Dolly, Candy chose her best friend, Sarah Ann Kennedy, who was up at Newcastle Uni with Candy and created *Crapston Villas* for Channel Four around the same time.

Usually, when a director starts showing you how to play a part, it's frigging irritating. Like, if you want to act, why didn't you become an actor? And it's not as easy as you think, as you're proving right now. And, you don't have

94

to wave a sword or mount a sand dune at the same time. Or clutch a script without rustling it. But in the case of Sarah, it was more a case of "be me", not "do it like this". The likeness is uncanny. I thought it really was Candy at first. The tone, the timing, the inflections. But that was the genius. Cast someone who knows you so well they can be you in a make-believe world – believably.

For the second series, the price of success was more episodes and more artists. The balance of brilliantly crafted script and slapdash drawing was pivotal. Candy had to hover over people, telling them not to make it 'right'.

"*No!* I want it to look a bit wrong. Not wrong, but how it is. A bit wobbly round the edges, mirroring the frantic uncertainty of the main protagonist. Oh, never mind. It doesn't matter why… please just make it a little more… difficult!"

Zaentz and Bakshi had bought the rights to the Tolkien classic. It was not popular back then, but they wanted to make an amazing movie out of a unique book. They saw the cinematic potential. I wonder what would have happened if they'd waited ten years; certainly, the curio they somehow conjured would not have existed. Digital was what the world of fantasy had been waiting for. Narnia, Harry Potter, how different would it all have been if we'd never got

Candy, with award

95

beyond the wheel? Beyond polystyrene, *The Land That Time Forgot*, Colour Separation Overlay and back projection. Yet it's the impact of the limitations that make so much of that old stuff compulsively watchable. Not sentimentally but because it is what it is and always will be. At the time it was shit-hot modern. As was the first blunderbuss.

Christopher Reeve looks faintly ridiculous flying about as *Superman*. Like a suspended action man doll. Yet at the time, we queued twice round the Odeon, Leicester Square to see him defy gravity and disbelief. What has changed is our expectations. We've become jaded.

When I was allowed to watch *The Lone Ranger* on the TV next door at Diana's in the sixties, the screen was as big as the one at the Odeon, Leicester Square. Just like Geoff Southgate's TV in Alpheton, where we watched England win the World Cup, was in "glorious Technicolour". I could smell the turf; senses straining, imagination plugging the gaps. In reality it was in black and white, on an eleveninch screen and, in the case of *The Lone Ranger*, in a gloomy sort of khaki and white, and the sound was monophonic and weedy. And yet it wasn't. It was fantastic. The 'William Tell Overture' never sounded so good and, when The Lone Ranger rears up his horse and says, "Hi Ho Silver", boy goes to heaven. Boy writes play called *The Farm Boy*. Boy gets holster and silver gun for Christmas. Oh boy.

Of course, the old stuff is all over YouTube now, and we can fly through the decades like index-finger astronauts; but what we can't truly get – or emotionally appreciate – is what it was like when it first happened. Being there, wide-eyed and gobsmacked.

When Yuri Gagarin, the first man in space, cavalcaded down the A4, past St Peter's Primary, and the whole school was allowed to go out and watch (even the recovering Kenny Morris, who'd been run over trying to cross the A4 and broken his leg), there was an aura of surreal modernity unlike anything I've experienced since. Bubble-gum cards, vast murals of Jesus predicting where to catch fish, Monica Rose predicting hits and misses on *Juke Box Jury*, Grandpa's 9.5mm camera, television cameras invading our house like Daleks so Joyce Grenfell could film *A Family at Christmas*, the Ford Zephyr up the road, my Ford Zephyr Dinky car, *Thank Your Lucky Stars*, fizzy tablets to make your frogman Action Man swim underwater in the bath, Roofy's son's sheath knife, the HBomb, earwigs under paving stones, spiders down the plughole... if that wasn't sci-fi, what is?

Why the Church murals? Well, we had to go to St Peter's Church twice a week, in neat crocodiles, to smell the varnish and stare at the stained glass and be told about miracles. About Jesus zooming up to heaven or bringing dead men back to life. Cool shit. I used to think Father Christmas was Jesus' dad.

Well, it had a kind of logic. Big generous bloke with a beard. The information came so thick and fast it was hard to process. Surrealism served up as reality. Small wonder we all smoked weed in the '70s. It was a bid to discover some kind of normality.

Years later, I tried to capture that six-year-old's world:

"Helen Shapiro was a young girl,
She made it big in a small world
Years ago,
Shadows falling on a bubble-gum card,
Frosty morning and the gum goes hard
Years ago.

Six years old,
Everything I'm told is pretty meaningless,
Goodnight, god bless.

Six years old,
Everything I do is really effortless,
Goodnight, god bless. Sold

Sold".

That sort of thing.
From my song 'Sold'.
All in the mind.
Art for fuck's sake.

12: Art for Fuck's Sake

The closest I came to any kind of formal artistic training was at Latymer, which is to say I had no formal artistic training at all. There were some natural talents lurking about, but they owed as much to the art room as I did to Stanislavsky.

Music was the same. Geniuses like Raphael Wallfisch, the cellist, was contemporary but, if he learned to do that in class, my name's Keith Moon. Music lessons were curricular necessities. There was little or no pressure on anyone to excel so, unless you were taught privately, or were in the choir or school orchestra, it didn't really matter. The great Charlie Morgan, who drummed for years for Elton John, may owe some of his progress to the music room, but I doubt it. I only say that because my abiding memory of music lessons is of thirty boys relieving their pent-up frustrations by banging things.

The droll Mr Harman adopted an attitude of dry resignation while the dynamic Mr Thornett tried to show us how to sing very high by pinching his forehead and rolling his eyes towards the ceiling. This definitely worked for him, but not for the sage-like Lane-Ryan, who's dulcimer had slid off his knees when he nodded off to sleep. He could sleep through anything. Even Mr Thornett's top C.

The alto dulcimers were in great demand because you got to bang them with a round rubber stick instead of a useless, frayed wooden one. The other dulcimers couldn't even go "tink". There were only eight alto ones so that at least stirred us enough to have a wrestling match but, if you were lucky – or unlucky – enough to get one, you quickly lost interest anyway. The wrestle was the main thing. Not the descant.

It's hard to play a descant when no one has mastered the main melody. So two strains would emerge, or in fact several, producing a grinding, rasping, industrial clatter more akin to the woodwork shop. Add to this the indefinable sound of several recorders blown so hard they either made no sound at all, or just bubbled a bit at the end and shrieked like bronchitic cockerels, and your ensemble was complete. We were actually given sheet music and encouraged to read it, but we were just as likely to eat it, especially as music lessons always seemed to be the last lesson before lunch, and we were already light-headed.

Mr Thornett was a cool dude, and did a great job with the choir, and taught English pretty well too, while Mr Harman found his mojo round the school orchestra. It's just how it was at Latymer. Drama and theatre were the thing.

When I suggested taking Art O-level, eyebrows quivered precipitously – not because I lacked talent, although I'd demonstrated little in that area – but because, for someone with Oxbridge tattooed on his forehead, it just wasn't 'serious' enough. Art was an option for losers who were predicted to fail Maths. Ridiculous. Music was the same. Do music outside proper school; don't compromise bunsen burners and the Alps. This was still the age of 'subjectism', when we were expected to be either artists or scientists. I wanted to do Biology with English. Can you believe that wasn't allowed? It fucked up the timetable, and your head apparently. A few years later you could mix arts and sciences willy-nilly. We embraced a lot of progress in the late '60s, but not chaos theory.

As for the art room, Reg Pye would arrive with the most enormous length of dowel, crack it down across three trestle tables, then bellow, "Right gentlemen!" Really conducive to knocking up a sunflower or two. Meanwhile Mr U, who had something of the flower about him himself, took a more pastoral approach. Both talented enough artists in their own right, they didn't seem overly keen on sharing their prowess with others. Unless you count Mr U's enthusiasm for life drawing.

It makes the eyes bulge with disbelief now but, when I was in the prep, still only nine, he sent an apparently innocent letter to my parents asking if it was OK for me to stay behind after school for twenty minutes while he sketched me. Max's parents were similarly approached. "Hey, why not? Seems a nice dude. This is the swinging '60s! What do you guys think, Mr and Mrs Max?" "Sure, if the boys are cool with it". Cool being the word. Or fucking freezing more like.

Three days later, I was alone with Mr U on the top floor of Rivercourt House. Max had been reserved for next week. Had my parents missed the word 'life'? Or just misunderstood? "Take your clothes off please". Charcoal and paper at the ready. The adjacent river was particularly high and brisk that afternoon and the windows were open. "What?" "Just take off your clothes. So I can sketch you". "Which ones?" "All of them. So I can sketch you". Oh I see. He doesn't want to sketch my school tie or my house shoes, he wants to sketch my frozen willy and my drooping shoulders. Fine. Anything to please. This must be part of the curriculum.

It seemed a miserably long way away from kiss-chase and Connie Lane. "We know something you don't know".

Jeezus, here we go again. Why do people fucking spring these things on the uninitiated? In a way it was no more or less compromising than the first morning at St Peter's. Just a different type of awkwardness.

I took my clothes off. Folded them on a chair. Socks stuffed into house shoes. Then just stood there, feeling that lonely, sick feeling you get when you've gone for your first night away from home and you're missing your mum. Mr U was perfectly polite and pleasant. He gave no indication that he had any interest in me beyond improving his draughtsmanship. And it was certainly drafty.

Time was doing somersaults again. How long? Twenty hours, it felt like. I reported back to Dad. No harm done, but the exercise was not repeated. Max only made one fleeting appearance too. Maybe that was Mr U's way. Cyclical. Don't obsess. Who knows? Maybe he didn't. Poor old sod. Years later he ended up in big trouble.

I mention all that because it was symptomatic of the age. With progress and liberalism, came some serious waywardness. Meanwhile, across the corridor, an obscene stickler for tradition, a man known as 'Bunny', was sharpening bamboo canes with a penknife before laying into the upper thighs of his favourite naughty ten-year-old boy. The boy has since changed his name, and who can blame him.

Years later, I discovered art for myself. By breaking rules, not following them. I'm untrained as an actor, a guitarist, a singer, a songwriter, a breeder of guinea pigs, a dog handler; and now as a writer of memoirs. I was lucky to meet lots of brilliant, creative people and I soaked up stuff like a sponge, but there was something else at work – a kind of stubbornness, a conviction that if you wanted to do something badly enough you could and a stoical belief that nothing comes easy.

And a willingness to trust my own judgement. I mean, if *you* don't know what you've done is any good, why ask someone else? Of course it's subjective but, whether anything is basically up to scratch or not, is down to the artist's quality control check. Someone might loathe your grunge punk but, if it's what you intended, and you like it, you've succeeded. Time is the best second opinion. Dream hard, work your bollocks off, ask yourself difficult questions and wait.

Acting is a bit different. You're in a cooperative. If the production is basically shite, your ingenious performance will only partly compensate; but if your painting is basically shite, you can't blame the assistant director. Or your teacher. Unless the teacher is you.

These ideas became clearer when I took the plunge of running an art club at my daughter's primary school. I'd painted before – heartfelt water-colours

– but only as a hobby. One or two I'd sold but acting and music were tough enough professions without adding a third. Amateur suited me fine. In the real sense. For the love of it. Not struggling to pay the rent with a hundred canvases in a cramped bedroom as Bill Bowyer had done in the early years.

In fact, Bill didn't inspire me at all, for all his brilliance. It was his sons, Francis and Jason, who did that, and not so much through their art as because of what they were and how they lived and how they related to the things they drew.

At one point, Jason became Fulham Football Club's official artist. Deeply unfashionable back in the '80s but he wanted to capture the inexplicable: his love affair with that curious mix of structure, movement, tradition, chaos, humour, success and failure – something that has come to be known as 'Fulhamish'. He rejoiced in the faces, the quirks, the eccentricities, the 'lore' of the terraces.

And just as Jace was drawn to the natural habitat of football supporters, he fell in love with gorillas and went to Africa to watch and sketch them. He always preached drawing. Always go back to drawing. The toughest discipline of all.

Cottage Celebration by Jason Bowyer

Art on the floor

Like comic timing. Be serious, they said to my sister. Why waste time and talent on sketchy drawings and weird comedy scripts? But that was the point. Candy was doing something she understood, something *of* her, and therefore something that everybody else could understand too. Jace painted Walberswick because he loved the place, and he loved it because it was a part of him. And that's what the seascapes tell us. They are self-portraits.

My dear friend, Ivor Thomas – whom I knew so briefly – taught me more by saying nothing than did a hundred art history lessons. Not that I had any. He would sit on his favourite stool in The Paris Hotel, Coverack, after a long day's sculpting in paint or stone, and just watch. And watching him watching was a wonder. The sparkle in the eye did his talking. Paradoxically, one thing he did take the trouble to say was how redundant words are, and to explain the difference between recognition and awareness. You know what it is, or at least you think you do, but can you draw it, or sing it, or find the right few words to describe it? Recognition. The world we live most of our lives in. Two-dimensional flashes of spontaneous memorabilia on smartphones, ever-diminishing returns. Shallower ponds and fewer ripples, stretching as far as the eye cannot see. Ooh, look! It's as beautiful as a photograph!

It was because I admired Ivor the human that I wanted to do what he could do; wanted to travel to where he had been; with paint and patience. The unknown. The untaught. The loved. His wife, Jo, said he knew he'd arrived when he no longer felt the need to paint or sculpt; when just being part of it was all.

Put me back in the jungle. Take me home. The orphaned orangutans. They can't explain. It is all sensuous. Untrammelled. Unanswered for.

"Rainbows do OK, they got the sky to cuddle up to, when they lose their way, when they've had their say for the while, sunsets muddle through somehow, they got a lot to do just now, but… it's easy for them, and it's so hard for me and you, to do the easy things".

From a song on the piano, '74, when I was just beginning. Again.

I know a lot of my paintings are compromised. I plan ineffectually and am frequently left panicking and flirting with disaster. The fine line between arrival and chuck it in the bin. But when they do work, at least I know it.

How do you write a song?

Well, exactly. No one taught Paul McCartney. It's like the song is already written and you just have to find it. Like hide and seek. A title, an idea, a place you want to go, a rhythm, some chords; start singing, see pictures, work hard, know when to stop… and start again. And then when you think you have a formula – break it. There is no formula. Only changing patterns, elusive fractals. It's not meant to be easy. We spend a lifetime looking for symmetry and order. Coffins and gravestones. Life's not like that.

With nothing but these home-made philosophies as learning tools, I entered the wild, wonderful world of the Wendell Park art room, where two groups of fifteen children, fives to eights, then nines to elevens, awaited my divided attention. Some would arrive flummoxed before they'd even begun. "I don't know what too doooo!" "Neither do I," my reply. "But you're the teacher." "Am I?"

And once they realised I was just like them really, and made mistakes, and only got better by getting things wrong, and liked to have a laugh, and looked bored if they swore – so much so that they soon got bored with it too – they would throw themselves into their work with such abandon it could almost overwhelm me. Technique? Well, I guess one may have evolved. But it was just

Kids' art exhibition

like extended parenting really. Some of the kids had maybe only one parent at home, and certainly not one who read to them regularly, or made a mess with paint, or discussed god, so the challenge was to be about fifteen different people all at once and give everyone makeshift one-to-one in a crowded room. Which was impossible really – and that's how I liked it.

Some amazing pictures emerged. And some I would take home, to finish or enhance – not to cheat, but to show them where they could go next. And if they didn't want me to, I wouldn't.

We ended up having an exhibition in the hall, big screens festooned with inspiring, vibrant artwork, mainly oil pastels and watercolours. Mixed media too. The local press came and we were in the paper.

Then out of this came more paintings of my own. Pictures with a story to tell – specially made for the kids – stories they would retell to the latest influx of panting painters. Leap onto a stool. I'll tell you! "Mr Chris says…"

Some of the stories had a kind of moral. They all had humour. I hope. This was art for the artist's sake. Send them home happy, and they're queueing round the block again next Friday. Bit different from the Latymer art room in the '60s, a place that came into its own mainly as a retreat for the upper fifth: somewhere to discuss Frank Zappa or make props for the school play. I want to, so I darn well will. I should, so I darn well won't.

It's all changed now of course. The wondrous Robert Orme, who taught me history in the '70s, is doing a three-part series of lunchtime lectures this coming March on *Contrasting Uses of Symbolism in Art* and all proceeds will fund a talented student to study History of Art in the Sixth Form. Now, that's more like it. Rock on Bob.

Robert Orme

I saw Robert on a bench in Furnival Gardens two years ago. I was cycling round the river to take my mind off the loss of my dear friend Mark Wilkin. So good to see him. Bob, I mean. Mark was a fine artist as well as a great drummer. More of him anon.

Seeing Robert made it feel like we were all there together, in 1969, in the early summer sunshine, forever.

13: Harbour Wall

This chapter is not so much about Coverack the place as Coverack the haunting. Ever since I went there in late summer, as a two-year-old, it's been a part of me; under the skin, sometimes beautiful, sometimes taunting, an elusive dream, inescapable.

"What do you do here?" said a friend, pacing round the village dreaming of a golf club. Not much. Well, in fact you do more than you could ever imagine, but only if you shut up and stop looking for something you'll never find. It often takes a day or three.

Looks like a postcard for a while. You're outside it. Not in. It waits like Narnia, wherever you may be. Until… through the wardrobe, off the sleeper train, through the moth balls, down the hill. Always there. Abiding, laughing, waiting for you. Summer, not winter. Dangerously attractive. Highs and lows, nothing in between. Too much for some. Too much romance. Too much reality. A holiday or just a coming home? Coverack looks gorgeous in the snow.

Oxford Circus. Rushing. Skeltering. Twisting and turning through shins and shoulders, running to stand still. Heat and dirt. Or maybe slush. Traffic. Carbon monoxide. The jungle we created, forged in agitation to keep us from distraction. I canter up an escalator, racing against myself, no surrender. Like the totem of a pagan, the harbour wall is with me. And Ivor on that corner stool, the crackling setting sun and the twinkling blue eyes, the smiling reassurance of impermanence – so that, however thick the traffic, however smug the fog, however self-assured the surge of prospering humanity, I will survive; I will come through it.

There were – still are – other things I cleave to, recall, dream myself into. Pre-school garden spider's web, the smell of Roofy's bargain perfume, Mum singing "Do you want the moon to play with?", the glow of a Suffolk oil lamp late on an autumn afternoon. Even singing 'Lord keep us safe this night' in my last term at St Peter's as we stacked the chairs on tables and prepared to wander home in the twilight. They work too; they are fit for aching purpose.

But the best in times of panic has always been the harbour wall. People jump into the sea from it, fish for pollock from it, focus binoculars from it,

Mum on the harbour wall

duck behind it when twelve-foot rollers crash above it in winter storms, lean on it, love on it, but most of all just… sit on it.

And then, when you are lost and it is many miles away, dream of it.

The moon is full, the tide is right: low on the beach by noon, high in the harbour by five. The sun has shone all day, the wind is from the south or west, gaggles have wandered from beach or cliff or pasture to settle on the warmed, familiar stone; chips from the Lifeboat café, wind-rippled beers, and blackcurrant and lemonades, on teetering tin trays gingerly conveyed across uneven flags by bare-footed heroes. I've swum from the wooden steps at the north end, across to the outcrop below the Old Post Office, sat on a rock awhile like a golden souvenir pixie, slunk back into the glorious salty chill, risen up the steps brine-baptised and pagan-perfect, sat on the wall with towel and beer and the hint of a shiver.

A little too much sun, a little too much salt, a trifle too much chill.

Never enough.

And this is the moment you keep tucked away in your soul in case of emergency at Broadcasting House. Or commercial casting sessions.

When you've been asked to be smart but casual, young but old, there but somewhere else. Homogenised casting for a digital age. Hall of holograms, jobs for the toys. When studio eight is more caffeine than oxygen, and the canteen sweats with theatre stories, and you shift on your chair like a neurotic raccoon in a cage, when you curse the day you said yes, and have forgotten how to say no: the harbour wall.

Just knowing that it's there. And will never go away. It holds back the tide and the tide of time. It waits for you like your mum after your first day of school.

It just is.

Your eyes full of setting sun, your lashes flash with shining – dark and bright and brackish. And your limbs tingle-drift, your shoulders shudder in slo-mo, and you know – this is *it*.

You wouldn't care if you died, you're *that* alive.

Coverack is – or certainly was – a working fishing village. A hard taskmaster back in the day, with a lifeboat so famed its Coxswain, Archie Rowe, was one of the first to appear as the subject of *This Is Your Life*.

At a time when celebrity was more earned than it is today, I was lucky to experience the unique Cornishness that Archie typified. A raw, ancient, sanguine innocence.

Coverack still has a huge heart, but it is an open secret now and the times I cherish most are those early days in the '50s and '60s when most of the cottages were lived in by Cornish people and tourism was a symbiotic part of Cornish life. You went to Cornwall because it was Cornish, not just because it was beautiful. And we had no car, so everything unfolded with a slow, mesmeric magic.

We stayed at Mrs Gordon's vegetarian guesthouse, Porthgwara – which is now an old people's home – where the huge garden was full of secrets and rolled all the way to the cliff edge, and we ran and roamed free with our friends Dave and Michael Woolf. Endless games of hide and seek. Lost and found. They were from Chelsea, near where the Stones lived in the early days, but had arrived through a wardrobe just like us.

Bed and breakfast could be had for a few shillings if you didn't mind being out all day. You were sharing someone's home and enjoying the best local food and authentic company. You slept like a log because the air was from heaven. If it rained, you got wet or sheltered under the Lambeague Hall. It was unclad wood back then, and provided weekly film shows, a retreat for the annual fête in inclement weather and, years later, a place for bands to rock out in the forbidding winter months; resident impresario Tom Salmon's *The Night of the Asteroid* festival springs to mind. And Reflex, who covered Police songs better than The Police.

If you wanted to go horse riding, you didn't pay unseemly amounts of money to learn how to do a rising trot on the end of a leading rein with a hat on. You caught the green double-decker bus from the old hut at the north end of the village. Branches of ancient trees thwacked against the upper windows, and you asked to be put off at Trelanvean.

Here you'd find Farmer Harris, a tiny, wizened man, with eyes as bright as moonbeams, and his son, who seemed as though he'd be able to ride the seventeen-hand bay bareback in his sleep.

The hay barns were festooned with kittens, too numerous to name. No Colonel Glens or Titanias here. Blackie or Ginger if they were lucky, but anonymity suited them fine. They were free. Names are so random anyway. And onerous. Animals don't care what they're called. It's your smell and the next meal they're interested in.

We had a dog called Pig once. I love pigs. They're sentient creatures proven in trials to be more intelligent than your average dog, and when was the last time you ate a Jack Russell for breakfast?

Anyway, a dog lady in a park picked me up on our choice of moniker; in fact Monica might have been preferable. Pig was a girl after all. "Pig?", she said. "Pig? How can you call your dog Pig?" "Well for a start, because it's her name and she answers to it and, second, because she doesn't care what I call her as long as I throw that ball.

I could call her Fuckface for all she cares". The lady definitely cared. Offended to the ruffled core. She huffed off. Never did know her name.

Farmer Harris also had a fleet of horses. A river of dashing, wind-ripped steeds which he would whistle in from the moors. Wow. This was *Lone Ranger* land. Harris Junior as Tonto, me as the Lone Ranger, Dom as Dick West.

I got to ride a plucky pony called Red Rocket. Mess with him at your peril. We were well met. I learned to ride him a bit like I learned to play the guitar. No hat, no boots. Love and pain. And Red Rocket had clearly learned the same way. Not the guitar, naturally. But I wouldn't have put anything past him. He endured, rather than embraced, saddles and stirrups, and made damn sure I knew he was doing me a favour. So watch it, cowboy.

Health and safety put a stop to all that. And today I doubt Farmer Harris would get away with trying to get my mother up on a horse so he could look up her pleated skirt.

He charged five bob an hour to ride his semi-feral steeds but, if no one else was waiting, you could stay out for as long as you liked. On warm, dry days, that would mean hurtling up and down a rutted field at a million miles an hour or trying to get Red Rocket to stop eating gorse, or being thrown off when he bucked and danced, then chasing him across the fields before

With Farmer Harris, Red Rocket and a real farm-boy

remounting and forgiving each other. On damp misty days, we'd just trek out through the spooky otherness, everything bathed in fragrant mist, field to field, under trees, through hedges, lost and drifting, except that the horses knew exactly where they were and always got you home in time for tea.

One day, out at sea, we were lucky to get home at all. Not only did the lady who owned The Harbour Lights café double as our taxi driver from Redruth, but Frankie Daw, the baker – who made the splits for your cream tea and was a member of the lifeboat crew – also rented us his outboard motorboat for the fortnight.

We learned to moor it and unmoor it, lash it to the cable, fill the engine with petrol – that to-die-for smell of salt and fresh grade one – and best of all wrap a rope around the top of the crankshaft then give it an almighty rip to get the engine roaring. Snatch hold of the rudder, ease your way out of the harbour and next thing you're cresting waves. Rise, splat, rise, splat, face full of surf. Deliriously delicious. Dad let us do all that. And the locals let him let us. They would probably have come to the rescue in an emergency, but they let you learn the hard way. Fucking up was all part of the holiday.

In these days of moaning and litigation, a lot of that has gone. There's a shiny railing at the end of the harbour and a sign advising you that the water that comes over the harbour wall is wet. We jump off the upper part of the wall now; can't keep a good wall down. Just don't wear stilettos when you carry your tray down the harbour, madam. There's no sign to say the wind might change. You can still get stung by a weaver fish and mobbed by a gull. Cornwall is still here for you.

Against Mum's better judgement, Dad took us out in Frankie's boat on a day when the murky mist was rapidly turning to sea fog, and not even locals were venturing out. Dad had probably inherited this self-determination from his mother, who had once driven the family VW Beetle round Shepherd's Bush Green in the wrong direction, insisting that everyone else had got it wrong. That's confidence for you.

Fog can mess with distance much as a TARDIS can mess with time. If you

Sentient Creatures by Christopher Guard

can't see anything, a miss is as good an inch, and a mile is incomprehensible. If you're suddenly transported to the age of Marco Polo, you don't waste energy wondering how you got there, you adjust.

We're probably only a couple of hundred yards out to sea, still in the bay – inshore – the sort of distance you'd happily swim on a fair day. But a white shroud has enveloped us: and then the engine conks out. I think Dad had been so busy saying, "fiddlesticks" and defying the locals, he'd forgotten to top up the petrol tank. Blimey. No sooner has the shroud descended than a chilly blow picks up, strong enough to cause us to drift in a – well, probably in a westerly direction, unless it's changed its mind like Red Rocket and suddenly turned east. Perhaps to eat gorse. Well, I don't know. All I know is it doesn't have the best interests of tourists at heart: it just wants to blow. Bugger.

Dad is not a naturally fearful man, but Dom and I both sense the tremor of doubt as he seizes the oars, rams them into the rollocks and proceeds to row manfully towards the – well, what? This is not a homing horse. It's a clueless boat, entirely dependent on humankind to direct it back to harbour. Bollocks.

Then Dad is sick. The sight of him smiling reassuringly as breakfast splutters fitfully from the side of his mouth, makes me feel sick too. I think I say, "Are you feeling a bit sick, Dad?"

There are several possibilities. Either we hit The Manacles and all drown. Or we arrive in France by the end of the week. Or Mum organises our rescue. Or we get fucking lucky and float back into harbour in twenty minutes, very much the worse for wear, but not dead. Mum and Candy are there to meet us, Mum hopping up and down like a trampoline artist and Candy, having picked up the bad vibes, screaming her bonneted head off. As for the locals, a knowing eye or two is cast our way. We know something you don't know. What? Nose.

And that was the joy. The adventure. The ignorance. The no health and safety. We were safer for it. And definitely healthier. Nowadays more people die on motorways than at sea. Some kinds of danger are acceptable, others are not. Me, I prefer to make my own mistakes.

Coverack was a place of stars. Everyone was a star. Brighter than the Albert Finneys and Joyce Grenfells back in London. They were just playing at it. These guys were real. Nowadays, David Baddiel might be seen ambling through the village or perched in the pub. And as a boy, I used to play with The Director-General of the BBC on Mill Beach. David Copperfield and Tim Davie. The last time I saw Tim he was playing volleyball with his lads on Meres Beach, on the other side of the headland. Business as usual. We're all just bucket-and-spade boys at heart – bladderwrack poppers, sand-eel hunters, figures in a seascape.

The BBC is a giant, but Coverack is bigger. Brenda's Stores was more cutting edge than *Channel Four News*: a hub of vital information, the nerve centre of the known world. Brenda sold everything: papers; butter; cloth buttons; beach balls; '50s postcards; mead; lettuce; surfboards; insect repellent; ice cream; jellies. Jellies for your feet, to protect against weever fish. And if you did get stung, Brenda would conjure a bucket of warm salt water to dunk your throbbing foot into.

Information was free. "Save everything, forget nothing", could have been Brenda's motto. If someone asks for something you haven't got, get some. For next time, five years later. If it's gossip you want, don't ask, just mingle.

Early morning in the winter, any time in summer. Brenda's became world famous.

This muddle of a seafront emporium was part of a cluster of cottages, built around the mill and the mill stream, which included the bakery. Frankie Daw's bakery. Frankie hired us not only the outboard motorboat but also the yellow canoes that featured in our blockbuster *Pirates? Humbugs!* Now, instead of canoes, his grandson Chris hires out windsurfers.

You couldn't invent Brenda's. Hard to believe it's gone. You don't know what you've got 'til then. Like the four original bars, and the hatch and corridor, and the old, cracked tiles in the Paris Hotel. Rip it up and open plan it. Carpet and red veleveteen. What would that look like? Mystery solved. Mist lifted. Mystery missed. I miss the outdoor toilets too. Breath of fresh air.

Roskilly's farm products now sell all over the country. Ice cream, cream, jam, cider. We're lost. A family ramble to St Keverne across country has led us up the garden path. We don't know where we are. Like the boat in the fog, not far from anywhere but, in this subtropical tangle, as good as vanished. Trudging round in circles. "Mum, I'm hungry". No digital nursemaids. No apps. Dr Livingstone I presume? Or better still, Mr and Mrs Roskilly. They give us tea and cakes and cream and set us on our way. Courtesy of the farm. No agenda. Word spreads. Fate finds them out. Chance and happenstance.

You don't have to be famous to be a star.

Jimmy Tripp, Norman Carey, Nellie Balls… they're all in the little churchyard now.

Ivor painted some of them. 'Rogues' Gallery', he called it. All still hanging on the wall of The Fisherman's Rest. Makes 'The Spotlight' directory seem redundant. Who needs a casting director when you've been perfectly cast as yourself?

Even better than the World Cup and *The Lone Ranger* in green and white, better even than *Tarzan Goes To India* in Eastman Colour at the Commodore, were the film shows at the Lambeage Village Hall. Stepping dreamily from the blue tingle of a long hot day to the dark and rattle of a makeshift cinema, all wooden benches and a projector as loud as the dialogue.

Outside, Technicolour reality as far as the eye could see: inside, black and white innuendo way over my head. *Carry on Cruising*. The lines blurred. Kenneth Connor, Brenda Daw, the lady with big hair from the Harbour Lights, Charles Hawtrey, the wild old mumbling sailor in the corner of the breakfast room at Porthgwara; were they all in on it? *Seven Brides for Seven Brothers* was not in black and white and was far more upfront about sex. Perfect fare for a rustic evening. Dad loved Howard Keel. He was definitely not the walrus.

Jimmy Trip

115

I think it was 1964 when we saw *Fanny,* with Charles Boyer. As the lights came up after the final reel, I heard gentle sobbing at my shoulder. It was Jane. Jane Wenham, who had recently separated from Albert Finney. She had come with us, with her son Simon, to forgive and forget. The plot was too much for her. Too close to home. And Coverack is not a good setting for a broken heart. Heaven when you're in love; hell when you're grieving.

Later it was the same for Mum. How to manage the memories and move on. Showbiz broke my dad's heart and Mum and Dad kind of broke each other's.

Dad crashed and burned; drove himself so hard as a writer. His favourite motto was 'per ardua ad astra'. In the end the work exhausted him while the big hit he craved remained elusive. Perhaps 'paulatim ergo certe' – Latymer's incongruous maxim – would have suited him better. Some trips to the pub with mum maybe. More time for each other. Slowly therefore surely. At least Albie was honest. He realised early on that he was not monogamous. No therapy. Just candour.

I talk of the harbour, of bottling those sun-slinking moments, the intellect-silencing elements, so I can release them like a genie into grey city streets and sullen dressing rooms.

When I painted, it always tended to be Coverack, even when it wasn't meant to be, like recreating my muse time after time in different rooms. The same girl wherever you are. I'd start a wild seascape in oil pastel, nowhere in particular, and feel the pull, the parallel world, morphing me home. I didn't want to paint the obvious.

Coverack is almost too beautiful to paint really.

Best just to be there.

And shut up.

I could talk of Coverack for ever. But let's try to say goodbye for now. And see what happens. Through the Goonhilly mists, through the wardrobe, across the universe. It cannot truly return because it never goes away.

It's just a question of turning up the lights.

Sitting on the Harbour Wall by Christopher Guard

14: Islands

Cornwall is akin to an island. Once you cross the Tamar, you're effectively in another country, geographically and spiritually. The Scilly Isles actually have their own microclimate and a host of genuinely subtropical flora and fauna. I went there once; reminded me of Jamaica. Humid, jungular, star-spangled, exotic, beaches like little jewels.

Perhaps the most exotic light to illuminate Pleydell Avenue shone from our lodger, Tete Ayito Tago. With the same fantastic maverick spirit that had led Dad to return to Wormwood Scrubs as a free man and invite convicts home for Sunday lunch, he was determined to do something about race discrimination. He was like a one-man band freedom fighter, taking up just causes at will, and writing about them in his own light comedy, sub-Shavian way.

This was when the United Kingdom was still hanging women – and men too obviously – until the Ruth Ellis case finally brought an end to state-sponsored strangulation.

Thank fuck.

Well, could you do it? Or slit a pig's throat? Not on my watch. Homosexuality was still illegal, and it was perfectly OK to put "no blacks or Irish" in the small ads.

As Brexit has just illustrated, the fear of foreign invasion and alien otherness is never far from the national consciousness.

Before he became a film star, Alan Rickman assisted on a play at the Royal Court called *Other Worlds* by the beautiful Robert Holman, which was based on the true case of a gorilla who, in eighteenth century Hartlepool, was hung as a French spy.

He'd been a ship's mascot and was washed up after a wreck, sporting a striped blue-and-white shirt, and snazzy black pantaloons.

Of course, he couldn't speak a word of English so it followed naturally that he *must* have been French. And he wouldn't answer any questions so he *must* have been a spy.

And he was hairy.

Mind-boggling. Where there is ignorance – to misquote Margaret Thatcher

– let us sow lies. Fear and bullshit go together as neatly today as they ever did. And after some of the tosh that has been bandied about recently by so-called Western leaders, we may as well go back to ducking stools and trial by fire.

Hardly anyone came to see *Other Worlds*. I saw it four times, spreadeagled across as many seats. They'd be queueing round the block now. It was directed by Richard Wilson, pre-Victor Meldrew from *One Foot in the Grave* notoriety, and featured Oscar winner-to-be Jim Broadbent; both just as talented then as they'd always been. It's just that hardly anyone had bothered to notice.

Dad put an advert for a lodger in a couple of sweet-shop windows – Sid's for one, where I bought my bubble-gum cards – requesting applications only from what we now call BAME. It didn't actually say "No whites, racists or scumbags", but Dad was determined, in his own defiant way, to level the playing fields of Stamford Brook. The majesty of the levelling was beyond our wildest dreams.

Enter – from Ghana, via Heathrow and Hammersmith – Tete: tall, jet black and supremely elegant. He was studying for a law degree and was destined to wed several beautiful wives and sire a vast family and become something very high up in the Ghanaian government. He was so cool. He used to wear his fabulous, flowing gold and green tribal best on Sundays. Dom and I called him Tetty Potatoes and bounced on his bed, often early in the morning before school after he'd been up half the night studying. He never minded. Tolerance personified. Huge heart, warm laughter. It's hard to think of anything bad to say about Tete. Except it was a real drag when he left.

For Mrs Wilkie who lived at Number Two, we may as well have had a French mascot staying with us. She and Ron would lie awake at night fearing for our safety. Well, Tete *was* gorgeous. Maybe she had erotic dreams about him. Ron too. She leaned over her front gate one day, and asked Mum – and this is pretty well how it went, with awkward pauses: "Mrs Guard…? You know that man… Well, we were wondering… Ron and I… er… does he use the same toilet as you?" Not much you can say to that. Were they still alive, I imagine they'd have been equally concerned about the Turkish invasion of Yorkshire in 2016.

I suspect they'd not read *Hamlet* but there are definitely more things in heaven and earth than were dreamt of in their philosophy.

Soon there were unfamiliar spicy aromas coming from the spare room. I can smell them now, as if they'd wafted through time. Our next lodger was the charming Pratip Kumar Chaudhuri and we are back in touch again.

Because one of its sub-plots is race and slavery, I'm reminded of *Return to Treasure Island*, the series I spent five months making alongside Brian Blessed.

Aired in *The A-Team* and *Robin of Sherwood* slot, it was not really a series at all but a serial, even longer than my *David Copperfield* teatime production twenty years earlier and needed watching carefully from week to week.

It had a regular cast but, instead of hurling them into separate, self-contained stories, it rolled on, with cliffhangers: one big ten-hour adventure.

It's not an excuse, but I think that affected viewing figures. It was too hard a watch for some, especially in biting off chewy chunks of history like the slave trade.

Not that it wasn't successful in its way. The US following was loyal and complimentary, especially towards Brian – who gives the performance of his life – and towards the sweep and ingenuity of the narrative.

John Goldsmith brewed up a more than worthy successor to the original.

My job as a grown-up Jim Hawkins was mainly to be heroic but the nuanced love-hate relationship with Long John Silver is excellently written and was a privilege to play. My goodness, Brian was good.

The perception of Brian Blessed as some kind of roaring, carousing, Oliver Reed-ian maniac is absurd. Eccentric, yes. Out of control, never. He is deeply zen, very fit and possessed of a sharp native wit.

The bombast is a part of the whole, but more as a homing device than anything, a default setting for dreary moments. You don't fight with a sword, on one leg, in hot clothes, in temperatures in the nineties by staying up all night drinking.

And when a man capable of filling the Albert Hall with his titanic baritone gets up close and sotto, how threatening is that?

Piers Haggard, the director, was brilliant at conducting the one-man orchestra, reining in and releasing Brian like he was juggling mercury or performing nuclear fission.

The enemy of the show was time. It was nearly abandoned before I came on board and, despite the Disney brand and budget, the schedule was tight; and this meant that, for the entire seven weeks we were in Jamaica, we needed two crews working in tandem. Not a second unit, but a full second crew with the experienced Alex Kirby at the helm. The sun rose like a bolt at seven and dropped like a stone at six. Every moment in between was precious. When not swimming in shark-infested waters, I was hurtling across the island for an interview with a corrupt governor or chasing a two-timing bastard through the jungle with a flintlock. My days off were gradually swallowed up. Saturdays, Sundays and everything in between. "Any chance Chris?" Agent called; overtime confirmed.

Not that I cared about the money: my sanity was at stake. Evenings and lunchtimes were taken up with choreographing fight scenes, or meeting my next horse or, if there was a moment, learning the sodding lines. No booze, no weed, no reggae, no beach clubs for me. This was on the cusp of the AIDS pandemic, but the world was still partying free. It's a wonder no one got sick. The only serious casualty was Artro Morris, who played the Reverend Morgan and fell victim to a burrowing spider.

The one afternoon I did have off, I went walkabout from the hotel in Falmouth. I wasn't supposed to, because of insurance. I met a young student. He told me he wanted to get his agricultural science degree so he could revolutionise the Jamaican economy. Luxury crops like avocados were discouraged by the US. Cuba was just a stone-skim away, and the intervening waters were heavily patrolled by the US Navy. You didn't want Jamaica getting ideas above its station, becoming economically selfsustainable and politically independent. That was why the massive illegal trade in cannabis was tolerated. The fertile blue hills were alive with the stuff. Better a black market and bananas sustaining a small economy than growing luxury crops and getting bolshy.

The Navy were in town once. After we'd moved to the beach hotel in Ocho Rios. Jeez, were they scary! Musclebound, ship-bound, testosterone-charged, neurologically compromised yankee-doodles, drinking the bars dry for three days of shore leave. You didn't want to discuss politics with them. Or French spies. The scariest thing though is that colonialism hasn't really gone away at all.

The slave trade has ended but not slavery.

One day, I was filming scenes with Peter Lloyd, a wonderfully cultured Jamaican actor with a brilliant singing voice. He had sung Lionel Richie's 'All Night Long' at the hotel the night before, between the ubiquitous reggae sets, all smooth moves and silky tones. Now here he was playing Abed, the flogged slave, tended by the humanitarian Jim Hawkins in the old slave quarters of a real sugar plantation.

The scenes were raw and real and meant a lot to us both, but it was our time-warped, anachronistic surroundings that stirred me most. These were not just old slave quarters – makeshift rows of single-bedded huts – but real modern slave quarters, ostensibly unchanged and very much still in use. The local estate workers still slept in them. And naturally the estate was owned and managed by a white man. This was the mid-80s. 1980s, not 1780s. With the US navy patrolling intimidatingly in the bay. Jaw-dropping.

The truth really hit home when two beautiful female Jamaican supporting artists latched on to me as I was getting into a unit car. "Can we…?" They had done already – before they were spotted by their beady-eyed landlord. "Sure."

They sat close on either side of me, and they wanted answers. "How come we ain't been paid?" The accents were American, but they were locals.

"Hey Swordman! Why you do this?" – a collection of polaroids

"You haven't been paid?" "We want our money." Shit. Only the day before, a dude had drawn a gun on the third assistant. Fair enough. If I'd been in my hometown at the edge of the jungle, being yelled at by a demented Welshman, I might have done the same.

The upshot was that the landowner, a foul man with a withered arm, had arranged to have all the supporting artists' money paid directly to him, on the understanding that he would then distribute it among the workers. Bollocks he would. Like the US Navy, he wanted to ensure that indigenous upstarts didn't get ideas above their station; so he hadn't paid them at all. I told Piers Haggard, who was totally astounded. He immediately moved to see justice done. The landowner was questioned and the hand that doesn't feed you bitten. So, well done those girls for kicking up. Look the other way, and the bastards will have you.

One evening after a long day thrashing about in the jungle, an excitable lady approached Brian in hotel reception. Rich Americans popped over to Jamaica for the weekend. They were everywhere, usually with more money than sense. Certainly more money than self-awareness. Clotted bottoms in designer bikinis, sweaty orange toupées with matching coiffured eyebrows, wind tunnel facelifts, that sort of thing. Delusions of glamour. We were knackered. Brian was still on one leg; it was a palaver unstrapping and strapping the other one, and he still had tomorrow's fight scene to rehearse.

"Oh, excuse me but are you the Long John Silver of the Hotel?" The polite answer would have been "fuck off" but, with spontaneous zen, Brian simply muttered, "Yers". "Oh, you are?" "Yers". Anything to take his mind off the numb leg and the ticks. "Could we have a request?" "A what?" "Come *on* Brian, let's get out of here". "Yers". "Would you sing 'Happy Birthday' to my little grandson? He's four". "Yers." And he did. So loud and abruptly the woman nearly fell over, and birthday boy shrank whimpering into her skirts. Brian sang it all, every last pulsating note of it. Then as suddenly as he'd begun, went completely quiet and limped across the lobby as if nothing had happened. Dropping jaws in his wake. Brilliant. That's how to deal with presumptuous weekenders. Sing at them.

A few weeks later, by which time I'd have happily laid down and died, I was in the jungle as usual, waiting to do a long shot. I thought I was alone apart from a squawking walkie talkie, all togged up in frilly shirt, buckles and sword belt, waiting for the signal to run like a maniac towards wherever the camera probably was, when I became aware of a presence. Motionless as a meditating Blessed. Serene as the blue marijuana hills. "Hey! Swordman! Why you do this?".

A Jamaican lad of about twenty stood nearby, red-eyed, subtle, wry, sanguine, forever stoned. Living off the garden. How long had he been there? Forever probably. I had no answer. "Action!" screech-garbled the walkie-talkie. He surveyed me with pity and a faint smile. He was right. Why you do this? Because I know something you don't know. Except I didn't. I vowed to go back one day, with no sword, and plant avocados with the agricultural science graduate. One day…

I was Tete and the French spy and Johnny Cox at Sunday lunch. The alien. The odd one out. Unable to explain what I was. No chains but speechless. A foreigner.

In no man's land. This man *was* an island.

***

Bear with me a moment; I need to ramble. Feel free to disagree.

Shakespeare's great, late play *The Tempest* is set on an island. Some scholars say it was inspired by Bermuda, others assume it was somewhere in the Mediterranean. Maybe it was Jamaica; not that Shakespeare ever went to Jamaica: at least I assume he didn't. But if Jesus went to England, I suppose anything's possible. Jesus got about a bit, like Buddha, learned about life, not just the meaning of it. Same with Will the Bard. Kicking his heels, anonymous, wandering, wondering. He didn't write his first play until he was twenty-six. Royalty is born famous, but for the rest it's at least partly hazard.

Traditional history is about fact, figures and logic. The great plague is much easier to write about than COVID. It's done, it's dusted, it fits. Retrospectively, it was always going to be that way; it's easy after the event. The reality was what we're suffering every day as I write – not having a bleeding clue. And the more plans you make, the more likely you are to go stark-staring mad. 'Good leaders' are those who pretend to know what's going to happen next, then lead people over cliff edges. An honest admission of doubt may not be popular but it's better in the long run.

Some people think Kit Marlowe wrote Shakespeare's plays. I think he probably just wrote bits of them. And why does Jesus seem to contradict himself in the *Sermon on the Mount*? And why is the Sermon in Matthew, but nowhere else? Perhaps because it's based on probability and imagination. Some have suggested the mount was a fictional setting nominally chosen to incorporate some of the words probably attributable to Jesus. I'm not saying I believe that; we believe what we want to believe. Probably. And the greater the confusion, the more zealously we seem to deny it and cleave to some assumed fit-all truth. Why else do people get so cross about religion? Perhaps Shakespeare did go to Jamaica. That's where he got his ideas for *The Tempest*. Or maybe he just went to Cornwall. We could have shot *Return to Treasure Island* in Cornwall instead of the Caribbean; simpler logistics and similar terrain.

And the Cornish have a similar relationship with time. Boats and props always arrived promptly in Montego Bay, just not necessarily on the right day. No problem. Or as they say in the land of the piskies, "Right orrrn!" It's an island thing. The sea sets the sails.

"Imagine there's no countries, it's easy if you try…" Try explaining to a bird or fish about Brexit, or any nominal national boundaries. "Yeah, so it's like this Mackerel-Face, you're allowed to swim here and get caught there, but not to get caught here if you come from there. Bonjour, Madame Mouette, you just crossed the Irish border, can I see your papers please?" Ignorance is bliss. Or if you're a writer, maybe just stay home and dream.

Of course, Will wrote the timeless soliloquies and all that, but I reckon, whether he was holidaying in Falmouth, Cornwall or Falmouth, Jamaica, Kit was left behind to write all the pedantic stuff. Will was a star so, just as poor old Joan Maitland shadow-wrote the extra lyrics for *Oliver*, so Kit knocked off the boring Lords' scenes and, in particular, Francisco's cough-all-the-way-through-it speech. Yeah, so thanks for that Kit Marlowe. Sir, he may live… or in my case, die.

Probably Will just stayed in England. Once you get that first number one, you're running to stand still. He had an imagination like The Beatles anyway. Like a brilliant child. All he needed was a few hints and fairy stories, some sparkling scraps and dockside gossip. Technically flawed, historically inaccurate, and utterly mesmerising. Sod the detail. It's the way you tell 'em. He didn't need to go to Prospero's Milan to feel Milanese; or to get washed up on a desert island surrounded by creatures he'd never met to describe them. "Where the bee sucks, there suck I". "O I have suffered with those that I saw suffer". Imagine. Maybe Dad was predestined to appear as Edgar at the end of 'I Am The Walrus'. It was all Shakespeare's doing. My dad and John Lennon? Of course, what's so weird about that? "We are such stuff as dreams are made on."

When I was twelve, my form master, Mr Knight, wrote this in my general report: "Sometimes he is so lost in the world of his own imagination, he seems apart or even aloof from those around him." Hmmph. At the time, that stung. I wanted some normal. But maybe he was right. I wasn't being up my arse because I'd been on TV, I was just miles away. Mum said, when she was staring vacantly out of the window, she was working. No Mum is an island.

15: Hobbies

I got the bird bug from my cousins; that was before birdwatching was the trendy obsession it is now. Back in the early '60s, it was up there with linocuts and stamp collecting for sexiness.

In fact, stamp-collecting was hip by comparison.

We had a friend called Frank who gave us stamps. He'd been a Japanese prisoner of war, then become a hoofer in West End musicals, before joining British European Airways as an air steward. He'd appear suddenly at the playroom window, hollering and gurning. Out of the blue. Literally. Frank's here! Suntanned, usually. Bronze scar tissue. We'd leap out of our skin.

He'd had a horrible time in that war camp, and still seemed to be on the run. His silliness drove Dad mad but we loved him because he gave us coins from wherever he'd just been – some with holes in – and ridiculously big stamps, and sometimes he'd take us to see a film in the West End. *The Parent Trap*, with lovely Hayley. The worthless exotic stamps would sit alongside the wildlife cards I fished out of the Brooke Bond tea boxes. All loose back then. Teabags and moon landings yet to come. The first teabag on the moon. I hated tea to drink but loved the aroma of the leaves, black and mystical in an oblong box. Your scrunched-up little hand reaching for a bird of paradise or a crane. And the big blowsy cornflakes packet. A plastic Comanche buried deep in the flakes and waiting to be painted. The crunch, the discovery, the emergence, the free giftness. Sold.

My cousins, Peter and Nicholas, lived with their parents, Vera and Eric, on Watford Road in Sudbury Town. Well actually, at the foot of a gently winding hill, called Homefield Road, that seemed almost rustic to me. Just a twenty-minute tube train ride away. Take the Ealing Broadway branch of the District Line from Stamford Brook, change onto a Piccadilly Line train to Uxbridge at Acton Town, ten-minute walk at the other end.

Incidentally, years later, my friend Stuart – of whom more soon – lived briefly on Homefield Road and, although the childhood memories flooded back, it was hard to believe that these were the same streets that had conjured a magical little mystery twenty years earlier. Not that the streets had changed. I had.

Mum and Dad turned their dreams into vocations; Mum's sister and brother-in-law, Vera and Eric, took a more cautious route. Eric held down a steady job, nine to five (I never really did know exactly what it was) and Vera, talented writer though she was, kept house, and hosted coffee mornings, and tended the children in timehonoured tradition.

When Robert Mitchell, Vera and Mum's dad, died in an avoidable mistake during an appendix operation, Mum was only three.

There was no welfare state back then, just charity or bust. Eric provided a hitherto missing stability, happy to turn his dreams into cherished hobbies.

Whereas at Pleydell Avenue, the heady world of showbiz could be a humdrum grind, at Watford Road, the commonplace became exotic and thrilling.

Peter and Nicholas were older by a few years and so had an irresistible exotic aura for us younger kids. Everything they did was exciting. Games of Monopoly or walks to the hillock at the top of Homefield Road. It was the shock of the old, not the new. The magic of the mundane. Even taking Bibby her lunch took on an exciting otherworldliness. Bibby was Mum and Vera's mother, by now partly bedridden and a little forgetful, and even her lunch tray was fascinating. Everything had to be just so. As precise as the spec of James Bond's new car. Even down to the number of peas. Seriously. Small is beautiful.

Eric loved his garden. It made his relentless tube commute bearable. The house being on a corner, the garden was large and spreading, full of nooks and curves; and up at the farthest end, it had all the curiousness of Mr McGregor's, in *Peter Rabbit*. Tales of the Unsuspected.

I remember crawling through the blackcurrant canes, via the tomatoes – those undersmells, deep in the palate and all-enveloping – unseen by Eric, as he poked at a pungent bonfire, towards the cedar-scented shed where Nick kept his jungle pharmacy (little, corked bottles of cochineal potions, lovingly labelled, for soft toy emergencies). And the guinea pigs, Josephine and Cicero, another wonderworld we discovered in the suburbs. Wheep wheep wheep! Hutches and runs all homemade by Eric. He made them for our guinea-pigs too. For the fertile Guinness and Blossom.

Rupert Bear annuals were everywhere. Innately quaint and English, yet sort of dangerous too. The tight, trite rhyming couplets, those busy suburban creatures dressed in school caps and scarves, visiting a Chinese conjuror in the middle of Nutwood – a village I imagined to be somewhere between Sudbury

Robert Mitchell

Town and Wendover – the intoxicating Tigerlily (whom I actually managed to fancy), Mr Bear smoking a pipe, in tweeds, in summer. Boy, he must have been hot! Every bit as surreal as Prospero on his desert island, spouting unrhyming couplets about monsters with two bottoms and conversing with thin air. Foreign parts. The dread of the strange. The eternal bogeyman. An Elizabethan audience that still believed in witchcraft and ghosts, Hartlepudlians who thought a gorilla was a Frenchman, Sunday Express readers who believe that Europe is the enemy. Thank God for Nutwood. And a sofa to hide behind. We will not exterminate you! In Mr McGregor's garden, the rabbits are the aliens and Mr McGregor the colonial status quo. He *will* exterminate you and his wife will put you in a pie.

It was all part of the mix. Eric's bonfire, Rastus mouse, Josephine the guinea pig, the jungle potions, the soporific lettuce, the blackcurrants, Mrs Bear, Vera's delicious puddings (apple snow and bitter chocolate trifle. "Bit of everything please, Vera!"), Cluedo, Miss Scarlett, Bibby's peas…

I still have my bird diaries, along with the real diary I wrote until May 1962, the year I sat the Latymer exam.

The moment I set eyes on Nick's diaries I was hooked. Standard address books, with birds indexed and illustrated alphabetically, along with dates, maps and observations. Sublime self-publishing. "Feb 2nd: Spotted a lonesome dabchick on Rickmansworth Ponds. Sundry mallard and tufted duck in attendance."

Nick spotted with a flourish. I started painting my own little watercolour illustrations. Not great but zealously rendered, all in the name of art and science. I became a member of YOC, the Young Ornithologists Club, junior branch of the RSPB, the Royal Society for the Protection of Birds, ubiquitous now, but a curio back then. I wore my black and silver YOC badge on my black school blazer lapel, alongside my black and white Fulham Football Club badge. So cool. The sublime and the ridiculous? Not to me. Which was which anyway?

At football matches, I was told I didn't look like someone who'd be interested in birds and, when I was watching rare, distant avocets on a wintry Havergate island at the age of eleven, I certainly didn't discuss football. Bless Bill Oddie and Chris Packham, but I preferred ornithology when it was the quaint domain of suburban eccentrics. Now it's everywhere.

And here lies a symbiosis, seamlessly linking my lapel badges. I struggle to explain to success-hungry Chelsea supporters up the road that I actually preferred being in Division Two to being in the Premiership. When we were looking up not down. And you got to eat chips in Grimsby and drink ale in Wrexham. And it was cheap. The Premiership is OK, but the romance came from being lowly and achieving the unexpected. Like being lowly and watching swifts, high in a searingly blue sky. The unreachable. Swifts only touch down to nest. Everything else is aerial. Even mating and sleeping. Imagine that. Sleeping on a thermal, then waking up and having a fuck at two hundred feet. Birds come to us. They go to Africa then come back to Acton.

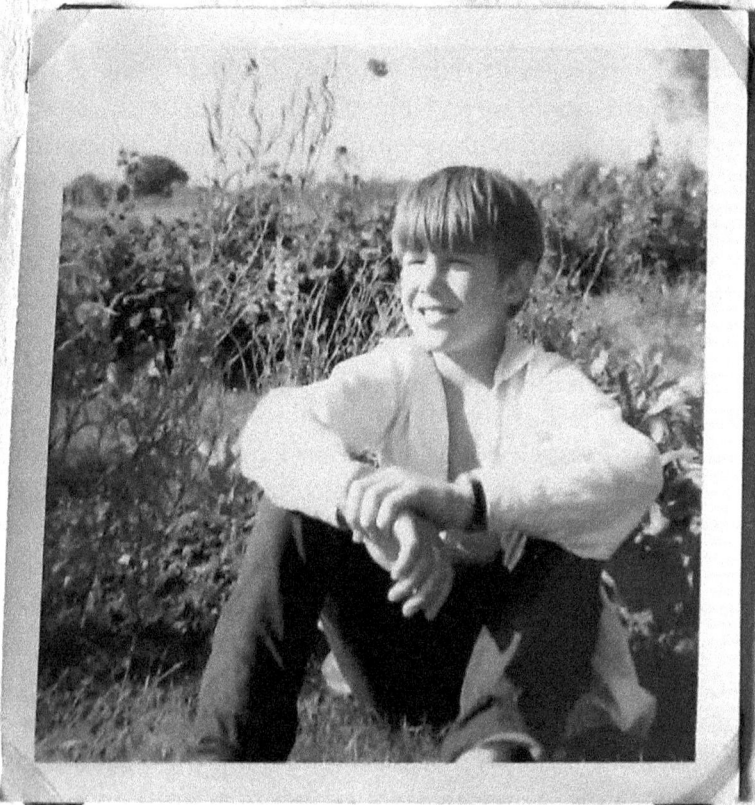

(When reading this book, one will find individual numbering of pages under each letter. The system works with the low numbers on the right hand pages and then one reads the next entries back on the left-hand sides if more entries were necess-
-ary.)

ORNOTHOLOGICAL

DIARY, 1968.

WRITTEN and ILLUSTRATED

by Christopher Guard,
Y.O.C. member,
age 14-0.

They charge nothing and have no respect for trade tariffs. They are free as birds. Try explaining Brexit to a mating swift.

We went on long walks in the Chiltern Hills, Vera, Eric, Peter, Nicholas, Dom and me. With a picnic that I always ate too fast, and binoculars that were a wee bit wide for my deep-set eyes. What on earth is the thrill of shooting animals and birds? How noxiously dull. How pathetic. Capture them alive and free in the barrel of your binoculars, whisper excitedly as you focus tremblingly on the object of desire. A view, a capture, a moment. "Got it? Did you? There! Now, see?" Unmistakeable. Low light but no doubt. The fluttering movements gave it away. Redwing. Three of them. Joy. Ten more miles, via Great Missenden and Amersham, flash of a sparrowhawk, couple of buzzards, a jay, several kestrels – no red kites back then – then home to the diaries. Write up the day. Describe your passion with precision. Game of Waddington's Go, glass of milk and chocolate digestives. "Goodnight, God bless".

Recently, since Vera and Eric died, Pete and I have been on more bird rambles. Pete has great ears. He can identify an otherwise invisible bird by its song. Once you know it's not far away, you can start to look. However unlikely.

Pete has great taste in music too. Bought a few 45s back in the day. Not many, but the best. I loved the B-sides: 'She's a Woman' – McCartney playing around with the onbeat – and 'No Particular Place to Go', by Chuck Berry. Went down great with Newberry Fruits – they always had Newberry Fruits. And Pete grew his hair long.

I can feel myself inching towards Acton. Not Acton Town. That's a world unto itself. A changing place. A tube station, where you cross the platform before rumbling on to Nutwood. Like the station at Mark's Tey where, on a Friday night, we changed from the mainline train to the one-track wiggly line and were collected at Sudbury by Fred the pig farmer and set free in Alpheton. Wide-eyed wheelbarrow boys. Turfed out into meadows.

Over the last century, more than ninety percent of Britain's meadows have vanished. Sugar-rich paradises for bees and a thousand other invertebrates, gone. "Among the meadows hay cocks, 'Tis beautiful to lie. When pleasantly the day looks, And gold like is the sky". John Clare. Mum loved him. He was at one with nature and wanted to let us know that all was well with his world. And ours. Why sophisticate perfection?

The changes happen so gradually. Insidiously. While we're too wilful and wanton to notice. Then one day, there are no more pygmy shrews or grasshoppers in your life. Digging for victory won the war but it was bad news for biodiversity. Nowadays, the charity Plantlife is reversing some of the mayhem. Other organisations too. Even Prince Charles. Proactive rewilding. We may not need meadows to feed livestock anymore, but we sure need them for our health and sanity. They protect against flooding too. Water meadows hold a lot of water. A lot of carbon too. Recently, some idiots built bungalows on reclaimed water meadows. Oops. Better reintroduce more beavers. They'll dam you up and sort you out. The insurers sure won't.

"Guard, you're not concentrating. Answer the question." "What was the question, sir?" When I said inching towards Acton, I meant…

I love halfway places – not quite here, not quite over there. Railway sidings and compost heaps, the steps from street to cinema, the last drag on a cigarette in Ravenscourt Park before passing through the school gates. No wardrobe. No two hundred pounds as you pass GO either. Get Out of Jail Free card if you're lucky. When Eric went to town, he changed from Piccadilly to District lines at Baron's Court: half-way. And as the toilet at Watford Road was halfway up the stairs, that became its name. "Just popping to Baron's Court." Oddly reassuring and it saved the class-riddled debate about what to call the bog.

Toilet, lavatory, loo, john, throne: the one obvious place that doesn't get much attention in gritty soap operas. Why? To enhance its air of mystery? There's enough programmes about food; everywhere you look someone is stuffing themselves with something. Forgive me, but the digestive tract is just one long tube really, so how come so much focus on the top end and none on the bottom?

'Ready Steady Shit'?

Poo was a useful metaphor in the Wendell art room. Mixing together every colour in the palette does not produce a rainbow. It makes brown.

Acton is full of musicians, and rehearsal studios, and musical history, and music schools and ghosts. One band rehearsal in a dive in Churchfield Road and I was hooked. Fronting up a new wave punk band, scream-singing for four hours, floating on air the next morning, ears ringtingling. I'd fallen in love. With the bass thrum in my feet and the snare slap in my head, with the crunchy togetherness, the singing from the hips – arse clenched to hit the high notes – the catharsis. What did this remind me of? This musical wilderness, this calling, this mythical road.

Nick was three years older than me. Sixteen when we went youth hostelling in the Cotswolds: Nick, me and Nick's friend, Laurie. It was OK to youth hostel at the age of thirteen back then, just like it was OK to get lost all day in the Suffolk fields or walk half a mile to school in London with Diana when you were six.

Our plan was to spot birds, admire the scenery, stay in a few drab hostels then end up in Oxford, where Eric would collect us. Eric drew excellent maps and made impeccable plans, but this plan went awry. Through no fault of the maps.

To my delight, Nick went through a metamorphosis in those balmy Cotswold lanes. This was a new reckless Nick, barely glimpsed at home. Once it had dawned on us that we could do pretty well what the fuck we liked as long as we sent the odd postcard home and didn't get murdered, Nick's ambitions looked beyond the immediate constraints of studying yet another yellowhammer in a hedge. We were high on oxygen and sunshine, and pretty well anything and everything was making us laugh. Laurie had no sense of humour whatsoever and was gripped by paranoia. The less he understood what we were laughing at, the more we laughed. We hadn't a clue anyway. In the end he cut and ran; well, caught a bus to a railway station after two fretful days and nights, and was never seen or heard of again. Not by us anyway.

In his stead came a sweet, wild replacement: a house martin, injured but healthy, that we found lying in the road. We eased her delicately into an open rucksack and took her with us on our travels. As a mascot. An angel. She inspired us and made us fearless. Instead of just walking to the next hostel, we started sticking out our thumbs and, as fate would have it, the first truck to stop was headed for Cambridge. We went to the end of the line. Just for the hell of it.

And then it happened. There was something in the air. Like Thunderclap Newman. "Call out the instigator… and you know that it's right". Two girls, hippy teens, older than us, smoking roll-ups, or spliffs maybe, semi-feral, on a mission. Hair like straw, feet like velvet, padding with gentle purpose to the promised land. We followed like rats behind the piper. Were we following them? Or following where they would lead? The Cambridge Folk Festival. It tasted so good.

We wandered all through the night, from bale to bale, from small stage to tiny stage, breathing in the free delights of music untethered. Live and unutterably magnetic. Slept in a marquee overnight. Tom Paxton, The Tinkers, and so many I'd never heard of but who found their way under my skin forever. More festivals would come – both as punter and musician – but this was the biggest and the best, because it was the first. Totally out of the blue. Festival virginity lost. The house martin was still with us. She came along for our ride, hitched our lift, heard the music, even made it back to the station where Eric did finally manage to round us up and ferry us back to Nutwood.

House martins are exquisite flyers. They live to soar and float and ride the thermals. Like swifts do. We had planned to release her as soon as she was well. We kept her overnight at Watford Road. In the morning she was dead. The strain of suburbia was too much for her. So much to worry about. Keep on keeping on, sacred wings. Never forgotten.

Road to Somewhere by Christopher Guard

16: All Roads Lead to Acton: Part 1

I seem to have covered more music than I meant to in the *Hobbies* chapter. So I think I'll write Acton Part One as Acton Part Two and vice versa. Do the acting stuff first. If that's OK.

In the '60s, you rehearsed with Joss Ackland or Francesca Annis in drafty church halls in Putney. In the '70s, all that changed. A vast rehearsal block was erected in North Acton, boasting eight floors of green rooms, and mirrored rehearsal spaces, and lifts. And one whole floor for the cavernous canteen. It was a revolution and became known as the Acton Hilton. No longer limited to the company of your own bijou cast, suddenly you could expect to meet pretty well anyone you might imagine. From Lulu to Ludovic Kennedy. Babs to Barker. Sykes to Sugden. An autograph hunter's paradise. Security was tight of course but not as tight as Television Centre. That was ridiculous.

Unless you were permanent 'staff', you didn't get a pass at TVC, so you had to be ticked off at the gate by some officious giant hellbent on *not* letting you be in *I Claudius*. "Where do you think you're going?" Being young and Celtic didn't help. One well-known Celt, having been heavily interrogated at the gates, and refused entry because his name was not on a list and his eyes were fiery blue, spun his car round and promptly headed back to Wales. "Fair enough, if I'm not welcome". All hell broke. Agents, assistant floor managers, apologies, Nemesis. The story has been attributed to Anthony Hopkins. I hope I've got that right. Anyway, he was not alone. Lists were hit-and-miss affairs and actors came and went. In this case, went. Getting into church halls was a doddle. You only had to get past God. Television Centre *was* God and it was zealously guarded.

One of the keys to a painless production is to know where your actors are. So it made sense to have everyone captive in the same concrete block. A sort of cross between a circus, a hotel and a zoo. The Vienna Hilton was similar, though less socialist. When we were making *A Little Night Music*, the entire cast and crew, apart from Liz, Arthur and the mighty secretary, were ensconced together.

Acting stuff: As Pip in *Great Expectations*

Then when the cast and crew of *The Man in The Iron Mask* – Ian McShane, Sylvia Kristel et al – joined the ensconcement, it was hard to cross your own bathroom without bumping into someone you knew, let alone take a lift.

I was only in Vienna at all as a result of bumping into people; at Threshold House in this case, the BBC office block on Shepherd's Green where I'd been cast as David Copperfield. All things posh and classical seemed to emanate from this anonymous building. The great Herbie Wise cast me in *Vienna 1900*, a year before I was to work with him on *I, Claudius*, because he happened to be passing an open door at the end of the day.

I'd been up for something else – *Churchill's People*, possibly. I seemed to go up for that quite a lot but never got to play any of the people. "Hey! Remind me of your name!" That was all Herbie said. For now. The next day he rang my agent. Meanwhile Sondheim and Hal Prince had decided to relocate Night Music to Vienna and when Vienna 1900 was aired in the US they would be watching.

There I was acting my knickers off as Dorothy Tutin's son, and inevitably attempting to waltz, and I was cast on the spot.

So, I ended up by the Vienna Hilton main lifts, chalking up possible teams for a Night Music v Iron Mask football match with Ian McShane. We'd only known each other five minutes.

Good footballer, Ian. Manchester United trials. The match never happened but the idea was typical. Think it, say it, do it. A natural adventurer. We would meet again many years later on yet another island. Burgh Island.

Filming *Lovejoy*, with Chris Jury, who played Deadbeat alongside me in the Doctor Who story, *The Greatest Show in the Galaxy*, and Caroline Langrishe, to whom I'd been fictionally married twice already (in *Les Miserables*, with the *Psycho* legend Anthony Perkins, and in *Dead Man's Folly* with Peter Ustinov as Poirot). The island is full of noises – it certainly was. Nowhere to hide on Burgh Island.

While I was still in Vienna, the first episode of *I, Claudius* aired and I happened to see a review in an English national. I'd almost forgotten I'd been in it. Playing Marcellus was interesting enough, but he'd been poisoned by Livia at the end of Episode One and, apart from getting paid, I didn't expect the show to figure much in my life after that, especially as the review was so utterly dismissive. It said it was dull and confused. Anyway, for me it had been just another BBC gig. I did so many in the '70s. And I was making a Hollywood movie with Liz Taylor at the age of twenty-two. What did I care?

How wrong can you be?

When I returned to London in December – all blue-eyed and Alpine – someone in The Cross Keys asked me if I'd seen *I, Claudius*. "I What?" "*I,*

Claudius". "I, er, well… I'm in it." Jeepers. The show was the hit of the year. Of the decade. Of forever, even. Once Hurt, Jacobi, Sian and co had hit their stride, the nation was bewitched. Episode One had been but a catalyst. "In it?" "Yes, poisoned in Episode One." "Brilliant! Well done!"

Hits can come from the least expected places. During the following year, while *Night Music* struggled for distribution, *I, Claudius* was repeated to further rapturous approval in the UK and sold all over the world. BBC royalty cheques have been a lifeline. Even today, they trickle in – slowly but steadily – down to eighty-nine pence for the sale of *The Professionals* to Micronesia. Who'd have thought it?

The Hollywood movie didn't bust any blocks and the BBC triumphed again; by taking risks, by trusting in quality, by trusting it*self*. Mess with it at our peril. We're in safe hands though. Tim Davie has a Coverack-shaped heart. As for *Night Music*, Flossie Klutz won an Oscar for Best Costume Design and I'm still in touch with Larry Guittard and Sandi Livingston. Divine, sublime people with transatlantic senses of the ridiculous. Thanks forever for those intros, Vienna.

Traditionally, most BBC programmes went out one after the other, not all at once, and the Radio Times reflected this. Scheduling was aimed at specific audiences and *Blue Peter,* for example, would be kept well away from *Play For Today,* and *Churchill's People* from *Top of the Pops*. But in the canteen on the top floor of the Acton Hilton, everything happened at once. Pan's People ate spaghetti, Eric Morecombe's pipe smoke wafted across your salad, Peter Duncan bounced by, hot from something daring, and Les Dawson's tray narrowly missed Penelope Keith's ear – all at once. As you oozed out of the lift and joined the canteen queue, the view was akin to an animated Hieronymus Bosch painting. Or Salvador Dalí crossed with the Dandy. Salvador Dandy. A cornucopia of household names and everyday objects, juxtaposed in a completely extraordinary way.

In a miasma of carrot steam and ubiquitous blue tobacco haze, were stalwart dinner ladies – heads down, ladling like heroes, impatient, unassuming, seen it all before. Souper-stars. When they did occasionally look up, their eyes were the size of saucers.

Other faces were framed in television sets – David Frost's certainly was – others seemed uncharacteristically small, like David Bowie's. David was probably there for a *Top of the Pops* rehearsal. Or a BBC play. I'm not sure. I could look it up but if I keep looking things up, I'll lose the flow again. Will Self says if he can't remember something, it's best left unremembered. Anyone can look things up. That's not exactly what he said but, whatever he said, I can't be bothered to look it up. In case I lose the… yes, well, I agree with him anyway. This isn't a history book, it's a deranged, time-travelling, old brain. In no particular order.

Bowie was already in the lift when a cluster of thesps squeezed in beside him. They didn't say "excuse me" because they had no idea he was there. Like one of those creatures in the Rupert Bear annuals, deliberately hidden in a painting, limbs entwined in branches, eyes as knots in tree trunks, petals for ears. You stare and stare and eventually they find you.

The lifts were ridiculously small. I half expected Groucho Marx to join us; "Is it my imagination or is it getting crowded in here?" The thesps were telling theatrical stories, one each, all at once; more material for the outro of 'I Am the Walrus'.

David was a sublime mime artist. Had he trained under Houdini? He seemed to lose corporeal substance altogether and become part of the lift wall. I wasn't staring, just empathising, but he did eventually find me. The atmosphere changed minutely. No eye contact but I like to think he knew I knew. So skinny. Almost invisible. Huge presence. I didn't tell anyone. We were probably in *The Duchess of Duke Street* and David Bowie was in the lift.

Hunky Dory.

In a way, those lifts were time travellers. Different eras, different worlds, rocketing towards the canteen in the sky. The great leveller. Like Prospero's island, where dukes rub shoulders with natives, and goddesses dance with dinner ladies, and Ariel conjures banquets, and all humanity is one. Ariel would have made a good *Top of the Pops* choreographer. All that seat-of-your-leotard last minute stuff. Quick! 'Tiger Feet' has gone to number one and there's been a shipwreck on the north shore. Change the routine. Forget Ferdinand, get those lords hopping. Forget 'Banana Rock', by the Wombles. Yes! Tigers not Wombles! Didn't matter if you were David Dimbleby or Flick Colby, you all ate the same carrots. Breathed the same steam. The canteen is full of noises.

Bowie in the lift reminds me of Le Bon on the train. Not with Rastus Mouse on his way to Nutwood but in the ordinary buffet compartment, with his feet up, languidly writing in longhand. The last time I'd seen Simon, I barely knew who he was, and even now I didn't know him to talk to. Here was a fragment of the all-singing, all-leaping entity that was one of the 'other boys of Rugby' in *Tom Brown's Schooldays* – like a meteorite that had broken away from an amorphous mass and become a famous planet. But just as no one had noticed Bowie impersonating the wall of a lift, so no one noticed Le Bon impersonating nothing in particular. Ordinary World. Best form of disguise. No one nowhere.

I was on a Fulham football excursion, up to somewhere northerly. May have been Manchester. Or Bolton. Or Oldham. I noticed Le Bon obliquely.

Didn't say anything. A conversation blew into my head but it died before my lips had parted. Last thing he wants. Me too. I was in football mode and he was in slo-mo. "Oh, er, Simon, you won't remember me, but, blah, blah, Flashman, blah, Fulham, blah". No Chris. Get your beers and move on. I was a bloody idiot. I only mentioned Simon to one person – like Pete might have quietly told me there was a siskin in a tree. (Even though he couldn't see it yet).

Anyway, ears pricked up and, next thing, there was a steady flow of twitchers sidling through the buffet and back, feigning nonchalance, eyes cast hard left or right – just to get a glimpse and cast an opinion. I needn't have worried about whether or not to accost him. Some were of the firm opinion that it wasn't Simon le Bon at all; others that if it were him why was he in the second-class buffet carriage, with no shoes on, staring out of the window and scribbling? And there's the rub. Just as you can't tell a willow warbler from a chiffchaff unless you hear its song, perhaps because Simon le Bon wasn't singing *Wild Boys*, verification was impossible.

It must be tough for stars who look like themselves. Or trade on one look. No hiding place for Ken Dodd. But David Suchet? Poirot is a disguise: walk, moustache, accent, all covered. He can get away with it in Tesco. Likewise, Le Bon. He wasn't in disguise. No big hair, no mic, no makeup, no cavorting. No "How tickled I Ham!" Just a dad on a train. How can that possibly be Simon le Bon? Brian Blessed singing 'Happy Birthday' in Jamaica was a unique hybrid. There he was, as the famous Long John Silver, pretending to be someone who sounded a bit like Brian Blessed for a woman who hadn't heard of him.

I spent a lot of time in North Acton. Sometimes I swear I saw myself leaving just as I was arriving. I would travel the three miles from Stamford Brook on my Maxi Puch moped and, later on, on another 49cc gem, the Honda Novia. I like machines that work. I don't care how simple they are. Low maintenance, high mileage, light and luggable. These days I like feet best. Bunions I can deal with, mechanical failures not. Encumbrances are such a drag. I'm not even wild about clothes. On, off, on, off, choose, think, wash, dry, yawn.

I had a dream that I was an otter in a former life. No joke. I envy those creatures. Waterproof coats, quick as silver on land or sea – or rivers in the case of our native critters – feisty, flexible and free. No Ancient History essays, no canteens or lines to learn, no typewriters, no school caps, no art.

The dream became a song, one of those summers when I was flirting with astral plains and the back of beyond. "You call me Christopher, you send me off to school, in uniform, and second form, it's second best to slaughter… I am an otter, child of the sea, I am an otter, wild and free, I am an otter, what else could I be?" Kind of like Steppenwolf. But on a moped. *Born to Be 49cc.*

Piers Haggard OBE, Herbie Wise, Peter Hammond, Alan Bridges; I was lucky to work with those mavericks, in the days when the medium was still morphing from theatre tradition, via live television, to single cam. The advantage of the lumbering multi-cam set-up was that you got the live, people-driven vibe of theatre, together with the precise, scripted movement of cameras. Like waltzing with adrenalised Daleks.

Fawlty Towers is typical of an era in which minor mistakes were absorbed seamlessly into the whole. Energy and spontaneity were what mattered and this suited stage veterans like Andrew Sachs perfectly. The same was true of *I, Claudius,* some of which is filmed in a proc arch, 'landscape' way, so that the actors can fully abandon themselves physically. At other times, the cameras come in dangerously close – almost too close – to capture the innermost workings of the minds: Livia scheming, Claudius fretting, Caligula lusting. It looks dated and yet gloriously modern now because, at the time, it was testing the bounds of the medium to the limit. Like Bakshi with *Lord of the Rings*, limitation created dynamic tension, and from that was born the cult.

Piers Haggard loves a challenge. From his film debut, *Blood on Satan's Claw,* to six months overseas location filming on *Return to Treasure Island* was a big leap. But then so, in its way, was *Pennies from Heaven*, the ground-breaking Dennis Potter masterpiece. Not a horse or ship in sight, but unchartered territory just the same.

As had been *The Chester Mystery Cycle,* a bunch of thirteenth century biblical plays, originally performed on wagons in the street, now transferred to Studio Eight of Television Centre, with a budget-busting ten days studio time. The expense was not because of the star-studded cast but because we were using colour-separation overlay – or chroma key as it's now known – for every single scene. The technique had been used before – *Doctor Who* and Hammer experimented with it in the '60s – but for every scene? Only Piers would have taken that on.

Rehearsals at North Acton were straightforward enough. For three weeks, we just imagined everything: costumes; sets; props. Tape and poles to mark out the sets as usual. So far, so good.

But then we had to film it. Normally when you arrived at your studio for a day or two's recording, you'd be greeted by sofas and chairs, chandeliers and doors, cobwebs, triffids, police desks – that sort of thing. But not this time. What greeted us in Studio Eight was an ocean of green. We'd been warned of course. The cameras will reject green. We shall all wear anything *but* green. Then the technicians will superimpose green-free images on to whatever they like, in this case two-dimensional medieval paintings.

Thus, when Sir Michael Hordern's God is ordering Cain from the Garden of Eden, I simply have to run from one green place to another via a couple of other green places, so it looks like I'm running between some trees and up the garden path; which was about right. Whereas in rehearsals your marks had been a different colour from the floor, thus enabling you to see them, in the studio, the marks were in green, thus enabling you not to see them. Well, you could just about see them if you looked carefully enough but, when God's in a raging fury with you, you don't stop to admire the floor. We'd have been better off rehearsing in the dark.

While I was zigzagging between imaginary shrubs, Sir Michael Hordern was in another part of the studio pointing his ungreen finger supposedly at me. Unfortunately, the finger had no idea what my intended route was. Instead of God at his mystical best, it was more like the colour blind leading the colour blind. Maybe God hadn't got round to familiarising himself with all the colours he'd just made. If black and white was good enough for *Doctor Who*, maybe we should have tried that. Grey separation underlay.

In the end God said, and I quote, "Oh for bloody fuck's sake, this is ridiculous!" and went back to his dressing room for a lie-down. Or to heaven. To berate an angel. I suppose, having gone to all that trouble to create the world in Technicolour and 3D, it must have been a disappointment to see it reduced to childish artwork and green.

Piers was indomitable. We came through. It was easier to recognise the difference between green and green at slower speeds, especially if you looked down occasionally. Thus, when Tom Courtenay's splendidly low-key Jesus was carrying his cross, he was a) travelling quite slowly and b) looking at the floor. Miraculous.

I liked Tom. We talked football during rehearsal, looking out on North Acton tube station. Hull supporter. I saw Fulham play up at Boothferry Park twice. Beer was cheap and the company cheerful. Special one-track football train. Reminded me of the Suffolk wiggly line. Different dialect. I think God and I were the only southern males on the *Chester Mysteries*. Otherwise it was the cream of the northern mafia. A veritable treasure trove of restive talent. Phil Jackson, Ken Colley, Brian Glover, Jimmy Hazeldine, Keith Chegwin, you don't mess with that lot. The vibe was a sort of dark, chuckly, otherly comeraderie. I flattened my vowels.

Coincidentally, Kevin R McNally – also destined to wax piratical in *Pirates of the Caribbean* – made his first TV appearance in this green extravaganza. He'd won the best acting gold medal at RADA, as had my cousin Pippa Guard in the same year, and his reward was the role of the soldier who gets his ear cut off by Peter. Or Tony Haygarth. This was fairly straightforward as the ear was its normal pinkish colour. Less easy was delivering the lines "He hath mine ear, mine ear he hath" with a straight face. Kevin excelled. No one laughed. He played the pain perfectly. Deadpan pain.

That's the mark of a great actor. Making a crap part interesting. Maybe if I'd played the "Sir, he may live…" speech in mortal agony, people wouldn't have coughed. But better still, cut the speech. Like the ear. He hath my speech, my speech he hath. Well, Shakespeare didn't write that bit anyway so who gives a toss?

It was good to see Keith Chegwin again. He used to sing and play the piano with his brother in the green room. He played Abel. I had to slay him. He was a good actor, but pop was calling.

The best thing about the *Chester Mystery Cycle* was getting into the *Top of The Pops* studio. We had to hang about a lot in one of the four 'relaxation' assembly areas – Red Assembly I think it was. Not Green, though it might as well have been. My hair was long and Cain wore some pretty funky medieval clothes, so I was easily mistaken for a member of The Sweet or even Legs and Co and had no problem drifting confidently past the floor manager and getting a glimpse of Tina Charles, singing about how much she liked to dance. I don't think I'll cover that one. I'd not seen Tina since the Two Twenty café Latymer days. *Top of the Pops* was 'it' back then. *Play of the Month* was decidedly not it but it got me in. Thanks for the ticket, Cedric Messina.

It was strange seeing Piers in hospital. No, it wasn't a mental hospital, although, after ten days of green, I'm surprised we hadn't all flown over the cuckoo's nest. A mental hospital is probably where I should have been and Kevin could have played Randle McMurphy. Maybe he has. Not sure.

Anyway, Piers was in a hospital in Almería, in southern Spain. Following four months of exemplary leadership, he, like the rest of us, was feeling the heat. Literally and otherwise. Not that he had to hop about on one leg in a hot coat or wear frilly collars and knee-length boots. In fact, by the time we were in Spain, Piers had taken to wearing nothing but a skinny, brown leather thong which, from a distance, looked as if he was stark beige-bollock naked.

Another way of keeping cool was by riding a freedomloving, Spanish horse, complete with pommel and snaffle, cowboy style. At the end of one particularly hot day, Piers – not a natural horseman – said he fancied a gallop. He was a fine swimmer and, when we were out at sea, he'd hurl himself into the briny at lunchtime like a Nordic merman. In fact, time and tide permitting, everything that Jim Hawkins did, Piers liked to have a go at it too.

Getting into the saddle was easy. Sandals and thong. No encumbrances. Like Farmer Harris' son riding bareback on the seventeen-hander. Except this time the rider was bareback and the horse was Spanish. Holding the reins was easy too. As was yelling "Ya!" and giving the horse an unnecessary kick. They don't need much telling these Andalusians, in any language. Anyway, "Ya!" was clearly Spanish for "gallop fucking fast and don't stop until I tell you"; "stop!" being the most important bit. Piers didn't. Tell him to. Stop.

We were in a fort, part of a set that had been used in early Clint Eastwood movies. It had four walls about fifty metres apart. Some supporting artists were still on the ramparts, which were barely supporting their weight, waiting to be told to come down and go home. Piers was too excited to say anything. Or rather, to rein the horse in. They're very obedient if you tell them. But not if you don't. Maybe it just hadn't crossed his mind. The horse, suddenly confronted by a wall, had the good sense to stop itself. Thirty to nought in two seconds. Thong to pommel in less. There was a high-speed testicular collision and Piers lost consciousness. It was seriously not funny. He turned green, flopped to one side and it was briefly rumoured that he was dead. Which he wasn't of course. Piers wasn't going to waste time dying.

When I visited him in hospital two days later, a bright spark had hung some plastic aubergines at the foot of his bed. Piers was wide awake, discussing shooting schedules and enthusiastically inviting us to inspect the damage. It was certainly impressive. As if chroma key had been set to reject everything except deep purple.

Just days later, the young catering assistant turned the catering wagon over on its back on the way back to the hotel. He'd fallen asleep at the wheel. He was staggering about at the roadside like a zombie, cut, bruised and miles away. That's how tired we all were.

On the subject of Deep Purple, I sat next to Ian Gillan on a flight between Madrid and Cardiff. By now most of *Return to Treasure Island* was in the can, and those of us that were still able to walk had been allowed to go home. *Living Wreck* springs to mind.

I was very fond of my *Deep Purple in Rock* album, purchased fifteen years earlier from King Street Music Stores. Or was it The Spinning Disc? Home of Smiling Beard. Anyway, my selection was met with derision in certain quarters. While poetic progressives like King Crimson were adored, and Jethro Tull were eclectic enough to pass muster, out and out heavy rockers like Black Sabbath invited suspicion. If you didn't aspire to be deep and meaningful, forget it.

But Ozzie wasn't that kind of songwriter. What was he trying to tell us anyway? Did it matter? He was trying to tell us that he didn't give a shit, and he was having a ball not giving it. Which suited me. I couldn't get through an essay on Henry's marriage to Ann Boleyn without a blast of 'Paranoid'. Or

'Hard Lovin' Man' by Purple. Or 'Speed King'. Turn it up for fuck's sake. And turn Gladstone down. *Disraeli Gears* notwithstanding. Cream that was.

Gillan was taciturn. Almost invisible. Gradually, I realised who he was, quietly said "hello", shared a recent anecdote, ordered a beer, offered one to Ian. "No thanks", he didn't drink. Neither did I – if I could help it. Best to keep off it on tour. By the time we'd landed, he'd ordered a beer and a brandy I think it was. I asked him where he lived these days, just out of interest. He looked at me as if to say, "don't be daft, I don't share stuff like that!" Fair enough. I jumped into a time machine and moved in next door to the whole band.

As Acton would have it, the house I live in, as I write, is attached to the house where Deep Purple lived prior to their first American tour. Blackmore and his girlfriend had one room upstairs, Jon and Nick shared another, and Rod and Ian shared the third. All else was communal. Kind of how it still is. Except there's a loft conversion now and lots of young New Zealanders sharing it. I confess I looked some of that up. The band moved on in '68. Last time I was on a plane from Madrid to the UK, Hugh Grant was sat beside me. Great singer, Ian Gillan.

In '72, I'd appeared in an episode of *Z-Cars,* playing Sergeant Lynch's estranged son, but not crossed paths with Fancy Smith, aka Brian Blessed. We first met on *I Claudius*; at the Acton Hilton, naturally. Brian was clean-shaven, a versatile and much-loved actor, but not yet the national 'tresh' he would become.

Judi Dench said recently how she hates being called that. Tresh. Like it freezes her in time. Almost freezes her out. I agree. She's Judi Dench, always has been. That's her secret. A rebel remains the same, it's everyone around them that changes. Stay true and you end up being called weird or eccentric or difficult. History is about perspective and opinion. What we take so seriously one moment usually becomes laughable in retrospect. Rebel on Dame Judi and damn the consequences.

Brian has a singular sense of humour. His default setting seems to be that all humankind is faintly ridiculous and everything else is a bonus. Like Ivor Thomas; a child in time, wise as a serpent, harmless as a dove, that *almost* smile.

Herbie Wise took his work very seriously. He gave of his best and got the best out of you. He was warm and shrewd, and chuckled gently across his half-moon glasses, but I don't recall a lot of laughs. On *Return to Treasure Island,* Brian and I sometimes had to resort to extreme methods to suppress laughter. Given the demands of the script and the impossible schedule, we were never far from the edge. However hard we worked, it was always against the clock, so that, by the time Piers was literally knackered and the catering wagon on its roof, it felt as if the world had stopped spinning and we'd all fallen off.

"Hey! Swordman! Why you do this?" My nemesis on the edge of the jungle. What day is it? Does it matter? A bit like how it feels now in the middle of this pandemic in Acton. And somewhere orangutans are still clutching at the crashing trees, disbelieving, eyes beseeching, gobsmacked by the inanity. "Hey! 21st Century Schizoid man! Why you do this?"

Filming for *Treasure Island* had begun in Wales, in a cold, cramped cottage out in the sticks somewhere near Cardiff. The atmosphere on day one was intense as Piers nuanced the love-hate relationship between Silver and Hawkins while the legendary Alf Joint hovered nearby, waiting to choreograph a fight and a housefire.

The sun was already setting when a bunch of pirates including the dashing Tony Osoba of *Porridge* fame, who of course lived in Acton – variously leapt from nooks and broom cupboards in an attempt to seize the coveted treasure map. Following some frantic swordplay, Hawkins then nobly extinguished the ensuing fire with his jacket before his trusty mate Silver hit him over the head with a crutch.

The stunt performer, Alf Joint, not only doubled for Connery in *Goldfinger* but, even more impressively, he's the geezer who dives off a cliff "all because the lady loves milk tray" in the Cadbury's advert. He's also in pretty well every action film ever made. And *Doctor Who* of course. My stunt double was Nick Hobbs, whom I next bumped into in Brenda's Stores in Coverack. On holiday. Typical Brenda's.

Just before Alf's fight, Silver has been deep in conversation with Jim, trying to con him out of the map, which is in a glass case on the mantelpiece. Meanwhile, a splendid actor called John Tordoff is hiding behind a door under the stairs armed with two combustible flintlocks. He's a bit nervous. We all are. Piers was hot on motivation and encouraged us to research the backgrounds of our characters. Thus, instead of just saying "Hah ha!" and starting a fight, you might think about it for several days beforehand.

While I was motivating myself to reach for the map – perhaps invoking a tragic relationship with my father – and Brian was motivating himself to be very still and devious – which he did bloody well – everyone had forgotten about John Tordoff, who was still in character and in the cupboard, perhaps reflecting on his difficult early life in Lostwithiel and why he also wanted a map.

At a tense, pivotal moment, with crew and cast hushed and Brian at his mercurial best, BANG! One of the pistols went off. Fucking loud in a small, cold cottage in South Wales, at four-thirty on a winter's afternoon. Or anywhere. The forgotten pirate suddenly burst from the cupboard. "What are you doing?!" said Piers. Good question. He hadn't meant to go BANG!

It certainly wasn't the fault of the props department. Roger Grocott was a gem. John's motivation had simply got the better of him. Perhaps it was those bowls of thin gruel he'd had to live on as a lad in eighteenth-century Cornwall.

"Sorry! Go again". Return to silence. And chill. But it was too late. The giggles had transcended the 'method'. Brian caught my eye with a deliberate glint. Piers took John to one side. Perhaps to talk him through his early life again, touching on the lack of opportunities for candlestickmakers after 1742, before ushering him back to the dark hole. When John finally got a chance to burst forth correctly and deliver some bloodthirsty lines, I'd completely lost it. He was so sincere, and eye-rollingly real, and shit-scared that he might do something else over which he had little control, I had to resort to self-harm.

While John prepared for his close-up, I asked wardrobe for a needle, which I dug into the palm of my hand every time my shoulders started to shake. Which was constantly. We were only there for lines off, so Brian was free to make mischief. I could hear every word he was thinking. Laughing loudly with his eyes. So quiet you could have heard a pin drop. Or a gun go off. Bastard. Damned shoulders. What a bloody mess.

My mum had been in *Blood on Satan's Claw*. Piers took the bold and delightful step of casting her in *Return to Treasure Island* too. As my mother.

Almería was blinking hot. I liked the dryness: it suited my asthma. But it was not to everyone's taste and seemed to crank up the burgeoning mania. It was just a shot away from Africa and felt like it.

Not only did we borrow Clint Eastwood's fort, but also some of his co-stars. Aldo Sambrell, who played Lopez, was in *The Good, the Bad and The Ugly*, *A Fistful of Dollars* AND *For a Few Dollars More*. He was in fact Spanish but Sergio Leone was Italian. As were most of the producers of Eastwood's Spanish ventures. Thus Spaghetti Westerns. Or paella cowboys. Spanish. Hence the amazing horses.

Or in our case, English, German and Welsh actors in a Spanish location pretending to be Mexico. Tortilla Pirates. Anyway, I can see his face so clearly. What a face. Big, bold, lived in, compassionate, expressive, sweaty. I think his voice was dubbed in the Eastwood movies but he said all his own lines as Lopez, an inmate of the Mexican prison where Jim and Silver were about to be reunited.

That happens a lot in the story. Being reunited. Then drifting apart again. Or being captured by a new bunch of desperadoes. It's a ten-hour twisting tale of bluff and counter-bluff, complete with scuffles, cuddles, cliffs and kerfuffle. Maybe I should have worked in PR.

Piers was in his element. The prisoners were up shit creek. Prone on hard prison beds, stacked like pasties in a baker's oven. We haven't seen Silver since he was armwrestling nutcases in Tortuga, then suddenly up he pops in Mexico and tells Lopez where to park his arse. Bad Lopez has not only been exceedingly rude – calling Jim a "puppy still wet behind the ears" – fair enough – but has also grabbed him violently by the throat. We're in big, eyeballing close-up and Aldo is in deadly earnest. You don't work with Eastwood unless you mean it. Ask the sublime Ken Colley, who was a superb Ben Gunn and who worked with Eastwood on *Firefox*. He said the set had an indefinable aura. The legend emanated. You learned just by breathing in. (McShane had some of that cinematic insight too. He just *gets* cinema, at every level).

Lopez's first line is "So, Hawkins…". Pretty straightforward, but Piers had motivated Aldo so effectively he really was beginning to go slightly mad; just as a hot, claustrophobic Mexican probably would.

The mutual respect was tangible. Here were a legend of British television and a stalwart of Spanish cinema, both eager to please. And therein lay the problem. It went like this: Lopez grabs Hawkins; excellent start. Hawkins looks shocked but defiant; good so far. Lopez eyeballs Hawkins; brilliant. Hawkins is impressed, Lopez sweats, Lopez looks desperate. Great. Hawkins continues

With Mum and hats in *Return to Treasure Island*

149

to look defiant, the tension is palpable. Piers is transfixed. A distant cockerel crows. Lopez draws breath. I like it. Lopez says, "So…"

Lopez says, "…so…" again. Lopez says "…Lopez!"

What?! "CUT!" says Piers.

Aldo knows perfectly well what he's done wrong: he called Hawkins 'Lopez'. It's motivation syndrome. BANG! CUT! The actors are so real they don't know what they're going to do next. Just like in real life. Go again… oh dear. Exactly the same thing happened. "So… Lopez!'" "NO! CUT! You are Lopez, HE is Hawkins". "Yes, yes Piers, I know". And he did.

If it hadn't been so tragic, I'd have laughed. Brian too. Here was a fully grown man who could speak perfectly good English, having to be lectured on the difference between the words 'Lopez' and 'Hawkins'. "I know, I know. I'm sorry, Piers".

In the end, Piers took him away – way into the distance where you could quite clearly see Piers mouthing, "YOU are Lopez, HEEE is Hawkins. HEEE is Hawkins, YOOU are Lopez".

We got there in the end, but only after I'd sweated more buckets than Aldo, and learned the true meaning of prayer. "Please, dear Lord, if you love me at all, in the name of all things bright and beautiful, please let Lopez say 'Hawkins' this time". It worked. Thank god.

Why the fates should have singled out my mum's brilliant and dear friend, Arthur Bostrom, to talk gibberish, heaven only knows but, before Arthur created the role of Inspector Crabtree in 'Allo 'Allo, Piers had already decided that he should play Don Felipe in Return to Treasure Island, with a traditional Spanish 'ceceo'.

Back then, we thought it acceptable to represent it as a lisp. We know better now but that's what we did. Anyway, it's eathy enough to thay, but you should try it. And Piers, consummate professional that he is, was watching Arthur's lithping lipth like a hawk. I mean how many times can you say "Yeth Thuperintendente" a) without laughing and b) without wishing you hadn't agreed to the fucking lithp?

With the best will in the world, sometimeth you jutht can't help yourself. "We established a lisp!" insisted Piers. Fucking hell, I only said one 's' without a lisp. "CUT!" Oh dear. Arthur rallied, as only a superintendente can, and survived long enough to roll down a dusty hill and have a fight with Hawkinth. And from there, it was downhill all the way really. When Inspector Crabtree says "Good Moaning!" it's meant to be funny. Tho! Lopeth! Don't go there.

***

Most of Episode Seven of *Treasure Island* was filmed in the mountains near Madrid, the city where Geraldine Chaplin lived. She still does sometimes. I played opposite her in a BBC production of *My Cousin Rachel*, which was directed by Brian Farnham, who also directed me in a *Poirot* episode alongside my brother, and made his name directing *Rock Follies*. Geraldine has that same liquid star quality as Lee Remick and Julie Christie. Shyly disarming in the flesh, magnetically alive on screen. Simultaneously still yet animated. It's something that can only partly be learned. She was a joy to work with.

I always say I peaked at twelve, because as David Copperfield I just *was*, I just did, I just dreamed. I knew what I was doing; it was no fluke but I was not nagged or over-directed. Just set free to do a job. Great screen actors have that in adulthood, an ability just to be there, like it was always meant to be that way.

Geraldine had a wonderful defiance. Rickman had it too. An innate sense of social justice wherever he went. Kind, charming, considerate but cross him at your peril. Human first, star second and, at best the two indivisible. Geraldine nipped home and back from North Acton one day. To turn the stew down in the pressure cooker. OK, she could afford the round trip to Madrid, but how cool to be that grounded. Air fares, but no airs and graces. Her dad's own daughter. Talent, tenacity and timing.

Geraldine wasn't around much to promote *My Cousin Rachel*; she was in demand. So it fell to me to pitch up on an early edition of *Good Morning Britain* at some unseemly hour and chat live with Selina Scott. I say chat. Jabber more like. I haven't the faintest idea what I said; made the fatal mistake of glugging gallons of coffee, then flying off at a caffeinated tangent more out of control than Piers' Andalusian horse.

Selina had screen presence, no question and, at that time, was nearly as famous as Princess Di. Her opening line, once I'd *un*settled in my chair and failed to draw breath, was, "Christopher, tell us what 'My Cousin Rachel' is *all* about". A sensible answer would have been, "It's a complex story and you'll have to watch the show", with a charming smile. Instead of which, I tried to answer the question. What seemed like three weeks later, I was still rambling on incomprehensibly about Florentine heat and laburnum pods when she changed tack and asked what it was like to work with Geraldine Chaplin. Thank fuck. I didn't make that mistake again. Answering impossible questions, I mean.

Mind you, I got myself in a swamp without a paddle doing live breakfast television for *Treasure Island* too. I'd been lulled into a false sense of security by two familiar faces. My Latymer schoolfriend, Dave Yates, was at the door to greet me and my Rugby School friend, Russell Grant, was on the studio floor in a wondrous jumper. Two of the sunniest smiles you could hope to meet. And Anne Diamond was not Selina Scott.

All was going swimmingly until I described how I was turfed into the Caribbean from a speedboat by a couple of Jamaican locals. Into the shipping lanes. Where the sharks feed. And they're especially attracted to white. Which I was wearing. The lads were just obeying instructions. Someone in charge had said, "There!", pointing to somewhere near the horizon. The camera was on the Hispaniola, half a mile away. All I had to do was swim towards it for as long as possible without being eaten.

Amusing enough story but, unfortunately, Anne then said, "Well, I won't be going to Jamaica for my holidays!" which amused no one. During the commercial break, the phone lines were jammed with indignant Jamaicans berating me for compromising their tourist industry. Shit. I was advised to say something as soon as we were live again. Which I did. Jamaica is fantastic. And safe. And beautiful. The best holiday destination. Which it was. And is. So there. For days after, I prowled the streets of Chiswick fearing retribution for cussing the golden isle. Blimey. Paranoia is bollocks. It wasn't me anyway. It was Anne. In her innocence. And I didn't get eaten. Not by sharks.

Geraldine couldn't make it to New York either. PBS had bought in several shows and I travelled as part of a BBC promo team that included Denholm Elliot, PD James and Jonathan Powell. First class solo, or club class and take a friend. A week to see the sights and do some press. All pretty cool. Especially as Lesley and I had found a shop that sold soft toys of Maurice Sendak's *Wild Things*, and travelled back to London with armfuls of them. We also saw Annie Ross in a fab little jazz club in a dodgy part of Harlem, and inevitably flew like rockets up one of the ill-fated twin towers. Oh, and Margaret Thatcher was in town so there were a lot of helicopters flying about.

Unlike the Prime Minister, I just wanted to have fun: like The Beatles on their first trip to the States. Spontaneous, witty and blithe. No long-winded answers to silly questions, no tedious theatrical stories, just roll with it whatever. On the big press day, Denholm and Jonathan took the afternoon shift, while Phyllis and I kicked things off in the morning. Not quite as early as breakfast television had been, but early enough. I made a crucial change of tack. *No* hot coffee. A bottle of cold beer instead. I never drank in the morning, except maybe on a long football excursion – to Carlisle or Sunderland – but this was medicinal. Tactical. Chill, Christopher.

The floor of the conference room was awash with regional press: Apache Junction News; The Boston Phoenix; the Nutfield News; Smoky Mountain Sentinel and so on. We sat high up on a polished rostrum. Below us, a sea of vacant, worldly faces. We waited. They settled. My heart bumped. The veteran

Brooklyn MC drawled into the mic, "Ladies and gentlemen, your questions please – for the acclaimed crime-writer PD James!" I had to sit and wait a while longer. Well, actually for what seemed like about three weeks, and certainly long enough for the beer to wear off. I was getting the heebie-jeebies. Use it, boy, use it.

Phyllis was only asked one question but, unlike my attempt to reply to Selina, she knew exactly what she was talking about. "Ms James, do you draw on your real experiences as a barrister in your books?" "Yes", she said, and then went on and on – and on and on, and on and on… and I got shakier and shakier. The MC gave my leg a reassuring squeeze which made it worse. For fuck's sake, be yourself, just be real.

Until… finally, finally… "Ladies and gentlemen, your questions please for "da stor of *My Cozin Rachel* – Christopher Gord". Hopefully guised as something between a cheeky John Lennon and a cherubic Hugh Grant, I snatched the mic. Go for it. "Er… hello… um… I'd just like to point out that – er – I'm not a barrister and I have in fact just completed a short ban for driving while slightly over the er – legal limit". Which was true.

I'd never say that now. Times have changed. Lots of people drove over the limit back then. Mel certainly did. There was usually more petrol in Mel than in his mother's Mini. And he never got stopped. Different era. Fewer cars on the road, no mobile phones and the beer was weaker. Don't quote me, but maybe driving after two pints is less dangerous than driving while taking a selfie. Or shouting at someone on the other side of the globe. And the cars were smaller too, and not as powerful. No excuse, just saying. It got the audience going anyway.

Bless Phyllis but she wasn't a barrel of laughs. Brilliant but a bit earnest. Some people had nodded off. Maybe Thatcher was eliciting a similar response up the road. As for me, chairs squeaked, and eyes boggled as the jaded journos turned to face the charming git. I've not got much memory of what ensued thereafter. It was like having one huge hit and trading on it for years. Like Toploader – whom my band The Bloogs supported twice – with 'Dancing in the Moonlight'. One cover version and it was instant limo status. For me, it was more like 'Winging It in the Sunlight'; every time I opened my mouth, they unanimously found me uproariously funny. Maybe I was. A bright spark from the Washington Post asked me something like, "Mr Guard, in the short second paragraph in Chapter Eleven of *My Cousin Rachel,* there is no specific reference to the whereabouts of the laburnum seeds in the Florentine courtyard as alluded to in the final paragraph of Chapter Three. Would you say that is of special significance or simply an oversight on the part of Du Maurier?" Nice one. Had he learned at the feet of Selina? I wasn't falling for that again. Here's an unanswerable question for you and please take as long as you like to make an arse of yourself. No way. I said, again with transparent candour, "I'm sorry but I haven't got the faintest idea what you're talking about". More gales of laughter. A stooge is born? Blimey.

Afterwards, a huge man with a Turkish accent, who introduced himself as Prince Fantastika or something there were a lot of erroneous titles in New York – asked me where I had studied my interview technique. Seriously? Royal Academy of Seat-of-Your-Pants mate, and yes you can buy me a Bud. After that, I collapsed in a heap, like a medium slavered in ectoplasm after a particularly exhausting seance and left it to Denholm and Jonathan to mop up the mess.

If Jonathan Powell, who was head of BBC drama when we made *My Cousin Rachel*, had been in the post in the late '70s – given his penchant for modernisation and streamlining – an earlier project with which I was involved might never have been given the green light. I somehow doubt he'd have allowed Cedric Messina to make the entire works of Shakespeare.

Over the same time span as *Fawlty Towers* was conquering the world by making just twelve half-hour episodes, with a three-year gap, the mighty Cedric employed pretty well everybody in the English-speaking world. It certainly kept the canteen staff busy, and it gave me a chance to work not only with my cousin Pippa but also with Manuel, aka Andrew Sachs. During the break from Fawlty. As Stephano. In *The Tempest*. Again. But this time I got to play Ferdinand, and no one got to play Francisco. Hurray. And Sir Michael Hordern didn't have to point at anyone not in green. He merely had to conjure spirits and shout at Warren Clark. Much better. And Pippa and I both got a nice review in the New York Times for being truthful. There is a Prospero. And all roads lead to Acton.

It was while I was working on *The Chester Mystery Cycle*, long after we'd blagged it into the *Top of the Pops* studio, that I went to Windsor. Elton John's place. My brother knew one of Elton's personal assistants, Mike Hewitson, and one day, out of the blue, he said, did Dom want to spend the weekend at Elton's? He'd not long moved in, but Elton was away touring Europe and had said it was OK for friends to use the place in his absence. So we did. Well, you would. Vast mansion, rebuilt in 1947 after a fire. Obligatory tennis courts and cinema. A disco. Glorious pianos of course.

Kiki Dee popped over. The weather was grey and still. Not much happening. Like a Sunday in Vienna. We just hung out. Half asleep. Watching TV. Until… "Elton's coming back!" "Huh? I thought he was…" "Yeah, he's home-sick. Wants some English food."

Kiki had drifted away earlier; should we leave too? It was just me and Dom and Mike and the mansion, and a home-bound Elton. We had no car; it would have meant a lift or a cab and a train.

"No, no", said Mike "It's fine. He doesn't mind". I wondered if he'd mind duetting with me on the piano, co-writing a song or two. Which of course was the last thing he wanted. Music. He wanted silence. Sweet, homemade silence. And fried eggs.

Elton was great. Human as the day he was born. Like when I met Liz Taylor for the first time. You feel overwhelmed for a moment, then life just takes its course. All on the planet together. The more ordinary the better. We sat round eating egg and chips and brown sauce in the little staff kitchen then went upstairs to play bar football. In the games room alongside the huge boots Elton had worn in *Tommy*. I rated myself at bar football. Dom too. We used to play on the old lead-backed table in The White Hart up the road from Latymer, where those endless days with Mel sometimes began. Keg Beer. 'All Along the Watch Tower'. Fancy a wager?

Forget 'Pinball Wizard', Elton was a bar football monster! Too good for me anyway. I didn't take a game off him. Hopefully, the tour was a bit less stressful after that. Who'd be a rock star, eh? Not for the faint-hearted.

I was nearly signed to A&M records back in the '80s. Elvis Costello's drummer, Pete Thomas, was drafted in to play with me, with Greg from Bad Company on keyboards and my co-conspirators, Stuart Walton and his stepbrother Chris Lea, on guitar and bass respectively. Heady days. It was a close-run thing. In the end, they signed a band called The Thrashing Doves instead of us.

It was not the first time the music industry had picked up on my songwriting; or the last. The British record label, Independiente, followed me too. But the deal never came. Slippery world. I wonder if I'd still be alive if the break had come. Maybe I was lucky to be unlucky.

And yes, I've made it. Here we are in Acton, at the rehearsal studios above Chance Caterers, where Colonel Gadaffer Tape (more of him later) rules OK and Pete is in an all-night drum battle with Ginger Baker's son, Kofi; and the inventor of trip-hop, Jonny Dollar, is learning his trade in the analogue recording space next door; and we can probably move on to the next chapter.

Jonny Dollar was born Jonathan Sharp. His dad directed me in *A Woman of Substance* with Liam Neeson and Jenny Seagrove. Jon played keyboards with the Chris Guard Band at the Mean Fiddler. Jon died at only forty-five. RIP. Massive Attack forever.

17: All Roads Lead to Acton: Part 2

Acton has been full of musicians for years. Because it's full of industrial spaces and cheaper than Chiswick. Same reason that BBC Lime Grove and Television Centre were where they were. Money. Shepherd's Bush is trendy now, but it wasn't back then, when I lived in downtown Stamford Brook, and employment was a just short bike ride away. Pick up your dad's tools and away you go.

Florin C Pascu and Andrada Brisc were more than a bike ride away. They were in Oradea in Romania, their lives heading in separate directions, until Acton came calling. Together, they created the eclectic wonderland that is AB Music Academy, just up the road from where I live now, where students from all over the planet, from the age of three to eighty, learn everything from ukulele to classical singing to drums, on the same street where I had recorded with Indians in Moscow fifteen years earlier. Can't believe I'm turning down Eastman Road again.

The Safestore was a vast, old factory building, very basically converted, where you could rent a so-called storage space and do whatever you wanted with it. Complete with free electricity and industrial toilets on the deep concrete landing. Perfect for a band. Pete and Stuart built the studio with what Pete dubbed 'fruit of the skip' everything found and recycled.

The powers got wise in the end. Realised they could make a fortune. Metres went in and the rent went up. But for a few halcyon years, it was heaven. A bit further up Acton Vale, Drum Tech arrived – the inspiration of Francis Seriau – which mushroomed into bass tech and guitar tech and a veritable emporium of musical learning and knowhow. Soon, there was a perpetual stream of loping, guitarlugging musos wending their way from Acton Central station down through Acton Park. It's people who make the music, the buildings just reverberate.

It was music that led to the oddest and best of all the interviews I've done: the *Doctor Who* one on the Wirral. The Bloogs had just played 'The Psychic Circus' and one of the questions we – Sophie Aldred, Chris Jury, Andrew Cartmel and me – were asked was something like, "Did you ever imagine, in that clay pit, all those years ago, that you'd be sitting here together like this, on the Wirral, twenty-five years later?" Due to an oversight, we only had one handheld mic between us. I reached for it. I wanted that question. Tiny pause for breath, then I just said "Yes". Firmly. I'd learned my lesson. All that interminable rambling and *faux pas* at ungodly hours. No more.

Great band The Bloogs. Ross Brown on lead vocals, Stu on guitar, Tom Burden – cousin Pete's son – on bass, me on rhythm and Mark or Gustavo Matteus on drums. Our single, 'Sideways' had had daytime airplay on BBC Radio Cornwall's David White Show, and the legend that was Mark Wilkin, who drummed on the original recording, got us on David's *BBC Introducing* show, followed by a gig at Bunter's in Truro. On the way, we met a van stuck on a narrow bridge and were forced to take the pretty route. But not to slow down. The narrower the lanes became, the faster we went until eventually the inevitable happened and all three Bloogsmobiles piled into each other. I half expected the Keystone Cops to turn up.

We didn't stop for long. We were late. No serious damage. Charmed life.

Oh, and thanks for the cool bass depping, Sarah Hunt!

We wrote 'Jumping off the Harbour Wall' to celebrate. The high bit of the wall, over and above the railings. Unstoppable. Sper-frigging-splash. "I ran into The Paris, where I had a word with Cerys. I said 'Hey, don't be embarrassed. Get some waterproof mascara, sink a few mojitos, get some sand between your feetos sweetheart, kiss the setting sun before you make your final run". Er, did I say "...that *was* Mark Wilkin?"

That still doesn't work for me. Mark is an *is*. Always will be.

The Bloogs

Daniel Hacker is an 'is' too. He used to come to my art club at Wendell, when he was seven, and I showed him how to play simple things on the guitar. He once said I taught him everything he knew. That's a bit daft. Well, maybe back then. But not now. I couldn't teach the perspiration. That was all Dan's doing. The genius for hard work, the rebellion and the truth.

The way he looks now, he could be walking through the gates of Latymer in 1970. Not an impersonation of a '70s hippy, but the real thing. Dan's paid his dues. Argued with teachers, walked out of lessons, travelled through time. He's eighteen now, and as good a guitarist as I've ever played with. Fashions come and go, the song remains the same. Dan lives near Acton.

News flash: during lockdown, sales of flared trousers have increased by twenty per cent. Verbatim.

Colonel Gadaffer-Tape was actually called Roy. Old school music biz: vivacious circus roadie, dodgems, end of the pier, cash on the nail.

His assistant, Phil, would open the creaking wicket gate like something out of *Oliver Twist*. Secretive, otherly, smile of the undergrowth. Perfectly legitimate business – nice, bright rehearsal space, recording facility, credible clients – but Phil always made you feel like you were up to no good, just because you'd knocked on his door.

Which reminds me of a gig I did with Malone – the brilliant Simon McInerney, my brilliant daughter, Daisy, and me.

Kite, our previous incarnation, had been spotted by Gary Crowley and played on his Sunday show, made it into his *Hall of Fame* like Suede before us, then stalked by sundry labels. We had a residency at the gorgeous old 'Twelve Bar Club' on Denmark Street (RI fucking P) where everyone from Dylan to the Gallaghers used to pitch up.

Then we morphed into Malone and hit the road.

We were somewhere between Camden and Euston, outside a gaunt, grey pub of about five floors. Five and a half maybe. We'd arrived unassumingly for the sound check at around five-thirty and taken the liberty of ringing the doorbell. One of those horror movie silences ensued, as if everyone from Bela Lugosi to Fenella Fielding was creeping about inside but not letting on. The building seemed to sway as the wind picked up, hurling dust and pigeons at us like gothic confetti. Not yet dusk but utterly deserted. Not a human in sight. A bit like everywhere is now in the middle of a pandemic, except that back then there was no reason *not* to be about; people were still allowed to sneeze on each other. And sing in bars. Supposedly.

This was just an unpopular door at a bad moment. We rang again; a bell rope would have been more appropriate.

And again. Vibes definitely exist. We all felt them. Suddenly a sash window was hurled open a hundred feet above us. "What the fucking hell do you want?" With sublime presence of mind, Simon retorted, "Madam, we are but humble minstrels, come to ply our trade!" Which was fair enough. This was a music venue, not Vlad the Impaler's castle. "Well, you can fuck off!" And the window banged shut, causing a dust storm and scaring the shit out of the pigeons.

As no other windows were open, we discounted the possibility of boiling pitch and gave it another minute. Eventually, a cowed youth who looked like Phil's nephew opened the door. Bolt, creak, slide, shove, creak. His only words were "Watch out. She's in a bad mood". You're not kidding.

Fortunately, by the time we'd had a feedback check and re-stuck the gaffer tape onto the wobbling mic stand, the creature from the banging window had sunk half a bottle of something soothing and Polish and turned back into Mrs Jekyll. "Alright boys? What can I get you?" "A pint of what you're not having, please madam."

Roy had a black bubble perm, like Colonel Gadaffi, and a notice board. When Pete Thomas and Gregg Dechert turned up, he thought we were going to make his fortune. Pete had been on *Top of the Pops* and Gregg was touring with Bad Company. "Got any inspiration?" Roy would say as we trouped in promptly at ten. We were professionals. We had investment from A&M and proper management. Roy had mouths to feed and nostrils to satisfy. Black fingerless gloves, woolly scarf, deep desk, cigar stub surrounded by artful dodgers and budding Jonny Rottens he hoped and prayed and waited. He had Kofi Baker. As insurance. Just in case. Son of Ginger. Great DNA. I wonder, were Phil and Kofi related?

Roy had put a hand-scrawled ad up on his notice board. "Gaffer tape, only £1.75 a roll". Hundreds of them had materialised from somewhere. Fallen off the back of a ghost train. Big rolls, black and super-sticky. Perfect for repairing wobbling mic stands and making comedy moustaches. (We had a drummer called Cheeserat once. He wore one.) Bubble perm, gaffer tape. Bubble perm, gaffer tape. Colonel Gadaffer-Tape! Roy became known as the Colonel and he never knew why. He loved it.

Roy and Phil were superb, natural roadies. They did the PA for me at Fulham Football Club, under the Riverside stand, for a show to raise money in the pre-Fayed days. Covers like 'Satisfaction' and 'Alright Now'. Roy scrawled another note after the gig. Phil handed it to me. "You owe us fifty quid. Or else". Quite right. I did. A pleasure to do business with you, Colonel. Cuddly toy and a goldfish.

***

Malone

I felt bad that we didn't get the deal with A&M. For me of course, and for Chris and Stu and Robbie and Liz; but most of all for the Colonel. He kind of stayed in touch; hoping against hope that fate would yet do a *volte face*. But the moment had passed. As fast as the limos had rolled up outside Chance Caterers, the chance had gone. EMI, Virgin, they all had a look. Thumbing the wads, waiting to see who'd make the first move. It just wasn't our day. We lost in the final to the Thrashing Doves. Like Fulham lost to West Ham in '75.

After all that outrageous fortune, the shindigs on the way home from Carlisle and Brum, beating Everton, defying the odds, it really had felt fated. And yet, we only went to Fulham at all because Robbie the dog was sick on that Fulham Palace Road bus. And we only worked with Pete and met the Colonel because I got chatting with Neil in the little off Licence at the end of Alkerden Road in Chiswick. "Some bloke comes in here – to do with the music industry". That was Robbie. Not the dog. Robbie McLeod, Elvis Costello's tour manager. Neil gave him my cassette tape. Few hours later, we were talking business in The Cross Keys. Bill Bowyer playing darts. Not with Dad of course. Happened so fast. And ended as quickly. I'm still in touch with Robbie. He's off the road now of course. Not retired. Never retired. Because of COVID. Something has to give. The Thrashing Doves got a million quid.

I always wear the same pin badge. It's a swallow and I transfer it almost religiously to whatever top I'm wearing. I have loads of pin badges. Bought or given. Pushed into the wall of my jumble-room. Mainly birds. But an otter too. I was an otter in a former life, remember? I used to wear the red kite one a bit and I still love red kites, but they've made such a remarkable recovery they're probably doing OK without me. The swallow I've lost several times. Falls off, gets washed, trodden on, whatever. One time it went to Cyprus on the sole of Stu's shoe. I'd given up on it; but these birds know better than me. Three months out of the egg and they're winging it to Africa; then they come straight back to the same barn six months later. How the hell do they do that? I suppose a bit like a child hears a song in the womb then recognises it in the car eighteen months down the road. Hypnotic osmosis. Stu had trodden on the upturned badge in my music room – where we decamped after the Safestore got wise – and taken it on holiday. He sent a picture. Wish you were here. See you soon. Swallow. I was so happy.

I have a special pocket too. Officially it's called a watch pocket. That little extra one above one of the main side pockets. It's my plectrum pocket. I have to play with a Jim Dunlop nylon 1mm. Nothing else gets that mix of tone and scratch. My primitive so-called style. Evolved from gaps in my knowledge as much as from learning. I don't want to know everything. My dear uncle Barrie Guard is a brilliant musician. Classically trained; wrote the music for the *Darling Buds of May* and hugely successful in the pop industry. "Why not play the whole chord, Chris?" "Because a) I can't and b) I like it like this". It suggests melodies that the whole chord doesn't.

Barrie was Cliff Richard's musical director and recorded Elkie Brooks and Bonnie Tyler and did lots of amazing work for the Performing Rights Society. In the 60s he used to stay over at Pleydell sometimes. Huge shock of hair and a drum-kit in the back room. Clarinet too. He was in a band called The March Hare, with Peter Skellern who went on to have a huge hit with 'You're a Lady'.

And I always have that plectrum in that pocket. Plus and this is equally important – two small pieces of lapis lazuli, my birthstone, and a guarana capsule. I rarely use guarana any more. It's natural and harmless but too much of it buzzes your head off. It's nice just to know it's there. In case of emergency. Up a tree. You never know these days.

I love playing in bands. I hid for a while, writing for younger singers, playing rhythm guitar and doing backing vocals. That worked brilliantly in The Bloogs. Ross was a perfect collaborator. I kind of wrote *him*. He would describe his troubles or joys and I'd channel them into songs he could sing from the heart. Bit like Daltry fronted up Townshend's writing.

That's how I wrote 'Sideways'. People ask what my songs are about and how I cannot write about my own experiences. Well, I do – sometimes. But often not. Ask Sondheim or any writer of musicals. It's no different from writing a script really. Putting yourself into someone else's shoes. In fact, being an actor feeds into the process quite neatly. You feel it none the less just because it's someone else's experience. Shakespeare didn't have to go to Jamaica to write about enchanted islands. Or be a Danish prince to worry about ghosts and liars.

The song I uploaded to Spotify today is a timely example. What sounds like a paean to lost love was actually inspired by a photograph of me lying on Boulders Beach in South Africa, looking over my shoulder at a coy jackass penguin looking away as though I've done something to offend her. It was all meant tongue in cheek originally, but someone said today that the song as it is now, made them cry. Blimey. I hope not with laughter. That's what comes of slowing it down, transferring it to the piano and getting a great female singer to sing the second half with me. Thanks penguin. How did you know?

"Was it something that I said, must have slipped out of my head, on the blind side of my heart? Was it something that I said, made you twist and turn your head, on the blind side of your heart? We don't know what we're doing, we don't know who we are. I didn't really mean it, at least we got this far. At least we got this far. We did, we do, we are".

I painted the penguin too.

My muse.

I just had a text from Lara, who lives next door. She works at Bush Hall, just up the Uxbridge Road. Glorious Edwardian music venue. Bit quiet at the moment but plenty of virtual stuff going on. Videos and Zooms and what-have-you. Someone had left a wallet on her hedge. Was there a Kiwi, called Troy, at number thirteen? Well yes, they're all Kiwis except the Australian.

How nice to have a chat on the street. Everyone's invisible most of the time. Lovely day too; spring peeping through the frayed edges of COVID winter.

Lara and I discussed her cat, Fluffy, and even my book – this book. I was bunking off really; should have started writing an hour ago. Then I got chatting to Mikaela, at number thirteen, after I'd returned the wallet. Troy was so happy.

These things happen when you break your routine. Like me when I took the wrong keys, when I went to the paper shop, the day I was supposed to be filming the video for 'Blind Side', and got locked out, and had to leave without half my stuff and no breakfast. If you're putting all your worldly goods into sundry vans during a pandemic, of course you put your wallet on a hedge.

The Kiwis are heading home. Such a drag. No sooner had they arrived in the UK than Brexit and COVID struck. Travel insurance covers most things but not stolen dreams. But they're full of pluck. Is pluck a cross between pleasant and fuck? Should be. Unlike this island, their island is virtually COVID free at the moment. Fewer people, true. But lucid leadership may have helped too.

Writing this book is keeping me sane. Land of confusion. Or *The People That Time Forgot?* That was the film Dom and I called *The People Who Forgot What Time it Was.* In case you forgot. At the Regal, Hammersmith. Light years ago. Hilarious at the time. Not so sure now. The UK seems more like the island colony, and New Zealand the mother country; certainly after talking to those enlightened sparks next door. I told them about Deep Purple living in their house. They were well delighted. Mikaela's dad is a huge Purple fan. I'm going to miss them, even if they do party in Kiwi time. They play great music, and games I don't understand. Not through the wall anyway. Sounds like a seven-year-old's birthday party. Musical bumps and pass the parcel, pissed. At three in the morning. Shakespeare wouldn't have known about New Zealand, but he imagined it brilliantly. That's how god would have made the world isn't it? By imagining stuff.

The People That Time Forgot. What is this obsession with Union Jacks and suits? Otters and orangutans don't get it. They thought we'd be on by now. "We

Was It Something That I said? by Christopher Guard

163

should be on by now", *Time*, by Bowie. Dana Gillespie, who played Ajor in *The People That Time Forgot (*and Juno in *The Tempest* opposite Julie Covington as Iris.)*, has just released her memoirs. She didn't forget. Seventy-one. Perfect age to release a life story. I wonder has Julie written one. No-one sang 'Don't Cry For Me Argentina' like Julie. The first and the best. Sublime honesty. My mum loved her.

Doug McClure was another that was in *The People That Time Forgot*. I hero-worshipped him in *The Virginian*. Not too sure about him in sci-fi. The peach sundae was good though. Dom and I laughed a lot. Matinees. In the circle. The Regal, Hammersmith. No one else up there but us. Six boys in the front row of the stalls. Two usherettes. A torch. A commissionaire somewhere, maybe moonlighting from Television Centre. "Where d'you think you're going? Have you got a ticket?" We renamed some of the films. *The People That Time Forgot* became *The People Who Forgot What Time It Was* and Bowie starred in *The Man Who Fell Over*. And *Shout at The Devil* became *Shout at the Manager*. Well, it was seriously shite.

I told the Kiwis how I started writing this book, in the eye hospital, and about the working title, *Eye Am*. We all liked *A Dream of a Memoir* as a subtitle, and they liked *What Was That?* as a main title. I promised to stay in touch and send details of publication when it happens. If it happens.

There is a kind of surreal, understood, otherly, understated sense of the ridiculous that is exclusive to a certain breed of musician and that you either get or you don't. Kosmas Mylon, who has been playing bass with me recently is typical of the species. Born and bred in Greece, raised on a diet of *Monty Python* and heavy metal, he had only to say "Spamos" and we bonded for life. The universal language of the preposterous. It could save the world.

Stu Walton, from Indians in Moscow, was a past master. So deep was his awareness of the fundamental foolishness of all human endeavour, he had only to say nothing and volumes materialised. I would talk and talk, while Stu worked on, apparently vacant but in fact full to bursting. "Where was I?" I'd say. "I think you'd finished", said Stu.

Enough said.

It's no coincidence that George Martin worked with The Goons and Peter Sellers. Or that The Marx Brothers were all fine musicians. Or that Eric Idle's songs were key to the work of *Python*. Or that George Harrison funded *Life of Brian*. It was only because George said, "I like your tie" to George Martin that The Beatles were signed. What made them laugh was also what made them tick.

To quote Mum, "It's not the writing of the poem/that causes me the pain/ It's being the person who writes the poem/that's the strain." You don't become

Stu, Chris and Chris

The Beatles by being 'The Beatles'. Or The Silver Beetles. You become great musicians who happen to be called The Beatles because you had the courage to open your minds in the first place. Decca simply didn't get the joke. There is no formula. History is just a thing.

Stu came from a family of non-musicians. In his teens, he happened to pick up a guitar one day and discovered he could play. The apparent effortlessness of his inventiveness is a tribute not to dedication or ambition, but to a genius for absorption. Like a transcendent sponge. You breathe out, you breathe in. And the laughter – when it came – was sheer joy.

We'd be up at the Safestore – Stu, Pete and me – working on something serious like *Hell's Harvest* or 'Industrious', while a folder of our latest silly sketches did the rounds. Like an antedotal drug. A page of Pudding Bison Haircuts and Buffalopian Tubes, or Stand-Up Chameleons and Giraught Excluders. Executed with the same attention to paradox as the songs themselves. *The Punimals*.

Our sometime manager, Max Tregonning, suggested at one point that we ditch the dance rock and concentrate on comedy. He may have been right. But we weren't interested in genre. The more we tried to squeeze into pigeonholes, the less we felt like pigeons. For better or worse, we were pleasing ourselves. And it all stands up now. Some things can't be helped.

STAND-UP CHAMELEON

Punimals by Indians in Moscow

Ten years earlier, John Selby, Andy Dascalopoulos, Ralph Dunlop, Trevor Hobden briefly and I – four school friends and a brother-in-law – named our post-punk band Some Burglars in honour of The Police. When a woman called Tracy booked us into our residency at The Windsor Castle in Kilburn, she called us The Sun Burglars; even put it on the poster in a dingy window, alongside lunchtime striptease. Sometimes people just won't let you be silly.

We'd gone down the 'The' road already. 'The' was popular back then. The Jam, The Pretenders, The The, of course; which paved the way for no 'the's at all. As in Wham!, which made cunning use of the exclamation mark, and Duran Duran which made cunning use of repetition.

But why this obsession with the definite article at all? To 'the' or not to 'the', that was a question. Why not pronouns? Once we'd decided to become criminals, it came down to a choice between bandits and burglars. Bandits had featured in my six-year-old play *The Farm Boy*. The Bandits? Too obvious. The Burglars? Not sure. In 'Seen one' of my play "john selden sez I notes *some* riders" and later, in 'Seen one', "the milkman sez theres *some* ridersover there". Sic. What about *Some* Bandits? Or – hang on – Some Burglars! Yes! John Selby laughed so much I thought he was going to die. Then, when Tracy changed it to The Sun Burglars, he did. Well, of course he didn't, but he was so full of endorphins he wouldn't have noticed if his head had fallen off.

167

Some Burglars!

Tracy could have been related to three other people – or even been one of them. Not the Colonel of course. Not in this life anyway, but it could very well have been her, fifteen years later, who told us to fuck off out of that lofty window near Euston.

I never actually met Tracy, and that window may have been the closest I got, but I never felt the urge to argue. If she called you 'The Sun Burglars', what the fucking hell did you want to change it for?! The poster had gone up already. Maybe she was the aunt of the lady at the window, and they were both related to Phil and distantly to the Colonel. They were the stuff of recurring dreams, without whom the music industry would have collapsed and died. No prisoners – burglars or otherwise. Ladies and gentlemen – The Some Burglars! With an exclamation mark. Not just any old band.

Before the rowdy Windsor Castle shindigs, we would calm ourselves at a little pub round the corner. I don't remember its name but there were never any other customers, so it was nice and quiet. Maybe it was shut and they'd just forgotten to lock the door. In fact it probably was open because there was a phantom behind the bar who looked as if he badly wanted to say, "What the fucking hell do you want?" but couldn't actually be bothered.

It was one of those featureless '60s pubs that looked as if it was built from an Ikea flat pack. Maybe it was and they didn't assemble it until they saw a customer coming. Like an early pop-up. It did seem to shake a little. The novel DIY design included the smallest stage I've ever seen. Like something The Krankies could have graced. A small cube cut out of a flat wall, with enough space for a snare drum and a diminutive stripper. Except that strippers were clearly not on the menu. Well, nothing was much. A sign above the cuboid hole – almost bigger than the stage itself – read, in no uncertain terms – 'NO DANCING'. So that's what we called the pub. It did have a name after all: 'NO DANCING'.

The last gig I did, quite recently, was at the Half Moon, Putney. The Stones use it sometimes. Great, small venue for pre-tour warm-ups and parties. The last time I'd played it with a full band was with The Bloogs. David Hamilton put us on. For Animal Aid. This time, I bit the bullet and booked the place myself. The place was rammed. The onstage sound was great. My amazing youngest, Tallulah, opened for us. The band was rocking. What could possibly go wrong?

This: my front right dental implant fell out halfway through the first song. Maybe I shouldn't have bitten that bullet. I just about managed to catch it and add it to my plectrum pocket. Next to the guarana capsule. Blinking heck. I'd had a premonition this might happen. The tooth had been wobbling for weeks. I carried on. Bit lispy but I coped. Nobody noticed. Not a soul. Even the stills man. Not until the following morning anyway. After the gig, my great mate, Andy Robbins, rock aficionado and Fulham supporter, said he liked the look and I should keep it. Well, it's still available. I've had a plate fitted to replace it. I can scare the life out of you any time you like. *Return to Return to Treasure island*? Toothless old Jim, gone to the dogs, rumsoaked and sea-shantied. Yes dancing?

It's been hard since Stu died. I'm a lazy sod and left all the technical stuff to him. He could do everything: bass; guitar; keyboards; Cubase; lighting design; you name it. And he'd only just begun. He was singing his own vocals for a new project, and writing a book, and planning the next Anglo-Indian venture, and getting to know his young son… He said we could live a thousand years and still have things he wanted to do. It just sucks. Stu was a beautiful atheist, a natural green, progressive socialist, a worker, a trooper, a genius, a one-off.

Mark Wilkin

Towards the end, he gave more vent to his anger; patient Stu cursing the cunts. While they bickered about flags and masks, he just ran out of time. Thanks, God.

When Mark Wilkin vanished, he left two amazing sons to fill his shoes. Unfillable though they are. Mark lived and breathed his passions. Uncompromising, boundlessly energetic – whether in London or Cornwall – he pioneered bands, inspired students, read voraciously, laughed like a drain, never suffered fools and watched the world with a unique wry wit and wisdom.

One night, his band, Blues Connection, had supported Little Feat in Truro; he was giddy on the high and I was staying over at his house. My attempts to retire to bed were not just aborted, they were banned. "Let's write some blues songs! We need originals, not just covers". I thought, "Fuck it, nothing by halves" and wrote several. In fact five in as many hours. Until the sun came up a-crowing. 'Suicide Tide', 'Big Man', 'Blues Connection', 'Slow Car' and 'No Through Road'. Delivered fresh to your drumkit.

Tide-eyed and logless, we then headed for Trelan studio and recorded the lot in two hours. Guitar, drums and vocals. This wasn't blood out of a stone, it was diamonds in the blood. I just listened to some of it. Sounds surprisingly great. I slept like a harbour sunset that night. 'Golden Slumbers'. Mum used to sing that to me on summer evenings before she went off to be in *The Tunnel of Love* with Ian Carmichael and Barbara Murray, in the West End. I cried. Brilliant how McCartney rips into that lullaby. It's how I felt as the front door closed.

When I started fronting bands again, I realised how many of my own songs I didn't know. Swathes of albums' worth of the stuff. I'd been so busy writing I hadn't bothered to mentally archive everything. Just rolled on to the next song and half forgot the previous one.

It's different for an actor. You don't have to carry every part you've ever played in your head. You roll on to a new set of lines, the next mercurial cast, trusting in luck or astrology, while the alchemy of casting directors and the whims of fashion design your winding road. "We must keep in touch!" But you tend not to, not because you don't want to but because you literally can't.

I've often had that clichéd actors' dream of not knowing your lines, when you're suddenly back doing a play you were in years ago, expecting yourself to know it, and you know nothing. Not even one word. Not even what the play is about. And you try to look silently interesting. Backstage, there are shopping arcades or a railway station, together with the most unlikely people, like Julia, my obsession, or the barman from No Dancing, or Frank from the Japanese prisoner-of-war camp. And it's all so logical. Except that I can't find my script. I look in sliding drawers and at the top of shiny escalators. I don't even know what play it is.

When I saw Elvis Costello – thanks for the tickets, Robbie – with his random, spinning wheel song selector at The Albert Hall, able to remember any song from his vast catalogue, it got me wondering. I've not had that kind of success with my songwriting, but I sure can do myself the favour of learning my own songs, just in case. After all, at some gigs, people have asked how many of my songs are covers, which is a double-edged compliment if ever I heard one. As if the songs sounded good enough to be covers, but inconveniently reminding me that they hadn't been hits.

So, I set about learning my own songs. Not just the first verse or the backing vocal bits I'd been singing at gigs, but the whole thing, with the inner logic of how I'd written it. And as the memory muscle grew, so the whole back catalogue ghosted into view. It had to do with expectation. Expecting to remember. Expecting to see ghosts. I know I can and I will. As Rosie always said, my songs sound best *as* I'm writing them. Maybe the genie is happiest in the bottle. Just make sure you drink the contents.

As for this book, it's getting quite scary how much I can remember. The in-between stuff. The intangible connective tissue. Part smell, part sound, part touch, part haunting. Memory now. Mum singing 'Golden Slumbers', as the Pleydell Avenue sunlight shimmers across the lime tree leaves, and the reassuring scent of hair lacquer wafts on the breeze, and the tie on the ceiling – for now at any rate – is beyond my wildest dreams. Maybe *What Was That?* *is* a good title. It's growing on me.

18: Telling Tales

I can't lie. Well, that's not entirely true. My agent, Pippa Markham, used to say I couldn't dissemble – that was the word she used; which on the face of it sounds like a disadvantage for an actor. But an actor doesn't just have to pretend to be other people; an actor has to pretend to be cold when he's hot and happy when he's sad, even rich when he's poor sometimes.

When I started rehearsing *My Cousin Rachel* at the Acton Hilton, and we went to the pub after the read-through, I couldn't even buy a round of drinks. Here was the leading man, playing opposite a famous film star, with his pockets stuffed full of two-pence coins because he'd had to raid the small change jar so he could buy lunch. No joke. It had been one of those winters. No repeat fees, a stage job I turned down, another commercial I didn't get – I never got commercials – so you roll the dice, take a deep breath and wait.

I'd signed the contract for *Rachel*, the deal was done. But would the owner of the agency advance me any money? Ten quid? Nup, it wasn't 'policy'. He said, "Plonk plonk" to cover his embarrassment He always said that when he had bad news. So it was a pocketful of pennies and looking like a skinflint because I couldn't afford a round of drinks. Twice. I hated that. I love to be generous. Maybe that's why I didn't have any money. All I had I'd earned. No vast inheritances coming my way. That's one of the reasons I didn't take up that place at Christchurch. I was earning a living.

I put up a front until the first cheque came through. You put up a front when you go up for jobs. The myth is that acting is all fun and romance and don't you just love it all the time. That's an inherent lie; and the hardest part to play. Plonk plonk.

I've never really known what acting is anyway. Beyond play. Everybody does it. Adjust the front then face the world; reflections of other people's expectations – or your guess at what those expectations may or may not be.

If anyone has time to think of anything beyond the next selfie. Not so much a hall of mirrors as a wall of monotony. If every picture tells a story, how many pictures do we need? Like the stories in the paintings I did for the kids. One was enough for a whole afternoon. Just a moment. Leading wherever we chose. Ravelled or unravelled, timespun, undone, told and retold. Image and imagination.

A misleading miniature of Anne of Cleves and a presidential Tweet. Henry and Donald. Two despots with the same idea; if it doesn't suit me, lie. And deny. Basic playground stuff and proof that, however knowledgeable you may be – Henry was an academic brainbox – emotional intelligence is ignored at your peril.

Unfortunately, there are no cartoons of Henry's descent into petulant madness but there are plenty of Trump as a wilful child. And of Thatcher, all wide-eyed and friendless. Some Oxbridge undergraduates who don't make it into O.U.D.S. or Footlights join the debating society instead; then give dreadful performances in the House of Commons. You can have your voice changed but not your soul. That was the idea behind 'Lie To Me'.

"Lie to me if you have to baby, lie to someone else, but for god's sake baby, don't lie to yourself".

I could easily have turned this book into a work of fiction. Well, maybe not easily but I could. I still could. Like an acting performance – not so much changing into someone else as putting myself in someone else's shoes and reacting to whatever happens next. Change the names, change the places, inject a murder or two maybe, alter the era. See what happens. What if…

In the early '00s, I wrote a novel called *The Cost of Flying*. It was with the Maggie Noach agency and got as far as a publisher and an editor; even a change of name to *Flight of Fancy* – which I never liked, but they wanted something breezier. Then they asked me to hack it about a bit. They loved the first third: all the relationship stuff based in Chatwick, the brilliant little girl, the ornithological imagery, the nervous breakdown. But when it started turning into sci-fi and a complex surgical operation, they became confused. But that was partly my intention: it wasn't meant to be easy – to read or to write. It is, and was, what it is.

Suddenly, everything went cold. Maggie died. And I couldn't have written that. Complete shock. Too young. So sad. The book still lies there, half-hacked.

The publisher had been lukewarm until they suggested a genre. Magical realism. That made it marketable. Instead of writing something original and finding your market, the wheels of profit demand that the product fits the market. Until something original comes along again, like *Wuthering Heights* or *Ulysses* or *Trainspotting* or *Parable of the Sower*. Then everyone wants a bit of that.

The Cost of Flying isn't really magical realism. It's just a book, with an inner logic and an outer chaos, and that's how I intended it to be.

Around the time Maggie died, I heard someone on the radio describe a new book they admired as "like three books in one" because it crossed genres. Where had I heard that phrase before? Of course! Eighteen months earlier. As the reason my book wasn't quite working. Hmmph. I'll go back to the first draft one day and sod the lot of them. Me included. Do I sound bitter? I am a bit.

The first three letters of bitter. Edited. *The Cost of Flying*. That's what it's called.

It used to be the same with music. Now along come Black Country New Road and do what they like, when they like, change what they like, how they like, listen to each other, not labels – and everyone loves them.

Peter Wright. Not the darts player with the chameleon Mohawk, who dances sideways before matches. Although he's a point in case.

Darts. Tucked away in The Cross Keys on Friday evenings. The end of the day for William Bowyer and Ruskin Spear, RA. The traditional old pub game with a ubiquitous corporate makeover. The moment Peter Wright appears, his theme song 'Don't Stop the Party' booming, he's an instantly recognisable brand. Hard-sell fandom, a frenzy of hero worship, the roar of an invisible, pandemic crowd, daring you not to watch. Forget the tedious hours of practice, the sports psychiatrist, the hotel rooms. The picture tells the story. It may as well be the 'Milky Bar Kid', dolling out white chocolate to his posse. Irresistibility. Peter Wright dresses up, he jokes, he acts; a great sportsman as a circus clown, appealing directly to our inner child. You are permitted to have fun. It's playtime.

A completely different Peter Wright was in my class at St Peter's. He lived on the far side of the green, probably just with his mother. I barely knew him, which is what made it all so weird. Not that there was much to know. He just seemed to abide, taking school in his reluctant stride and happy enough simply to be delivered and collected each day by his mother. Anyway, subtext notwithstanding, I don't recall addressing a single word to Peter nor him to me, before… it happened. Before I was rebranded, out of the blue, one grey Friday afternoon.

At the end of the week, it was the wont of Mr Jones, our benign, normally cheerful headmaster, to roll back the dividing partition between the top two classes and read to us all. Supposedly, as a treat. He wasn't the greatest of readers and the stories were usually standard fare, like *The Famous Five* or *Swallows and Amazons* but on this occasion, his tone of voice and choice of fiction set a new precedent.

"Stand up Peter Wright!" Shift, ruffle, shuffle, stand. "Stand up Christopher Guard!" What? Had I heard my name? "Christopher GUARD! Stand up!"

St. Peter's at White City

Shit. What goes on? Stand up in front of the big girls in the top class for a start. Shock, flush, fret. Stand up in front of Julia, who was only two tables away and flushing on my behalf, her little nostrils characteristically flared, admiring me and my embarrassment in equal measure. I wasn't a shrinking violet; I'd represented the school at White City Sports, kissed Gloria Mora on the lips and had a fight with John Waller. But I wasn't notorious; just another boy. "Christopher Guard! What have you got to say for yourself?", as if the sight of Peter Wright staring at his knees was enough of a clue. And why did he have to keep saying my name? And why so loudly? And why was Peter Wright standing up looking furtive? I suggested that I had very little to say for myself, given the lack of context, which inflamed the previously gentle headmaster still further. He'd turned the same colour as Julia. And the day had been so grey up until then. Lovely, lilting, melting inconsequential grey. I was burning with shame. And hadn't even been accused of anything yet. It's that original sin thing. It must have been. Guilty until proven guiltier. I need to draw breath. Just thinking about it.

At some Victorian schools, after children had walked six miles across rut and furrow to the house of slate, bible and multiplication, they would be asked to hold out their hands as they walked through the front gate, not to be given a Milky Bar, but to be hit with a stick; the idea being to show them what might happen if they were naughty.

Like a promo. Like the trailer for *Asylum* at the Commodore Hammersmith. I saw it on Talking Pictures Freeview channel the other day. "Come to the asylum! To get killed!" That's all it says. Several times. An offer you can't refuse. "Three in the dress circle please and a hot dog, no onions". "Come to the asylum! To get killed!" OK – I confess! I'm bad! Badder than the bandits in my play. Just get it over with. Please. And take those eyes off me.

It was now over to Peter Wright, who was acting as prosecuting council, several witnesses and victim all at once. His story went thus: I – Christopher Guard – *him* – had told Peter Wright that, if he came into school last Tuesday, I would – quote – beat him up. What the fuck? What did I have to say for myself? "Nothing, Mr Jones". "Don't lie". "I'm not". "Don't answer back". I didn't. My face was now on fire. Flame was bursting from my arse and my ears had turned violet. Oh Julia! "Well?!" I felt like confessing. That's how the inquisition works. I'd have happily been hung for a witch to stop those girls looking at me. And Albert. Everybody.

Something came to my rescue. Maybe it was the song we sang at the end of every day. "May angels guard us while we sleep 'til morning light arrives… Aaahhmen". "You will both report to my office at break tomorrow morning". I didn't sleep. Not even a hallucinatory tie on the ceiling.

This was real.

What had in fact happened was that I had been given the starring role in Peter Wright's three act fantasy. Plucked at random from his casting directory and inserted into his script. Peter, on some never-revealed whim, had bunked off school on the Tuesday, then been too afraid to confess to his mother, and named me as the reason, as if I was running some kind of junior protection racket. Then the indignant Mrs Wright, believing the sun to rise in Peter's trousers, had seen Mr Jones in person, and demanded that I be brought to summary justice. Not that she knew who I was.

Irony had it that my sense of justice was now so keen, I put the brief hiatus outside Mr Jones' office to immediate use. I informed the surly Peter that, if he didn't come clean, I'd get Danny Judd on to him. Then he'd regret it. John Waller too. All hokum but I said it like I meant it. If I'd taken a lie-detector test, I'd have passed. Peter wouldn't have. Who said I can't dissemble? This was life and death. He acquiesced. Confessed all. His mother forgave him.

Happy ending. Except I never fully recovered. That's why I've taken the trouble telling you now. What a performance.

Bunking Off School by Christopher Guard

Unlike Peter Wright, Shakespeare borrowed a lot of his plots, and some of his structuring is a bit loose, but he had an insatiable audience to consider. Literary greatness is all very well but not at the expense of bums on seats. He was a player; his trade was illusion. It's what you don't see that counts and what you choose to believe. Prospero uses illusion to illuminate truth. Masques and visions to mirror the soul. Hamlet's dilemma is revealed to him by a play within a play. And with a play, he presents reality to the king. The Royal Academy of Dramatic Artifice. So where do we fit into all this in an era of uncertainty and fear? Do we cleave to tabloid lies? Suspend disbelief like a child? Leave 'normal' behind? Can we ever live for the moment? Can we 'act'?

Middle-aged professionals crawling around on all fours like babies in drama therapy sessions. Rich, successful and certifiable.

"When they see your innocent face, they form a queue to fill that space. Take good care of your empty room, don't let them in".

From 'Fear', inspired by the kids in the art room.

I loved doing *Jackanory*. For the handy money, yes, and for the lack of lines to learn, yes, and for the challenge of autocue, yes but, most of all, just because I loved reading stories. My favourite came to me via a call on the morning of the recording. No warning – just could I get into Television Centre asap because Hywel Bennett wasn't well, and they needed someone to read *Stig of the Dump*. Joy. Five fees – because the show was aired on five separate days – two days intensely recording a genius story, gratitude galore because I'd come to their rescue, and – best of all – no time to think. Thinking is overestimated. Ask Hamlet. Not the cigar. "Happiness is a cigar called Hamlet". Prince Hamlet was a disaster waiting to happen. Don't discuss. I stayed up all night with Hywel Bennett once, and some 'sparks' in a hotel in Dorset. We were making *Malice Aforethought* for the BBC and had given scant aforethought to the looming early call. Ouch. Like Mel, Hywel liked you to drink *with* him. Until dawn. He was great as poisoner Dr Bickleigh. Different kind of poison.

I had written a story called *The Water Dragon* because my daughter Rosie asked me to, in verse, Roald Dahl style. I just wanted to hold my kids' attention; no reader in mind but them. I happened to show it to *Jackanory* producer, Angela Beeching, and she said, "Write four more" and she would commission them and find an artist. I was living in Coverack – a good place to write a series called *Sea Creatures*: 'The Mer Monkey', 'The Sandwitch', 'The Sea Dog' and one other I don't think I ever finished. With the kind of bad timing that was becoming a habit, *Jackanory* came off air. Swept away by the same broom that did for *Doctor Who*. I read the same stories at Coverack School and at Wendell Park years later. Better in the flesh really. Small, real, rapt audiences. I liked going into Wendell nursery too, with a bunch of my paintings and random photos and just rambling spontaneously. Whatever held the attention. Sod the plot. Just play.

I played Roald Dahl, in a *South Bank Show* special. Now there's a thing. It's a real drag Roald wasn't fond of it because it was a cool piece of TV. It was the only time I worked professionally with Mel Smith, and the second time I worked with Sir Ian McKellen. It was made by the wildly imaginative Jack Bond, who was feted by Salvador Dalí and Andy Warhol and was once described as "the most irresponsible man on God's earth", after a bear and assorted psychiatric patients had escaped from one of his sets.

Melvyn Bragg was barely in it. Jack wanted undiluted Roald: a surreal, kaleidoscopic mix of life and work. I not so much *played* Roald, as reflected his maverick, gambling spirit. Jack threw me in at the deep end. On day one, I drove a vintage 1930s Bugatti at high speed, doubleclutching, through the back lanes of RAF Northolt, in a white tuxedo and trailing silk scarf, uninsured. The mechanic had assumed I'd be on a low-loader. Bond was appalled. So was the mechanic. The name's Bond, Jack Bond. "Of course the kid has to drive it. Get in Chris!" Life, limb and a hundred and fifty thousand pounds worth of car. You never think you're going to die. Even if you do. (Roy Kinnear did. That was terrible. And I nearly got eaten by sharks). But we're just playing, aren't we? We're actors. "Drive as fast as you can towards the camera, then, at the last moment, just before you kill the operator, turn sharp left". The bonnet went on forever. Screech.

The next life I was required to endanger was Tom Bell's. On a disused section of motorway. This time I had to drive even faster than 'as fast as you can', as close to Tom's motorbike as possible, then, just as we were about to crash, throw a wad of money in his face. He skidded, fell off, flew across the motorway and cut his cheek. Someone did anyway. Quite who did what stunts and when, I can't recall, but Jack didn't seem to care. He was enjoying himself.

Next, he put me in a Spitfire and turned the engine on. I was fully expecting him to tell me to fly it. Roald was in the control tower talking about the 'still point', the spot of absolute concentration, and I was hoping that I had one. Jack's friend turned up; it was his plane. He did the flying for me. Of course he did. In a terrifying kind of way, I was disappointed.

Mel Smith did a turn as a preposterous police constable, and Sir Ian fashioned the definitive, depraved, childloathing witch replete with blue spit. The show's climax featured a fantastic giant peach bouncing along the South Bank at night. Truly huge and magical.

Yes, it was a shame it didn't get Roald's blessing. Something irked him. Maybe it was just Jack. Or maybe it was Tom Bell insisting on calling him 'Ronald' to his face. Tom had a weird sense of humour. When Roald's alter-ego – me – pulls in at a garage in the Bugatti, the real Roald is filling his car with petrol, humble and otherly, the balefaced wizard. The look he gives me says it all. Jack was a rebel; Tom was a rebel. Roald out-rebelled us all.

The show was aired of course. I liked it. Still have it on VHS. I remember the night it was aired because I went to The Cross Keys afterwards. I'd happened to have been on BBC2 at the same time, in an *Everyman* called *The True Story of Frankenstein*, in which I played the doctor as a flawed innocent, close to Shelley's original dream. Jason Bowyer was in the pub. "Oh no!" he said. "We can't get away from you." Rock on, Frankie Dahl.

While I think of it, and apropos of rebels, I didn't take the Television Centre commissionaires at their word, make like Anthony Hopkins and drive straight back to Wales. I only lived a mile up the road; not much of a protest going back to Stamford Brook. I appealed instead to their innate sense of reason. Just because they were smothered in ribbons didn't give them *carte blanche* to instigate military campaigns. You could feel the tension from the other end of Wood Lane. They may as well have asked us to hold out our hands for a warning swipe with a stick, for not having a non-existent day pass; while billions of permanent employees could come and go as they pleased, use the restaurants and bars, park, shimmy, walk the walk.

There was no digital swiping of course, just lists in a glass booth and a bloke with a clipboard. Never women. No female war veterans. Tony Blackburn cruising past as the Gestapo debriefed another humble actor 'come to ply his trade'. "What the fucking hell do you want?" Well, it might as well have been. "*I, Claudius*". "You what?" "*I, Claudius*". "You're who? Never heard of you. How did he get that many medals for being a bastard?" "I'm in it. *In I, Claudius*". Up to my neck, apparently. I was on foot, with a soppy Roman fringe. He probably thought I was a *Top of the Pops* groupie. Again.

"Christopher Guard. Can you have a look? I'm playing Marcellus." "You're playing silly buggers. Get out of it." What the fuck? I exerted my imperial status. "Now look here, I'm in *I, Claudius*, directed by Herbie Wise, and I'm on your list. Go and have a look." "You'll have to wait." A Pan's person hoves into view. "No, I won't wait. I'm going to be late. Look! There! In there! Do your job, that's what you're paid for isn't it, or are you too busy ogling the dancers?" "Right, you little bastard, I've had just about enough of you!" Result? He started removing his jacket, with every intention of engaging in fisticuffs. In front of a Pan's person. Or was it a Leg and Co? Here was my chance. I ducked under the barrier and legged the fifty yards up to reception. Stop that Emperor! Livia did that. At the end of Episode One. With poison figs.

Getting into the zealously guarded BBC Club was even more of a challenge. Forget day passes, they should have issued lottery tickets. Every time you went, you had to be signed in again – and again – by a member, and there wasn't always a member about – just lots of thirsty disciples and some hungover Daleks.

My ploy was to partly change back into my day clothes, then advance swiftly on the check-in desk like a demented floor manager in search of an errant actor. "I've lost Christopher Guard! Have you seen him?" "Who?" In a flash, I'm in the club, vaulting the stairs, descending the tiers, lost in a throng of members. I never did find him. Me I mean.

The circular design of Television Centre was meant to ensure that, wherever you were and on whatever floor, you couldn't possibly get lost. But I got lost loads of times. Often met myself coming back the other way. On a different floor. And on a different day. Like a static, spiral TARDIS, where David Copperfield could bump into Marcellus on Tuesday and have a drink with Doubting Thomas on Thursday. Couldn't have been the beer. It was rubbish. Beer back then was much weaker anyway. I just seemed to defy logic. I was OK in lifts. But not when they went round in circles.

19: Working for a Living

Good work if you can get it. Something to fall back on. I'd like to be an actor but isn't it very insecure? My daughter sings nicely.

Do you know anyone…?

My good friend, Andy, of Some Burglars, could have been a professional guitarist. He's talented enough. His beautiful wife wanted to be an actress. She was hoping I could introduce her to Trevor Eve. She was starstruck. She came to a party at our house and couldn't take her eyes off him. Andy told me she was available weekday evenings and all day Saturdays. That's enough time to become famous… surely?

Depends which you want: fame or freedom. Fandom probably. The devil they knew. Andy runs a successful art shop now. And plays for the love.

Could I have been a painter and decorator forever? A teacher? A fisherman? I was all these things and more. In the gaps the public call 'resting'. That's a laugh. Resting is when you're gainfully employed, given a nice berth in a hotel, and all you have to do is learn your lines and pretend to be someone else.

Working is when you're waiting by the phone, and you're down to the last two and it's gone six on Friday, and you're losing hope, and you can't pay the red gas bill.

That's working.

Working is Dad cycling to the Labour Exchange in Power Road, Chiswick in 1958, with me sitting on the crossbar. Working is wondering why Dad is not his usual cheery self after he's had a play returned by Binky Beaumont. Working is pretending your life is normal when it's anything but. Working is an orphaned orangutan learning to be normal so she can go back to the jungle. Working is lying awake at night thinking about this chapter, and if the book is publishable at all.

Working is my sister slaving over a hot drawing board, alone, for three hundred and sixty-four days, then attending a wildly unctuous launch party on the three hundred and sixty-fifth. Working is making a comic strip called *The Animator's Year,* then sending it as a postcard.

And working is earning money. I don't know if it was insecurity that drove us. Me and Dom. I think it was just what children do. Raising extra cash to top up the pocket money. A shilling for me, sixpence for Dom, rising to one and six for me and a shilling for Dom. We weren't up there with the Krays but we did have one or two fiddles on the go. In fact when Dom was very little, I tried to convince him that pennies were worth more than threepenny-bits because they were wider, which would have been like trying to convince him that I was worth more money than him because I was bigger. Which I was, up to a point: taller anyway. And worth more money. But not for long. Not after Joe Losey cast Dom in *The Go-Between*.

Chris and Dad and Dad's bike

183

Bibby, Mum's mother, she of the peas, was naturally liberal, good at drawing and always happy to see us 'naughty boys'. To give Vera and Eric a break, she stayed with us occasionally, usually in bed because, nominally, she was bedridden. At first, I thought that meant she'd got rid of her bed. I liked the sound of that. I hated going to sleep and was always first up. I used to do the housework and take Mum a cup of real leaf tea in bed in the hope that she'd say "Yes" to us going to Battersea Fun Fair.

Bibby could in fact walk perfectly well but she was quite forgetful, so it was probably safer for her to be in bed. We knew where she was and so, to some extent, did she. I'm not sure whose idea it was for her to go to bed in the first place, Bibby's or ours, but it provided Dom and me with a willing and captive audience. Bibby loved singing and, when awake, was always happy to hear our latest duet. Usually something hastily knocked together on a Saturday morning after we'd blown our pocket money on a Corgi Mini Cooper from Wally Barnes. Real suspension and jewelled headlights.

Bibby's attention span was quite limited so one verse of 'Silent Night', even in July, usually did the trick. She would smile and clap and ask us to pass her purse, then give us a threepenny-bit or a couple of pennies and go back to sleep. We never stole from her. No way. No, the bad bit was that we knew she'd probably have forgotten in half an hour, so we'd nip back for an encore. Not the same song. *Holy, Holy, Holy* maybe. Religious stuff was the safest. I think she knew perfectly well what we were up to but couldn't always remember how much she'd invested in us the time before. She erred on the side of generosity. Thanks Bibby. We love you. The naughty boys.

Dad's parents were fully *compos mentis*, although Grandpa was more knackered than Granny, who still intended to traverse the globe, making interminable home movies in new dresses. Grandpa had a habit of turning his lips inwards when he kissed you goodbye, so that you couldn't see them at all. Then he'd make a strange smacking noise to signal the moment of whiskery affection. Lips were sexy you see, and sex was a bit of a nuisance, at least according to Grandpa's interpretation of the Bible. We had a knack of pulling the right face in the hall – a humble, resigned sort of face – as if we were happy in the sight of God whether or not Grandpa and Granny were about to give us half a crown. This was real work, cultivated over several years, and eventually honed to an art form. Five bob once.

Each.

Not that all our fundraising activities were based on greed and deception. We were encouraged to raise a lot of money for Oxfam and we certainly did. Our 'Zoo Museum' consisted of a Victorian silver propelling pencil, a rusty meteorite which weighed more than our giant rabbit, a fossilised sponge and one or two Children's Encyclopaedias opened at riveting pages like 'How magnets work' and 'The history of the wool trade'. Plus the cat if she was about, but she was usually outside near the fence so they may already have seen her. Lucky them.

The rabbit was under the bed among some dust, so was not always available for inspection: just like a real zoo, when it's raining and the warthog is in his house and won't come out. We would lure total strangers up the stairs, and when they'd had enough of admiring pencils and fluff we would demand sixpence. Most were so pleased to be released they coughed up.

Never to be seen again.

'Penny for the Guy' was extremely lucrative. Profits mainly to charity, but with a small percentage syphoned off for the workers. We deserved it too. We made proper guys: out of real clothes properly stuffed with lots of newspaper, patiently patted and sculpted into unnervingly lifelike form; and we had this cool old-man rubber face mask to complete the monstrosity. Shoes, gloves and attitude.

Mum used to 'have a turn' sometimes if she forgot he was reclining in the playroom.

He certainly hit the spot at Stamford Brook station, in a wicker shopping basket. Most kids just tied a balloon to a jumper, scrawled a felt-tip face on it, and hoped for the best. Not us. This was art. One bloke gave us a ten-bob note. Fuck. That was like robbing the Post Office.

One year Mick, Dom and I, victims of our own success, got lazy and abandoned the tableau in favour of living theatre. We dressed Dom as a guy. He wasn't too keen at first but he looked great, even more authentic than newspaper. We were coining it one evening when, as *rigor mortis* began to set in, the guy abruptly wrenched its buttocks from the basket and made a bid for freedom.

"Dom! Dom! Come back!"

Rumbled. Heads turned much as they had done when Jeeves did that upside-down shit.

What were we on?

More soothing but no less demanding was carol-singing.

Again, no half-cocked, vapid hopefulness for us. Guitar, tom-toms, maracas, harmonies. Rehearsed but relaxed. 'Away in a Manger', as Peter, Paul and Mary might have sung it.

Or better still, Donovan. 'We Three Kings', Dylan style.

One year – I must have been about thirteen because I knew at least four chords – we'd made our usual sort of collection, maybe seventeen shillings and fourpence, down by the river and up the roads in between, and had been about to head for home, when fate lured us up the steep steps of one of the huge, elegant houses in St Peter's Square. That's the one. Julia's square. Lennon even had to write a song about her. (Which it wasn't. It was about his mum. But seashell eyes worked for my Julia too).

What happened next was like when Mohammed Al Fayed took over at Fulham and suddenly all those pennies that we'd raised running marathons and playing in celebrity matches and doing gigs with David Hamilton and selling home-made fanzines seemed paltry beside the Mo millions.

Twenty years earlier, at the door of that St Peter's Square house, our angel was dressed in a towel. She was taller than Mo and had evidently been in the bath. Her hair was also wrapped in a towel, and she had an intangible 'something' about her. Far-away eyes beholding our glory as we rocked through 'Away in the Bleak Midwinter'. For a pregnant moment, we all just stood there. Mesmerised.

"Would you like to come in?" Huh? "Please, do come in". Like being lured by a steamy mermaid.

In we went. Dom, me, Mark and Paddy. Average age, about eleven.

"Take a seat."

Sumptuous. Floral chaise longues and golden side lights. Rock regal.

"I'll be back."

A bloke came into the room, silent but friendly. A 'nowwhat's-she-up-to?' look on his face. Tony Richardson, I think.

"Coke?"

"Please!"

"Ice?"

"Oh *yes*."

When Vanessa returned – for 'twas she, daughter of Sir Michael – deals were done, promises made, parents phoned; this was not an abduction. Would it be OK to take us to a Christmas party to raise more money for Oxfam? More money than we'd ever dreamed of. It was more than OK with the choristers. Peter, Paul, Mary, Dom, Donovan, me, Paddy, Mark, Bob. Go tell it on a mountain, over Hammersmith Bridge and far away. Kensington, I think. Or was it Chelsea? Anyway we travelled like rock stars in a limo, Vanessa even more excited than we were. Ssshh! Here was the plan: we tip-toe into the apartment incognito, Vanessa goes ahead and turns down the lights in the hall, then we burst into the living room like a gospel choir; singing, strumming, shaking and banging.

We went down a storm. The guests were several magnums of Dom Perignon to the wind and ripe for investment. Notes sterling that I wouldn't clap eyes on again until Mel was waving them. Our bucket didn't chink once. It sighed and simpered like a bed being made up with silk sheets. Flocks of money. I don't know how much we made – and it all went to Oxfam – but the crowd thought we were worth every tenner. What a snazz idea, Vanessa. Good things happen when you don't expect them. You make your own spontaneity.

We OD'd on more Coke, exited backwards to rapturous applause, then glided back to Pleydell in the limo. Good work if you can get it. Just don't make too many plans.

Bad work, best avoided, was my attempt to become a Cub. A trainee boy scout. I must have been about seven. The local troop met at the side of Stamford Brook station, in a smelly wooden hut. The lads at the green, my football mates like Duncan and Blair and Stoody-Woo, had given it a good press and I was keen to be part of something extracurricular other than piano lessons and writing plays about cowboys.

What a disaster. As I had only ever seen Cubs dressed in navy, with a yellow scarf, I assumed all Cubs looked like that. I was nothing if not enterprising. What better than my navy fisherman's jumper from the Seine Loft in Coverack, and one of Mum's new yellow dusters tied round my neck? Jolly smart. Except that, when I arrived, everyone was wearing a grey jumper with a green scarf, neatly inserted into a shiny toggle. Oh dear. Big laugh.

Scoring on the hallowed turf

Not that there was anything funny about Cubs. For a start, there was someone called Akela who was at least ten feet tall. She reminded me of the White Witch from Narnia when she visits London and scares the shit out of mere mortals. Supposedly representing wisdom and authority, Akela spent about ten minutes hoisting a vast Union Jack on a length of frayed string before telling us all to belt up while she said prayers. This was a nightmare. A feather duster, a Union Jack and now God. Help!

Next we had to play a game called 'British Bulldog' or 'Rule Shitannia' or something, which no one understood. The hut was too small for it anyway, so most boys just rolled around on the floor kicking each other. Brief respite came when a boy called Paul Howells, who was good at the piano and extremely naughty, headbutted someone in the face and there was an interlude for first aid. Not sure if there was a badge for stemming nose bleeds but there were definitely badges for knots. In this troop, knot practice involved tying each other up like Tonto in *The Lone Ranger* or tying yourself to someone's ankle and practising for the three-legged race. Not a sheepshank in sight, though I'm surprised no one tried a hangman's noose.

Before we were eventually allowed to escape, Akela hoisted the Union Jack again, implored the Lord to forgive us and asked her assistant to get the 'holy slipper'. The what?! Fuck my old toggle. This was a white plimsoll, white witch size. Paul Howells was commanded to bend over, then swiped by the bony old crone while we looked on like guests at a public execution. Maybe we'd do nooses next week.

Enough! Having spent three weeks begging Mum and Dad to let me join the Cubs, I then spent the rest of the week begging them to let me leave. Shame because I'd really liked the look of those 'Job Done!' stickers in people's windows. Bob-a-Job. Untapped source of revenue. A Scout came to our house one Saturday morning and Dad gave him a Bob-a-Job job. "Dig over that patch of garden please". Half an hour later, he'd done nothing except chop up worms on the crazy paving. No bob for that job. Dad was very cross indeed, especially as it was only a week since Titty the cat had been sick all over his typewriter.

I tried a paper round too, but the conventional avenues of youth employment didn't seem to suit me. I was more a Bibby and museum man. The round started at some ungodly hour when all good boy scouts were still in bed, dreaming of Nutwood and worms. The bag was so heavy, especially on Sundays when the new-fangled colour supplements ganged up against me, that I nearly dislocated my shoulder. The route took me from King Street down to Chiswick Mall, via lots of huge, insatiable houses, and back via Rivercourt Road to the sweet shop opposite Latymer of all places. My pay was to be one pound a week. Sweeping chimneys would have been easier. Having crawled through the dark for two hours every morning for seven days, I was told that I'd only be receiving twelve and sixpence on account of late deliveries, magazines damaged by letterboxes and Lord Aberdare not receiving his Telegraph at all on Tuesday. Bollocks to that. I resigned after three weeks.

Keep the change. Thanks very much. The change at the end of a shopping trip. That was more like it. Half a crown to get the fruit and veg from Shepherd's Bush market and, "If there's any change left over, can I buy a…?" Mini Cooper? Too expensive. Catapult? *No.* They were made of steel and leather and black rubber and fantastically dangerous. Split peas for my Sekiden gun? Yes, but don't mention the Sekiden gun. They were banned at school. Pee-yow, pee-yow. Anyway, I must have been at least sixteen by now. Too old for all that. Rat? Never too old for a rat. "What? Oh no. No more pets, Chris." "Pleeease. But Mum, I'll look after it; you won't have to do a thing." "But what about Jeeves? Jack Russells are ratters." "He won't go anywhere near the rat. It'll be in a cage. They're highly intelligent. And clean. And pet rats don't get diseases". All true. Rats are fab. Even in the wild. Their resourcefulness should be admired, not feared. All these empty pandemic office spaces turning into 5-star hotels for rats. Instinctive entrepreneurs.

There was fifty pence left over. The exact price. Which one? There were a lot. In a glass tank designed for newts probably. "This one?" Market man grabbed an albino by the tail. "No, that one". "This one?" "No, *that* one". "This one?" "No, *that one*". They were all the same to market man. But not to me. The one I wanted was particularly lively. Eventually, after some cussing, she was procured and put into a flatpack, white box. No Dancing! We already had a cage. The old mouse one. I was well chuffed; sat upstairs at the front of the bus smoking a Number Six while Monday scuffled around in the cardboard. It was a Monday and I *do* like Mondays.

The honeymoon period was brief. The reason for Monday's state of high alert soon became apparent. She had put on a lot of weight. Her cage was in a corner of my bedroom alongside my Boots stereo record player and vinyl collection. I awoke one morning to discover the bars bent asunder as though by Charles Atlas, and Monday nowhere to be found. Woe! Had she done a runner like Barney Warbit? Were they both roaming free somewhere, like the Lone Ranger and Tonto, putting the world of Stamford Brook to rights? A notice on a tree would have been redundant. "Have you seen this cat? Answers to the name of Titty." No problem. "Have you seen this lodger? Answers to the name of Tete." But "have you seen this rat?" What would Mrs Wilkie have said?

That night, something raced purposefully across my face. Then it raced purposefully up and down the wall, across the floor and finally under the heavy Victorian chest of drawers. The next night, much the same. This time I turned on the light. There she was. Big bulges to the hindquarters. Penny dropped. I read up on gestating rats. Rule one, leave her alone. Give her time. I moved out. Let her have the run of the room. Maintain the food and water supply, leave the cage open.

Four weeks later, the big day arrived. Carnage or creation? First time mums can be fickle. They might desert or even attack their young. Gingerly I lifted the chest of drawers. Baited breath. I dared to look. I dared… and there they were. The Marx Brothers. In the nicest, nattiest, neatest nest. Not piebald like their mum, but jet black; like their dad I bet. Eyes shining up at me like eight stones of onyx. We stared at each other forever; adapting – them to me, and me to them. Then ever so gently, I picked them up, juggling fingers, eased them into the cage, nest and all. Monday was calmness rodentified. She followed them home. Job done.

The nest was a work of art, featuring Mick Jagger's eye, a morsel of Donovan's kaftan and the corner of the flyleaf of *A Portrait of the Artist as a Young Man*. A mischief of rats. I sold the kittens, to 'All Pets' in Richmond. Upmarket. Pound each. Three pound fifty profit. Purr. Monday lived on. She used to sit on my shoulder when I went to the baker's or Wally Barnes Sports. Good as gold. No one noticed until they noticed. A bit like Bowie in the lift. Pieces of eight? Hardly. There was nothing to fear.

David Copperfield caused my TSB bank account to swell. I had four hundred pounds in there at one point. I felt I'd earned it not so much by acting as by negotiating the infamy at school.

"You're not at the BBC now, Guard!"

Tell me about it. The fan letters were more forgiving. One girl wrote that she had sixteen shillings in her moneybox and, when we were married, could she call me Lionel.

Truly.

Twenty years later, I tried my hand at professional painting and decorating. Not deliberately. That is to say I deliberately painted our house: little terraced place in Chiswick. I had no plans to rival Inigo Jones. But then the lady next door said, would I paint hers too.

Then Ralph, who was playing bass in Some Burglars, joined forces with me and we painted another. And another.

It was soon assumed that we weren't Burglars at all but proper decorators and, as our reputation spread, we were soon employed along illustrious Strand-on-the-Green itself. The posh houses. That was like being invited into Vanessa's.

This time it was a woman called Mrs Collingwood and the lady next door in Zoffany House. Mrs Flemyng I think. Or was it the other way round? Anyway one was an excellent artist and used to pay us from her ruffled cleavage while reclining on a chaise longue like Eartha Kitt. Heaven only knows what was on her mind. Come to the asylum. To get paid!

The other was a rubbish artist and kept criticising our gloss work, telling us where we were "not professional". She was a fine one to talk.

One day she invited us up to the fourth floor to show us her paintings. A stack of A4 canvases in a pile like a big deck of cards. Each uniquely lifeless and boring. We enthused of course.

Until she accidentally pulled out a dreadful picture of what I think was meant to be a raven on a wall, and hurriedly put it back again. I caught Ralph's eye.

Suddenly he flew down four flights of stairs and out into the verdant calm of Thames Road. He had literally wet himself laughing.

A few days later, we saw an Austen 1100 doing about fifteen miles an hour along Thames Road, driven apparently by no one. Just a wig, barely discernible above the driver's door.

It was Mrs Cleavage, no doubt reclining like Eartha Kitt and trusting in providence to get her home.

Pulling lobster pots is not for wimps. While I was living in Coverack, I helped a young fisherman called Paul Watts set up in business. We had one small boat and no hydraulic winch. Coverack had once been awash with professional fishermen. Now there were only a few left. Derek Carey, Willie Hunt, Phil Moore… and maybe, with a bit of luck, Paul. We were working eight strings of pots – that's ten times eight. Eighty pots. And every single one needed pulling, emptying, re-baiting and throwing out again. Every pull was like a deadlift in the gym and, once the pot was aboard, you had just enough time to empty it, rebait it and throw it over again. Don't get the rope round your legs while it's running. Men have died that way. Maybe not in summer – inshore like we were – but in heavy seas, especially alone, sometimes at night, with mouths to feed, it's happened often enough.

We played AC/DC on the boogie-box to lighten the load. Against a big swell, kelp across the lines, lugging like your life depended on it. And as the days went by, what had seemed impossible at first briefly became a way of life. It was only for three months but, if anything ever came close to making a man of me, it was that. "My arms and legs are breaking and my head's about to blow", from AC/DC's 'Carry Me Home'. By the time we'd moored the boat and dragged the tackle up to 'The Fisherman's Rest', there was never enough day left for beer or shanties. Just eat, sleep, and up again at dawn. Tough but so good for the soul.

Real work. Not like this. This finger-dancing, brainteasing, memory-bank-juggling dream of a memoir. I wonder where it will all end. It started on an operating table. I suppose, if I wait long enough, something else terrifying might happen, and I can end with that. Or maybe I could make something happen. Buy a pregnant rat. Or an axolotl. I've got my COVID jab coming up at the end of the week, so maybe I could have a reaction. Axolotls can regenerate their body parts. Even parts of their brain. If a leg comes off, it can reattach itself to the head. The Axolotl-Vaccine effect. Maybe something like that.

20: A Sort of Ending

Maybe I could die; that would be a good ending. But then, how do I write about it afterwards? Better not tempt fate. Maybe a soliloquy. "Not 'to be or not not to be'. 'Sir, he may live.' 'He may or may not be about to be not.'" No. Maybe not.

Anyway, I died once before, and it wasn't all it's cracked up to be. But maybe that's because I came back to life again. The doctor was certainly worried, and I did see a white tunnel. But is that dying? It's probably just having pleurisy and running a fever.

I don't want to catch COVID, but it feels a bit like vertigo sometimes and I want to jump off a tall building. Because everyone keeps talking about it and stressing us out with statistics. OK, OK – I give up! I'll catch it. Then I can talk from personal experience instead of dying of boredom. Like method actors who actually hurt and suffer so they can be authentic. De Niro getting fat for *Raging Bull*, Tom Hanks losing thirty pounds for *Philadelphia*, Buster Keaton hanging from clocks. Me being thrown to the sharks. Not sure what Stanislavsky says about death.

When I made Dennis Potter's *Joe's Ark*, reality-obsessed Alan Bridges used to twist Angharad Rees' feet in rehearsal to remind her of the agony she was meant to be in as a young cancer victim. And I used to run round the rehearsal room like a maniac until I was gasping for breath. When Oliver Reed died mid-shoot, that wasn't method acting it was just inconvenient. Method living. That's what death so often is: inconvenient.

You miss people, like I miss Stu, because you loved them; but as the years go by you miss them because they're not around to fix the lighting, and get your mic position perfect, and discuss this inane government over a cup of coffee. And take their son to the park. It's just a drag. Especially for the dead person.

I had to go back to the hospital a few times last year. My eye is OK, except they had to put a new lens in because retinal operations can cause cataracts and then those need sorting out too. Eventually the new lens will need lasering. It's boring more than anything. Unlike this book, it will probably go on forever.

It's amazing how the hospitals have coped. I've even got a dental appointment booked in next week.

Would you mind if I organise my own funeral? We're so nice about each other once we're dead. If I seriously pissed you off, I want you to be free to say so. In a harlequin suit. Or in the nude if you like. We ignore someone for ten years then pitch up at a crematorium all long-faced and sycophantic, in an ill-fitting suit that perfectly reflects our relationship with the deceased, and pretend we regret that falling out in the pub when in fact we haven't thought about it once. Until they kicked it. How rude is that? Being polite I mean. So, I'm going to choose all the music and design all the emperor's new clothes and write all the speeches. Then you can really say what you think.

Our dog, Dilly, is an atheist. She has no interest in religion whatsoever. She's thirteen but thinks she's three, knows nothing about death and has no intention of dying; which is as close to eternal life as I ever want to get. Neurosis is the enemy, not death. Of course the wheels fall off, and we ache and quake and gravity keeps on pulling but it's like with these interminable debates about COVID. Yes, it's shite, yes, it's terrible how many people have died but, frankly, if I'd never heard one stat or watched one COVID conference, what the fuck of a difference would it have made?

You do what you can, use your common sense and then write your memoirs or something. Anything. Build a snowman. It's been snowing today. Stu wanted to live forever because there was so much he still wanted to do. So, when I hear people groaning on, I feel for *him*. Because he died. And that just sucks. Like *It's a Wonderful Life* or *A Christmas Carol*. Don't just get soppy-sentimental at Christmas, live your fucking life.

I first kept a day-to-day diary when I was eight. And I still do. Not swathes of anecdotal soulfulness; the opposite. Just what actually, factually happened: the weather; the leaky tap; the council election result; the Fulham score; what we had for lunch; maybe a job interview; a conversation in the corner shop. I can't fit much in because they're just little appointment diaries, so it's all squeezed and scribbled and probably indecipherable, but they keep me sane, because I can go back and say, "Blimey, was that really the same week Dilly had her operation?" or "I didn't realise we were in Coverack in September that year" or "That was the day in the art room when Ryley pretended his cat had died", that sort of stuff. They were meant to be appointment diaries. Recording the future: far-off family parties; Television Centre appointments; house viewings; proper stuff, for futurewise people. But the gaps were bigger than the entries, so I started filling it up retrospectively. The future as the past. The present as a jigsaw with missing pieces.

I get up at 6.30.
to day, go to the toile
and start writing
in this Diary
we rehearsed two play
My Brother O w/friend
and I, and in the
afternoon. we do
them to six people.
Two things I am sor
to say, went wrong
I couldn't find a gun
so ~~tot~~ I had to use
a key, and the other
thing was, that
we t forgot about
the tray of coffee
And there were Choc
Ices in the interval
wich all the
children liked.

An early diary page

I am sorry to say I have missed a lot of diary but now I am starting fresh again not a lot has happened except I have got into the lower latymer I go in September and dad is taking me to see Mutiny on the Bounty this Saturday week. This week school exam week. a week.

Another early diary page

I'm watching the big, fat snowflakes through the window, drifting sideways. Let's make up an ending. I recently signed to a new agent. My first acting agent in twenty years. So it's just a question of time before I'm cast in something extraordinary, isn't it? A Whovian character, a dark, otherly type, called Crosstale, who can morph back to childhood to retrieve important emotional information.

The child is psychic and lucid and can provide the missing pieces of tragic jigsaws. Then Crosstale can return to adulthood and fix the midlife shit, not with hindsight but with foresight: the child parenting the adult. Things only appear strange out of context. History puts us in chronological boxes: life roams free.

Forget that. I'll definitely make the TV series, at some point. It's called *The Cost of Flying* or *The Wizard of When*. But first there is the concert at The Albert Hall, with the Romanian Symphony Orchestra. The acoustic solo album fully orchestrated. That was a great day. Well, three actually. Due to demand. Cut.

I just want to sit by the wayside and watch.

That's what I did.

How to do and yet just be.

That is the question.

Hammersmith Bridge by Christopher Guard

Epilogue: Am I In It?

So, now that I've sort of finished and read through what I've written, I feel like I've hardly written anything at all. Hands keep popping up in the classroom.

"Me, me, choose me!"

In fact, my old school friend, Ian Weitzel, did just that yesterday. He said "Am I in It?" on Facebook.

Well, no, not yet, but you are now Ian. Thanks for buying my painting.

Ian and I were often in it. In the doghouse. In Mr Mower's maths class. And, of course, that's worthy of mention. So, here's a more prosaic ending. Keep it real.

Attention spans are short.

Weitzel's Shoe on A4!

Guard ordered to write out a thousand times "I must not throw Weitzel's shoe over the fence"

I had my first Pfizer COVID jab yesterday.

My soul aches.

Mirror by Christopher Guard

www.ingramcontent.com/pod-product-compliance
Lightning Source LLC
LaVergne TN
LVHW011326080426

835513LV00006B/207